LAND VALUE TAXATION

Land Value Taxation
An Applied Analysis

WILLIAM J. McCLUSKEY
University of Ulster, Northern Ireland, UK

RIËL C.D. FRANZSEN
University of South Africa, South Africa

ASHGATE

Published by
Ashgate Publishing Limited
Gower House
Croft Road
Aldershot
Hampshire GU11 3HR
England

Ashgate Publishing Company
Suite 420
101 Cherry Street
Burlington, VT 05401-4405
USA

Ashgate website: http://www.ashgate.com

British Library Cataloguing in Publication Data
Land value taxation : an applied analysis
  1. Land value taxation
  I. McCluskey, William J. II. Franzsen, R. C. D. (Riël C. D.)
  336.2'25

Library of Congress Control Number: 2005927639

ISBN-10: 07546 1490 5

Printed and bound in Great Britain by Antony Rowe Ltd, Chippenham, Wiltshire

Contents

List of Figures

List of Tables

About the Authors

William J. McCluskey (co-author) is a Reader in real estate and valuation at the University of Ulster. He obtained his BSc (Hons) and PhD from the University of Ulster and is a Fellow of the Royal Institution of Chartered Surveyors. He has held various international teaching and research positions including Visiting Professor of Real Estate at the University of Lodz, Poland (1996-2000) and Professor of Property Studies at Lincoln University, Christchurch, New Zealand (2001-2002). He is a member of the Advisory Board of the International Property Tax Institute, co-editor of the *Journal of Property Tax Assessment and Administration*, and a David C. Lincoln Fellow of the Lincoln Institute of Land Policy, Massachusetts, United States from 2001 to 2003. His main professional and academic interests are in the fields of real estate valuation and more specifically ad valorem property tax systems, local government finance, computer assisted mass appraisal modelling and the application of geographic information systems. Within this context he has been involved in a number of international projects advising on ad valorem property tax issues including Jamaica, Northern Ireland, Bermuda, Poland, Tanzania and South Africa.

Riël C. D. Franzsen (co-author) is a Professor in tax and commercial law in the Department of Mercantile Law at the University of South Africa, based in Pretoria. He obtained the BLC and LLB degrees from the University of Pretoria and a LLD degree from the University of Stellenbosch. He has authored chapters in various mercantile law and international property tax textbooks, regularly contributes articles on property taxation to South African and international journals, and has presented papers on land and property taxation at various international conferences. He is a member of the Advisory Board of the International Property Tax Institute and a David C. Lincoln Fellow of the Lincoln Institute of Land Policy, Massachusetts, United States from 2001 to 2003. He has acted as an advisor to the governments of South Africa, Tanzania and Uganda, and also to the World Bank on property-related taxes specifically and aspects of local government finances generally.

Owiti A. K'Akumu (guest author) is a Research Fellow with the University of Nairobi's Housing and Building Research Institute. He holds a BA degree in Land Economics and MA degree in Urban and Regional Planning, both from the University of Nairobi. He is a member of the Institution of Surveyors of Kenya (ISK) and African Real Estate Society (AfRES). After graduation he served in the Government of Kenya in various capacities as Valuation Officer and Lands Officer before joining the University of Nairobi. He is an enthusiastic writer/researcher with an interest in land economics in general and land taxation in particular.

Abdul Hassan (guest author) is presently a Lecturer in real estate and land use planning at the University of the South Pacific, Fiji. He joined the Fiji Government service in June 1973 as a Senior Technical Assistant with the Valuation Division of the Ministry of Lands and Mineral Resources. Whilst with the Ministry of Lands he was promoted to Principal Valuer. In 1985 he was sent to United Kingdom to complete an attachment duty with Chief Valuers Office in London. He became a registered valuer of Fiji in 1987 and from 2003 a Member of the Valuers Registration Board of Fiji. He has completed a postgraduate Diploma in Land Management, Master of Arts and Graduate Certificate in Tertiary Teaching since joining the University in 1999.

Washington H. A. Olima (*guest author*) is an Associate Professor in the Department of Land Development, University of Nairobi, Kenya. He is currently the Dean of the Faculty of Architecture, Design and Development. He has some 18 years practical, research and academic experience in the field of property development, land management and property appraisal and taxation. He holds a Bachelor of Arts in Land Economics (Honours) degree and a Master of Arts in Housing Administration, both degrees from the University of Nairobi, as well as a PhD in Spatial Planning from Dortmund University, Germany. He is a full member of the Institution of Surveyors of Kenya. He has contributed chapters to various books, and also a number of articles in refereed international journals.

Preface

Land has been and still remains a favourite object for taxing authorities and the taxation of land, in one form or another, has been around for millennia. It is to some extent a 'natural' candidate as a tax base given its visibility and the unique feature of its fixed location. In addition, there has long been recognition of the fact that land, and in particular, the ownership of land is a repository of wealth. The inelastic supply of land and its locational attributes create a relationship that has a profound effect on the 'value' of land. This scarcity factor along with the efforts of communities can produce increases in value that are not, in any way, related to the efforts of the owner. It has often been argued that these community produced values should form the basis of a tax on property, returning such gains back to the community. In England, during the 13th century government funds were used to drain and channel water from the Fens and to build water protection structures. The owners of land that benefited from these works had to compensate the government through the payment of land taxes.

A number of books have been published in recent years presenting overviews of real property tax systems in various countries (for example McCluskey, W.J. (ed.) (1991) *Comparative Property Tax* System;[1] Youngman, J.M. and Malme, J.H. (1994) *An International Survey of Taxes on Land and* Building;[2] Rosengard, J.K. (1998) *Property Tax Reform in Developing* Countries;[3] McCluskey, W.J. (ed.) (1999) *Property Tax: An International Comparative* Review;[4] Bird. R.M. and Slack, E. (eds) (2004), *International Handbook of Land and Property Taxation*[5]). Some of these publications tend to be more descriptive than analytical and truly comparative, whereas others again concentrate on the theory of property

---

[1] McCluskey, W.J. (ed.) (1991), '*Comparative Property Tax Systems*', Avebury Publishing Limited, UK.
[2] Youngman, J.M. and Malme, J.H. (eds) (1994), '*An International Survey of Taxes on Land and Building*', Kluwer Law and Taxation Publishers, Boston.
[3] Rosengard, J.K. (1998), '*Property Tax Reform in Developing Countries*', Kluwer Academic Publishers, Boston.
[4] McCluskey, W.J. (ed.) (1999), '*Property Tax: An International Comparative Review*', Ashgate Publishing Limited, Aldershot.
[5] Bird. R.M. and Slack, E. (eds) (2004), '*International Handbook of Land and Property Taxation*', Edward Elgar Publishing Limited, UK.

taxation rather than how it performs in practice. Recently a number of publications discussing land value taxation, as a specific form of property taxation, have been published. In this regard reference should be made of Netzer, D. (ed.) (1998), *Land Value Taxation: Can it and Will it Work Today?*,[6] Connellan, O. (2004), *Land Value Taxation in Britain: Experience and* Opportunities.[7] Could yet another publication in the area of land value taxation possibly add any value in an area that has intrigued scholars such as Smith, Ricardo, Mill and Henry George for more than two centuries?

Despite the growing number of scholarly works on property taxation generally and land value taxation specifically, this book does add new perspectives and insights. It does not intend nor pretend to provide yet another reflective or profound theoretical overview of land value taxation as a tax system, but rather provides a practical synopsis of how a land value tax has been performing in a number of diverse countries under very different constitutional, economic and social circumstances. It traces the origins, merits, demerits, and in some instances the demise of land value taxation in countries ranging from developed (Australia and New Zealand) to developing countries (Fiji, Jamaica, Kenya and South Africa), ranging from small island states (Fiji and Jamaica) to large countries (Australia, Kenya and South Africa), and countries where it is the sole form of property taxation (Fiji, Jamaica) to counties where it is merely one option amongst other forms of property taxation (Australia, Kenya, New Zealand and, until recently, South Africa). In many respects this book is quite timely given the pressures coming to bear on the continued use of land value taxation. Significant structural changes in terms of the 'most appropriate' basis of the property tax are occurring at the present time. For example, South Africa is moving towards the adoption of capital improved value as the national uniform system of property taxation;[8] several territorial authorities in New Zealand have rejected the continued use of land value as a basis for raising locally based revenue in favour of a capital

---

[6] Netzer, D. (ed.) (1998), '*Land Value Taxation: Can it and Will it Work Today?*', Lincoln Institute of Land Policy, Cambridge, Massachusetts.

[7] Connellan, O. (2004), '*Land Value Taxation in Britain: Experience and Opportunities*', Lincoln Institute of Land Policy, Cambridge, Massachusetts.

[8] McCluskey, W.J. and Franzsen, R.C.D. (2004), '*The Basis of the Property Tax: A Case Study Analysis of New Zealand and South Africa*', Lincoln Institute of Land Policy Working Paper WP04WM1, Lincoln Institute of Land Policy, Cambridge, MA, United States, pp. 1-48.

value system;[9] the majority of local governments in the state of Victoria, Australia have changed from land value to capital improved value.[10]

Given these changes that are occurring across the world this book provides an invaluable insight into the practice of land value taxation today.

William J. McCluskey
Riël C.D. Franzsen

---

[9] Since 1989 nine local authorities have switched to capital improved value (the date of the change is in brackets); Dunedin (1989), Tasman (1991), Banks Peninsula (1992), South Waikato (1993), Invercargill (1994), South Taranaki (1994), Otorohanga (1996), Lower Hutt (1997) and Franklin (1999).

[10] McCluskey, W.J. and Franzsen, R.C.D. (2001), '*Land Value Taxation: A Case Study Approach*', Lincoln Institute of Land Policy Working Paper WP01WM1, Lincoln Institute of Land Policy, Cambridge, MA, United States, pp. 1-109. (see http://www.lincolninst.edu/publications).

Chapter 1

Theoretical Basis of Land Value Taxation

Willian J. McClucksey with guest authors Owiti A. K'akumu and Washington H.A. Olima

Introduction

Tax is a compulsory payment, usually of monetary form, made by the general body of subjects or citizens to a sovereign or government authority. It has the following special characteristics:

- it is paid without quid pro quo;
- it is enforceable in law;
- it may be levied against persons (natural or corporate); and
- it may also be levied against property.

Our primary concern here focuses on the last aspect i.e. taxes levied against property and in particular landed property. Indeed, we are not concerned with landed property per se. The scope here is limited to tax operations that are meant to capture land value. But taxes that are levied against property are not the only taxes that would capture land value. Even taxes levied against persons would at times capture land value as will be discussed later in this chapter.

Some requirements for a good tax structure

Adam Smith (1776) and Musgrave (1989) have identified some prerequisites for a good tax system. The following broad requirements are generally associated with a good tax:

- the distribution of the tax should be equitable, in other words every taxpayer should be expected to pay a fair share of the tax (i.e. the Canon of Equity);

- the tax structure should endeavour for fair and non-arbitrary administration. It should also be understandable to the taxpayer (i.e. the Canon of Fairness);
- when compared to the revenue collected, the administration and compliance cost of a tax should be as low as possible – in other words it must be economical to collect (i.e. the Canon of Economy);
- tax obligations should be based on benefits receivable from the enjoyment of public services (i.e. the Benefit Principle);
- tax should be levied at the time, or in the manner which is most likely to be convenient for the taxpayer (i.e. the Canon of Convenience);
- taxation should as much as possible avoid creating 'excess burdens' that would interfere with the efficient functioning of the host market.

The above conditions for a good tax system were meant to apply to taxes in general and therefore also with regard to property and land taxes.

Although taxes could also be used as instruments of socio-economic leverage, or for achieving various other non-fiscal goals, due care should be taken not to deviate from the above-stated principles for a good tax. In this context it is noteworthy that land taxes are quite often suggested as useful instruments to assist with land redistribution and/or land reform programmes.

The historical concept of land value taxation

Put at its simplest the concept of land value taxation rests upon the premise that only land should be taxed. As Youngman (1993) puts it, even this simple idea can create major difficulties in political acceptability and administrative limitations. In any society, there are three classical factors of production, land, labour and capital. The latter two have their costs and therefore their prices in terms of wages and interest. On the other hand, land has no cost of production, and if land was in unlimited supply people would pay little or indeed nothing for its use. However, land is not unlimited in supply, it is quite the opposite being fixed in supply. This fact creates demand for land in particular locations and therefore a value of land. Whilst land is generally accepted to be fixed in supply, the concept of alternative uses can create a supply shift, in that, supply for one kind of use rather than other kinds follows its own supply versus rent curve to the point where supply and demand equalise. The rent for land is said to constitute two components, firstly, its transfer or opportunity cost, which is the rent of the land in its next best use. Secondly, an amount attributable to scarcity or inelasticity of supply for a use in a particular location. It has been recognised that land was a free good as opposed to labour and capital that are never free. Therefore the market price of the products of land is determined by the cost of labour used in their production and capital equipment. On this basis the amount remaining for distribution as land rent is an excess (Lindholm, 1965; Douglas, 1961)

The history and economic foundations of land taxation are firmly rooted in the early 18th and 19th centuries. The Physiocrats argued that a particularly unique way to raise revenue was through the taxing of land (Quesnay, 1963 (1756)). Their belief in the sterility doctrine gave rise to the theory of 'impost unique'. Taxation of land was justified because of the productivity of land. From a social standpoint, therefore, the taxation of land had positive benefits. This group of economists tended to the view that since all taxes had to be paid out of rent, it would be sensible to replace all other taxes by a single tax on rent. In many respects the work of the Physiocrats laid the theoretical foundations that subsequent economists would construct their theories of land taxation. Smith (1776) famous for his canons of taxation made a number of important contributions to the land tax debate differentiating the land tax between a tax on agricultural land and a tax on ground rent to cover developed land. He found land to be suitable for taxation, since the tax would fall on the economic surplus and as such could not be passed onto consumers in the price of goods.

Ricardo (1817) suggested that the rent for land be the residual after paying for the costs of variable factors of production. His theory was largely based on the premise that a tax on land rents would not have harmful effects of the economy as such a tax would not inhibit production. Ricardo's theory was taken further by Mill (1824) who explained that a tax on the rent of land would not affect the industry of a country. In this regard he contended that as the cultivation of land was dependent upon the investment of capital, the capitalist was to some extent indifferent as to whether he paid the surplus, in the form of rent to an individual, or a tax to the government. Following on from his father's work Mill (J.S.) (1848) suggested that if the rent of land increases as a result of society, the owners of the land should have no claim to this 'windfall' increase in land value. The difficulty with this approach is based on the issue of clearly linking the increase in value to some identifiable societal improvement.

Henry George (1879) set out his views on the taxing of land (the 'single tax') in some detail in his book, *Progress and Poverty*. George was influenced by the state of the economy of the time and in particular, how development and progress in society was accompanied by high levels of poverty. His explanation of this phenomenon centred around the scarcity of land which was as a result of land speculation. The solution proffered by George was to replace all taxes with a single tax on land. This would have the desired result of making land more accessible to a greater number of people, raise wages, lower prices and in consequence raise the living standards of workers. In this regard, an increase in land values would be due to increased productivity which was closely related to increases in population and wealth. This rental income gave land its value and as such could be collected in taxes without decreasing the incentives for efficient production (Lindholm, 1965).

Proponents of land value taxation have cited a number of appealing properties, one of the main ones being its neutrality with respect to land use (Bentick, 1979; Tideman, 1982; Wildasin, 1982, Tideman, 1999). As Netzer (1966) argues, location rents constitute a surplus, and taxing these rents will not reduce the supply of sites offered, provided that landowners have been optimally using the land prior to the imposition of the tax. Economic theory also shows that under the assumption of perfect markets, a tax on any good with perfectly inelastic supply and non-zero elasticity of demand will be borne entirely by the supplier of the good; it cannot be shifted to its user because any increase in the price would lead to an excess supply of the good (in a competitive market the demand for units that are offered at a price above market price will drop to zero). Therefore, a tax on land has to be paid by the owner of the land (Skaburskis, 1995). Given that the supply of land is fixed, the tax does not have any substitution effect and therefore no deadweight loss, which makes it an ideal tax from an efficiency point of view. It is also argued that the real property tax (a tax on both land and improvements) has a number of negative economic effects on investment decisions (Mathis and Zech, 1982). It is alleged to discourage improvements to a site by reducing the economic return from such improvements. This reduction, in turn, results in a disincentive to maintain and improve buildings, the substitution of land for capital, causing urban sprawl, the utilization of buildings beyond the point at which they should be replaced and the speculation in land by holding it off the market. Advocates of land taxation argue that removing the tax on improvements and taxing only the value of the land would result in a restoration of the incentive to develop land to its fullest potential.

Ever since the publication of George's *Progress and Poverty* in 1879, the possibility of using land value taxation as a source of government revenue has intrigued economists and other tax specialists. The impact of George's ideas, whilst not widespread in a geographical context did effect the politicians of the day in New Zealand, Australia, South Africa, Jamaica and Kenya to introduce such a tax. Indeed, graded property tax systems, where land is taxed at a higher rate than improvements have been used in several Canadian provinces as well as several cities in the United States (Oates and Schwab, 1995; Brueckner, 1986; Wuensch et al, 2000).

The concept of land value

Classical economists have identified land, labour and capital as the three factors of production (Vickrey, 1999). Under 'capital' was implied all means of production that have been created through human effort while 'land' was primarily used to describe natural resources that were not created through human effort.

Land value in turn refers to the earnings accruing to land in the process of production. Where land is not put into productive use, the value will be based on the opportunity cost of not putting land in the production process. 'Opportunity cost' here refers to the next best alternative use that land could be put to. These earnings may be realized in loose form and expressed as rental income/value, for example annual, quarterly, monthly, weekly or daily rent. The earnings may also be realized in compact or discounted form and expressed as capital value. The capital value is the basis upon which the exchange price of the land will be considered. Land value therefore refers to a stream of income from land as a factor of production considered under a certain or definite period of time. Value in this case is tied to the income generating advantage of land. However, even land that is not put in the income generating process will still have its value derived on this basis by relying on the concept of opportunity cost. Opportunity cost would be subject to the prevailing land market conditions.

As a factor of production, land like any other commodity, is traded in the market. This means that the price (value) of land will be subject to the economics of demand and supply. In this respect, land becomes a unique commodity since it has unique demand and supply descriptions. Indeed, as a discipline, land economics is based on two basic concepts, namely:

- that the supply curve of land – as a commodity – is *perfectly inelastic*; and
- that the demand for land is *derived demand*.

Land is fixed in terms of geographical location. For that matter, all economic advantages provided by land must be utilized on site. Location is therefore crucial in determining land values because shortage in supply at one place cannot be made up for by surplus at another place. The value of land will be influenced by those economic factors pertaining to the area in which it is situated.

The immobility of land in turn influences its economic characteristics. Just as the land is fixed in geographical location, its supply too is generally considered as fixed. Because the supply of land is fixed, in theory, its supply curve is perfectly inelastic. This means that increases in the price of land from P1-P2 (as shown in Figure 1.1) arising from a shift in the demand curve from D1-D2 will not stimulate an increase in supply. The supply will remain the same no matter what the price increase is. This particular fact applies for land as a gift of nature that cannot be created by efforts of man. It also applies for land that has undergone capital investment by man. Some lands are uniquely developed to the extent that their supply is inelastic. For example, no matter what prices are offered for Fort Jesus in Mombasa, Kenya or the Pyramids in Giza, Egypt, there would be no increase in the physical supply of such lands. In theory, at least, this applies to all lands with only limited variation.

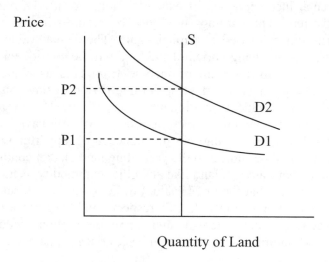

Figure 1.1   Demand and supply of land

The supply characteristics of land, as discussed above, have a significant impact on the levying of land value taxes. These taxes are levied on the assumption that they would not interfere with the supply of land and hence cause no disruption of the economic equilibrium. In practice, however, the supply of land for a particular use in a given area may change in the long run as more land is brought into that use. Even in the short run, land can be transferred within limits from one use to another, for example, through rezoning (e.g. converting a residential house to office space).

The demand for land, as such, is purely derived demand. Land is not demanded for its own sake, but virtually as a factor that is used for the production of goods and services. The demand for land will therefore depend on the demand for goods and services. For example, increases in the demand for housing will occasion an increased demand for residential land. Therefore, the demand of goods and services is what will determine the demand for land of a particular use. Since use is interchangeable, this will affect supply for that use and hence price. Demand for other goods and services and revenue from them will therefore determine the income accruing to the land for a particular use and hence its value.

Bases of land value taxation

There has been considerable debate as to whether the imposition of a land tax would have side effects or not. On the one hand there are those who hold the view that land taxation would not have any effects on the productive nature of land. On the other, there are those who hold the view that land taxation will indeed have an impact on the productive nature of the land. The introduction of a land tax may have foreseen and possible unforeseen consequences. It is therefore necessary to provide a brief theoretical basis for land taxation as such.

The view that taxation of land would not have any effect on the production characteristics of land is supported by two well-developed theories, respectively the theory of economic rent and the tax capitalisation theory.

Theory of economic rent

In micro-economic theory, economic rent simply refers to any payment accruing to a factor of production over and above payment that is necessary to keep it in production. The payment that is needed to keep the factor in production is known as 'transfer earnings' (Foldvary, 1999). Transfer earnings are payments that would remunerate all the factors involved in the production process at market rates. However, due to increase in demand a factor may earn more than transfer earnings. Depending on the nature of supply for that particular factor, payments over and above transfer earnings may be realised in the short run or in the long run.

If the supply curve of the factor is relatively elastic (i.e. the supply is responsive to increased demand), more factors will be attracted into the market to meet the increased demand and the surplus payment over and above transfer earnings would be eliminated in the long run. In this case the surplus earnings would be referred to as quasi-rent. Machinery and equipment, for example, would earn quasi-rent in the event of increased demand because they cannot be manufactured, assembled and delivered immediately to meet the increased demand.

On the other hand, if the supply curve of the factor is relatively inelastic (i.e, the supply would not relatively respond to increased demand), more factors would not be attracted into the market to meet the increased demand and the surplus payment over and above transfer earnings would persist in the long run. This is economic rent.

Land, being a gift of nature cannot be reproduced in greater quantities to meet increased demand (Foldvary, 1999). It is therefore, scarce by nature and fixed in supply. Any payment to land over and above the transfer earnings, is thus a surplus. As indicated above, transfer earnings essentially refer to payments made to maintain the current use of a factor (i.e. to ensure that its productive advantage would not be transferred to another use). Given that payment to land is in the form of a surplus, it is better to tax land – as such a tax will not affect the transfer earnings and thus will not cause distortions in the economy. By taxing only the surplus earnings (in respect of the land) that can be taxed without causing any interference in the market, a land tax conforms with at least one of the requirements of a good tax system: It minimises interference in economic decisions in otherwise efficient markets.

Tax capitalisation theory

The tax capitalisation theory is based on the assumption that whenever a tax is imposed on land as an asset, the capital value of the land is diminished by an amount equivalent to the capitalised value of the tax at the prevailing rate of interest. In essence it is assumed that subsequent land owners/buyers would first capitalise the annual tax then deduct it from the sale price. Hence the subsequent land owner/buyer would only pay a diminished price for the value of the land. The returns from such land would also be discounted net of tax; for example, capital value of land would be derived from rent less tax as an expense. In this way it is assumed that only the original landowner would bear the tax burden and that the tax cannot be shifted otherwise the burden would fall where it is not intended and cause disruption in the economy.

According to this theory the purchaser, or an investor in land would not be discouraged by mere imposition of tax. In this way, investors would not shift their capital to other sectors by way of tax consideration. However, the capitalisation theory presupposes the existence of the following conditions:

- an active land market so that values will reflect market forces rather than non-economic influences;
- the supply of land is inelastic with respect to changes in the returns on land, otherwise at least part of the tax would be shifted rather than capitalised;
- the pattern of future tax liabilities is foreseeable and fully anticipated;
- the government does not spend the tax revenue in a way that affects the value of services to the land
- the tax does not affect the rate at which returns to land are capitalised.

Tax as instrument of economic leverage

Various arguments have been put forward to discredit the proposition that a tax on land will not cause disruption of the economy as suggested by both the economic rent theory and the tax capitalisation theory. It has been argued that although the supply of land is generally fixed or completely inelastic to changes in price, supply for a particular use in a given area may change in the long run as more land is brought into use. Even in the short run land can be transferred – within limits – from one use to another (for example, converting residential use to office space or agricultural to residential) in a process known as occupational mobility of land. Although fixed in supply, land is capable of assuming alternative uses and although the physical limitation of land supply tends to have no or negligible economic significance, changes in its use may indeed be economically significant.

Many of the arguments against land taxation focus only on the negative aspects of the effects of a tax on land use as a fiscal tool. However, there is a further aspect to look at that could benefit the discourse on land taxation theory. Instead of limiting discussions to the merit of a land tax as a means of raising revenue, the scope of discussion on land taxation could generally be broadened to also include the non-fiscal aspects of land tax, i.e. its possible use as an instrument of economic leverage. There should be increased realisation that land as a primary factor of production and a land tax may therefore have potential as a strategic policy instrument for overall economic management. This would be especially so in developing countries where land constitutes a large proportion of factor input.   Land therefore maintains a significant influence in economic production hence by mere fiscal control of land use (factor input) the policy maker can directly influence the trend of economic performance for better results. However, the principles to which a good tax should adhere – as stated above – should not be forgotten in the process of attempting to attain non-fiscal goals.

Classification of property and land taxes

Taxes on property (including land) can be classified in three main categories depending on the choice of tax base. These categories are the following:

*   taxes based on the income derived from property ;
*   taxes based on area (i.e. property size); and
*   taxes based on rental or capital value (i.e. ad valorem).

According to this classification, there are taxes that are specifically levied in relation to land (e.g. annual land tax or a real property transfer tax). There are taxes that are generally levied on wealth/property and fall on land where land forms part of the property/wealth base of the taxable person (e.g. estate taxes or death duties). Furthermore, there are those taxes that are generally levied on income or expenditure and capture land (value) only indirectly in so far as land forms more or less important part of the income base[1] of the taxable person (e.g. income tax on rental income or value-added tax (VAT) on the acquisition of a house from a property developer).

---

[1] Income tax can generally not be equated to a land-based tax. An income tax targets income from whatever source. Where income is derived from real property, the tax will to some extent fall on the property and hence land could be an important object within the tax base. Land-based income is called rent. Rent and land value on the other hand are directly related since rent forms the basis of capital value. Taxing rent as a form of income therefore entails taxing land value. The main difference between annual rental value tax and income tax is that the former falls on hypothetical income while the latter falls on actual income. Secondly, annual rental value tax is a tax that is specifically designed to fall on rent while income tax is a general tax designed to fall on income and captures rent only where rent forms the basis of a specific income.

In some jurisdictions, mainly in developing countries, property taxes (be they on land only, or on land and improvements) are levied in relation to the size of the property. In some instances location and use will also be used to determine the tax payable.

For purposes of the discussion that follows, the focus will only be on those taxes levied with reference to the value of immovable property, and more specifically ad valorem property taxes.

Taxes based on rental or capital value

These are also known as *ad valorem* taxes. An ad valorem tax can be levied on an annual basis with reference to the rental or capital value of the property (e.g. a property tax), or it can be levied every time the taxable object (e.g. real property) is transferred by way of a transaction or otherwise (e.g. transfer tax). Capital value taxes could be based on a variety of bases, namely: capital improved value, unimproved land or 'site' value, improvement value only, improvement value plus site value, incremental value, etc. From these bases the following taxes can be generated:

Rental value

Rental value taxes are usually based on the net annual rent. In this case, a yearly rent that the property would most probably generate is determined. This we may call the gross annual rental value. From this statutory deductions or out-goings for maintenance, insurance, management costs etc. are made, resulting in a net annual value that is subject to tax.

It is important to note that the rental value tax is applicable whether the rent is realised or not in any one particular year. Even if the property remains unlet for a whole year, the tax is still levied because it is based on a hypothetical other than actual rent. This is its main difference from income-based taxes. The latter would consider the actual rent paid as the basis of taxation.

This tax has two main advantages. As it is levied on a broader tax base that includes land and buildings, it could, given the same or even a lower tax rate, yield more revenue than a tax on the value of land only. Secondly, it involves ease of assessment, as rents in one locality are comparable in a market situation. Its disadvantage on the other hand is that it has allocational defects. It may discourage investment in real property with investors preferring to invest in untaxed land uses or in the capital market.

Capital improved value

Most jurisdictions presently levying a property tax uses the capital value (i.e. market value) of the property for assessing tax liability. If the property consists of land and improvements, it is the single, combined value which has to be determined.

Unimproved land value

Unimproved land value tax or unimproved site value tax (USV) is levied on the capital value of the land assuming it is vacant. Any improvement on site is generally disregarded in the assessment of capital value. USV tax has several advantages:

- it encourages physical development in urban centres;
- it discourages ownership of land for speculative purposes;
- it is a simple tax to levy without many technical and administrative challenges; and
- the amounts to be raised can be determined in advance and therefore used for purposes of certainty in budgeting.

USV has been subject to certain criticisms especially regarding its regressive nature:

- it is difficult to determine how much of the land value is derived from the site or location value and how much from the reproducible assets and entrepreneurial expertise;
- related to the question of value is the contention that for the tax to be equitable it should be applied when land is first acquired; otherwise unearned increment is diffused through the purchase and sale of the property;
- it is regressive in terms of residential development because taxpayers with a lower income spend a higher percentage of their income on housing than do those on higher incomes. Subjecting them both to *ad valorem* tax therefore does not conform to the principle of equity;
- it is also regressive in terms of methods of assessment that tend to favour the rich against the poor; lower priced properties are many and change hands more frequently; assessors therefore may be

inclined to assess high-priced properties more conservatively than low-priced properties because sales comparables are scarce for high-priced properties that are owned by high-income earners;

- it favours large-scale development against small-scale development (such as owner-occupier home developers), who receive no income from the subject properties that they can in turn use to pay the tax; and

- it may involve allocational defects through a 'substitution effect'; the tax burden can be considered as 'qualitative' i.e. involving the choice of different types of uses, or 'quantitative' i.e. involving intensity of use. A qualitative choice is likely to deny other uses, which are equally important in the urban economy, their due share of land (e.g. when commercial use pushes out residential use); whereas quantitative choices on the other hand involve, as one example, cases where single-storey buildings are pulled down to facilitate the development of high-rise buildings under the same land-use category, a process that requires large capital outlay and may lead to unnecessary commitment of capital to real estate vis-a-vis development in other productive sectors lsuch as industry or agriculture.

Improvement value only

Taxes based on improvements, in contrast to USV, leaves out the site value and apply to the value of improvements only. This is appropriate in the case of the benefit principle. For example, if local taxes were being levied to finance and sustain services like waste collection, street lighting, road maintenance and so forth it would not be equitable to charge a site value tax. In this case, a vacant site adjacent to a site with a high-rise improvement on it would be paying the same amount of tax (assuming that both sites are similar in all other respects) yet the landowner of the vacant site would not have equal enjoyment of all these services. The level of development is an important consideration. A property with low-level development generally generates a lower demand for services than a property with high-level development.

Including the value of improvements in the tax base to finance provision of related services, may however discourage development. Secondly, valuing improvements on a regular basis for property tax purposes implies a more complex and costly process of valuation in comparison to USV. As improvements keep on changing every year due to new construction, extension or demolition, maintaining a capital improved system is administratively more cumbersome.

Site value plus improvement value

In some cases property taxes may be levied on both site and improvement values, as separate taxable objects. Although such a tax broadens the tax base, it necessitates assessed values for both the land and the improvements. Although some of the benefits of both a land only tax system as well a capital improved tax system can be gained, it is administratively costly and cumbersome to have separate values.

Other property-related taxes

Capital gains taxes

Taxes can also be based upon capital gains. In this case, if land forms part of the subject capital, land value will form the basis of the tax. Capital gains taxes include taxation of inheritance. This is a softer form of wealth tax because it is to be paid, not by the person who has worked to generate the wealth, but instead, by a person who simply stands to benefit from it. What is more, the payer does not have to find money to pay as it can be paid using part of the wealth.

Capital transfer taxes

There are taxes that fall upon capital (included) when it is being transferred. The transfer value would be the basis of the tax. Such taxes include stamp duty, real property transfer taxes and so forth. As far as these taxes may pertain to land as a possible or the only taxable object, they are unique in that they are only levied upon transfer of the land; unlike most of the land based taxes that are levied on regular basis, usually annually. The tax will not be levied as long as land does not change hands, irrespective how long it may take. On the other hand, it would apply as many times as land changes hands – even if these changes take place in less than a year.

Incremental land value taxes

Land tax can also be levied on the basis of incremental value. Under normal circumstances, land values tend to increase over time. This is because population continues to rise against a limited supply of land. Land resources therefore tend to become scarcer over time. Also, an increasing population means increased demand for goods and services that will engage land as a factor of production. The scarcity element or shortage in supply creates the economic rent. An incremental value tax is therefore a fiscal tool that is sometimes used for capturing economic rent from the landowners and redistributing it back to the broad community – especially in areas where unimproved land is held for speculative purposes.

Value Added Tax (VAT)

VAT is another general tax usually imposed on the process of production or consumption of goods and services. In some cases the tax base could be wide enough to capture taxable transactions related to landed property. Depending on the circumstances, the rental or capital value of land could be used to determine the tax payable.

Conclusions

Despite the apparent merits and demerits of a land value tax from a theoretical point of view, the choice of tax base is more often based on the very specific circumstances faced by the relevant taxing authority. Socio-political views, historic factors, as well as practical realities seem to be the deciding factors – as will become evident in the following chapters.

References

Bentick, B.L. (1979), 'The Impact of Taxation and Valuation Practices on the Timing and Efficiency of Land Use', *Journal of Political Economy*, vol. 87 no. 4, pp. 859-868.

Brueckner, J.K. (1986), 'A Modern Analysis of the Effects of Site Value Taxation', *National Tax Journal*, vol. 39, pp. 49-58.

Connellan, O. (2004), '*Land Value Taxation in Britain: Experience and Opportunities*', Lincoln Institute of Land Policy, Cambridge, MA, United States.

Douglas, Lord (1961), '*Land Value Rating: Theory and Practice*', Christopher Johnson, London.

Foldvary, F.E. (1999), 'The Ethics of rent', in K.C. Wenzer (ed.), *Land Value Taxation: The Equitable and Efficient Source of Public Finance*, M.E. Sharpe Inc., New York, pp. 184-204.

George, H. (1879), '*Progress and Poverty*', Modern Library, New York, United States.

Harvey, J. (2000), '*Urban Land Economics*', Fifth Edition, Palgrave.

Joshi, T.M., Anjanaiah, N. and Bhende, S.V. (1968), '*Studies in the Taxation of Agricultural Land and Income in India*', Asia Publishing House, Bombay.

K'Akumu, O.A. (2000), 'Land Taxation for Sustainable Development in Kenya', *Journal of Property Tax Assessment and Administration*, vol. 5 no. 2, pp. 3-15.

K'Akumu, O.A. (1999), 'Land Taxation Policy in Kenya', *Journal of Property Tax Assessment and Administration*, vol. 4 no. 3, pp. 3-15.

Lichfield, N. and Connellan, O. (1997), '*Land Value Taxation in Britain for the Benefit of the Community: History, Achievements and Prospects*', Working Paper, Lincoln Institute of Land Policy, Cambridge, MA, United States, pp. 1-69.

Lindholm, R.W. (1965), 'Land Taxation and Economic Development', *Land Economics*, vol. 41, pp. 121-130.

Mathis, E.J. and Zech, C.E. (1982), 'The Economic Effects of Land Value Taxation', *Growth and Change*, October, pp. 2-5.

McCluskey, W. (ed.) (1999), '*Property Tax: An International Comparative Review*', Ashgate Publishing Limited, Aldershot.

McCluskey, W.J. and Franzsen, R.C.D. (2001), '*Land Value Taxation: A Case Study Approach*', Working Paper, Lincoln Institute of Land Policy, Cambridge, MA, United States, pp. 1-109.

Mill, J. (1824), '*Elements of Political Economy*', Baldwin, Cradock and Joy, London.

Mill, J.S. (1848), '*Collected Works, Vol. III, Principles of Political Economy with some of their Applications to Social Philosophy*', University of Toronto Press (1965), Toronto, Canada.

Mills, D. (1981), 'The Non-neutrality of Land Value Taxation', *National Tax Journal*, vol. 34, pp. 1125-1129.

Musgrave, R.A. and Musgrave, P.B. (1989), '*Public Finance in Theory and Practice*', 5th Edition, McGraw-Hill, New York.

Netzer, R. (1966), '*Economics of the Property Tax*', The Brookings Institute, Washington DC.

Netzer, R. (ed.) (1998), '*Land Value Taxation: Can it and Will it Work Today?*', Lincoln Institute of Land Policy, Cambridge, MA, United States.

Oates, W.E. and Schwab, R.M. (1995), '*The Impact of Urban Land Taxation: The Pittsburg Experience*', Working Paper, WP92W01, Lincoln Institute of Land Policy, Cambridge, MA, United States, pp. 1-33.

OECD (1988), '*Taxation of Net Wealth, Capital Transfers and Capital Gains of individuals*', Organisation for Economic Co-operation and Development, OECD, Paris.

Quesnay, F. (1756), '*The General Maxims for the Economic Government of an Agricultural Kingdom*', in R.L. Meek (1963).

Ricardo, D. (1817), '*The Principles of Political Economy and Taxation*', Dutton, New York.

Skaburskis, A. and Tomalty, R. (1997), 'Land Value Taxation and Development Activity: The Reaction of Toronto and Ottawa Developers, Planners and Municipal Finance Officials', *Canadian Journal of Regional Science,* Autumn, pp. 401-417.

Skaburskis, A. (1995), 'Consequences of Taxing Land Value', *Journal of Planning Literature,* vol. 10, pp. 3-21.

Smith A. (1950), '*An Inquiry into the Nature and Causes of the Wealth of Nations',* *Vol. II,* Methuen, London.

Tideman, N. (1982), 'A Tax on Land Value is Neutral', *National Tax Journal,* vol. 35 no. 1, pp. 109-111.

Tideman, N. (1993), '*The Economics of Efficient Taxes on Land*' , Working Paper, Lincoln Institute of Land Policy, Cambridge, MA, United States, pp. 1-43.

Tideman, N. (1999), 'Taxing Land is Better than Neutral: Land taxes, Land Speculation and the Timing of Development', in K.C. Wenzer (ed.), *Land Value Taxation: The Equitable and Efficient Source of Public Finance,* M.E. Sharpe Inc., New York, pp. 109-133.

Vickrey, W. (1999), 'A Modern Theory of Land Taxation', in K.C. Wenzer (ed.), *Land Value Taxation: The Equitable and Efficient Source of Public Finance,* M.E. Sharpe Inc., New York, pp. 13-16.

Wald, H.P. (1959), '*Taxation of Agricultural Land in Under-developed Economies',* Harvard University Press, Cambridge.

Wildasin, D.E. (1982), 'More on the Neutrality of Land Taxation', *National Tax Journal,* vol. 35, no. 1, pp. 105-108.

Wuensch, J., Kelly, F. and Hamilton, T. (2000), '*Land Value Taxation Views, Concepts and Methods: A Primer*', Working Paper, WP00JW2, Lincoln Institute of Land Policy, Cambridge, MA, United States, pp. 1-18.

Youngman, J.M. (1993), '*The Role of* Land *Taxation in Tax and Land Policy*', Working Paper, Lincoln Institute of Land Policy, Cambridge, MA, United States, pp. 1-7.

Youngman, J.M. and Malme, J.H. (1994), '*An International Survey of Taxes on Land and Buildings* ', Kluwer, Boston, United States.

Chapter 2

Land Taxation: The Case of Jamaica

William J. McCluskey

Introduction

The island of Jamaica is situated in the Northern Caribbean Sea and is the regions third largest island after Cuba and Hispaniola (Haita and the Dominican Republic). The country is divided into three counties, Cornwall, Middlesex and Surrey and fourteen parishes. The total area of the island is approximately 4,411 square miles or about 2.8 million acres. It is 146 miles long and approximately 51 miles wide at its widest point. The terrain of Jamaica is in the most part rugged and the economic use of a large part of the island is dictated, to a great extent, by the size of the parcels of land, the elevation, the depth and quality of the soil. The surface of the island is extremely mountainous, particularly the central range which is known as the Blue Mountains and reaches an elevation of 7,400 feet above sea level. This terrain has been an important consideration in the development of the property tax system of the island.

Everywhere in both the developed and developing world the concept of taxation as a means of providing a budget for government is well known and is often an entity to avoid. In particular, property tax has had a long and notorious history. From the very birth of mankind there was a requirement to give to God in sacrifice one tenth (tithe) of the fruits, crops and animals produced each year from the land.

The maxims of taxation, as declared by Adam Smith in his book Wealth of Nations (1776) of equity, certainty, convenience of payment and economy in collection has long governed the imposition and maintenance of property taxation. Jamaica has had a long, interesting and diverse history of property taxation. It was first introduced in the mid 17th century under British administration and has reflected the social, economic and political climate of the country at the various stages of its history and development. The first tax imposed on land and real property was the Quit Rent. This tax was a nominal payment of one penny per acre. This was followed in 1956 by a property tax initially based on capital value. However, after three years of valuation field operations and the lack of completion of the first parish this approach was abandoned. Capital value as the basis for property tax was proving too costly and time consuming. The basis of the property tax was changed to land value and all rates and charges on land would thereafter be levied on this basis.

By 1974 the entire island was revalued under the provision of the Land Valuation Act (1956) on the basis of the 'unimproved value' of the land. This basis for the property tax system remains in operation today with only a few minor amendments made to the legislation (Lyons and McCluskey, 1999). This chapter examines the property tax system, the historical background of the tax, and will focus on a number of key aspects such as the tax base, legislation, the property tax rate, local government reform and the collection of the tax. It will also attempt to provide an explanation of the strengths and weaknesses of the current system and highlight possible changes with regard to the future of the tax.

Historical background to land and buildings taxation

Prior to 1903 four taxes were imposed on land under the provision of the 1901 Valuation Law:

•   the Quit Rent of one penny per acre per annum. This was a nominal tax on acreage to maintain ownership of the land by the Crown. Non-payment led to forfeiture of the land but there was the provision for redemption on the payment of a lump sum usually related to the value of the land;
•   the House Tax, which was a tax on the value of each dwelling unit;
•   the Crop Tax levied on cultivated land; and
•   the Graduated Holding Tax levied on all parcels of land.

The Quit Rent and the Graduated Holding Tax was paid to central government, while the House Tax and the Crop Tax was paid to the Parochial Board (parish council/local authority) in the relevant parishes. Tax collected on real property and land was shared on the basis of five twelfths to central government and seven twelfths to the local authorities. Property tax revenue at this time accounted for approximately 64 per cent of all direct taxes levied in the country.

A review by a select Committee of the Legislative Council on Real Property Tax in 1903 resulted in the then existing land taxation law being repealed except for the Quit Rent Law. In 1903 a new Property Tax Law was enacted. This Law imposed a single property tax rate of 8 pence in every £10 of capital value of all real property. Section 13 of the 1903 Law was considered to allow within this rate the inclusion of the 1d per acre Quit Rent. Additionally, all taxes including property taxes had to be paid directly into the Consolidated Fund, a situation that existed until quite recently when a change in the legislation now sees property tax revenue going directly to local authorities.

Funding of local authorities was provided for under the new Law by way of a General Rate and a Service Rate. Service rates paid for the provision of services such as street lighting, fire protection, sanitation and the provision of sewerage in Kingston and St. Andrew. The General Rate was in effect a compensation element paid to local authorities and used for infrastructure and economic development. The Law set the limits at which these rates could be charged.

The 1901 Valuation Law provided for the creation and maintenance of a valuation roll which remained as the fiscal cadastre for the 1903 Law. This roll was created from 'ingivings'. In essence, the Law required that all persons in possession of real property had to furnish to the Collector of Taxes of the parish in which the property was located a true and correct ingiving stating: the description of the property, the location, acreage, particulars of tenure, area under cultivation, type of cultivation, description of all buildings, dwelling houses, warehouses and factories on the property; stating the value against each item and finally giving a gross value for the entire property. Landowners were required to submit three values under this law:

- the annual gross present value of the real property;
- the actual or presumable net annual rental value of the real property; and
- the presumable net value of the ground forming the site of the real property in its natural and unimproved condition in its then present surroundings.

Revision of the 1901 Valuation Roll took place in 1911, 1929 and 1937. These revisions constituted copying the previous roll with the exception of those properties that had changed hands or had been subdivided. The 1901 roll was based on a capital value structure of 'self-assessed ingivings' by the landowners themselves. As Risden (1979) suggested, the 1901 roll was little more than a cadastral register, with the values in the majority of cases varying with the individual landowner's conscience. In the late 1930s the property tax system came under attack as its obvious inequalities and weaknesses were exposed. The basis of the roll being landowner's 'ingivings' meant that values varied with individuals estimates of value or their ability to negotiate with the Collector of Taxes who approved the values. This was further compounded by the fact that the values on the rolls were out-dated and the valuation staff did not have the expertise to properly determine the value of large agricultural holdings and commercial properties. It was these issues and anomalies that resulted in a resolution being moved in the Legislative Council that called for the establishment of a Commission to investigate and make recommendations in dealing with the problems of land valuation in the island.

Reports on the property tax system in Jamaica

A Royal Commission under the chairmanship of Bloomberg was established in 1943 to examine and report on the problems as well as to make recommendations as to what changes should to be made and the means of effecting these changes. The Bloomberg Committee's report was a comprehensive one and 'can surely be said to be the bow from which the arrow of a modern system of land valuation was sent forward.' The Commission further recommended the adoption of the unimproved value system (site value or value of the bare land) as the valuation basis for the assessment of property tax. This recommendation was further endorsed by other teams of international experts as a mechanism to discourage the holding of land in either an idle or under-utilized state.

Other recommendations included:

- a permanent Central Valuation Department be set up to deal with valuations for the purpose of taxation: the collection of land taxes to remain the function of the Collector General's Department (now the Inland Revenue Department);
- government to obtain the services of a Valuation Commissioner who has had experience of the practical administration and application of the unimproved value system;
- revaluations should be quinquennial;
- quit rents be abolished;
- property tax be abolished and that revenue from all rates and taxes on land to go to the local authorities;
- ingivings be required from owners that should show *inter alia* unimproved value and capital value of the real property.

These recommendations were accepted in principle but the government had great difficulty in obtaining the services of a qualified Valuation Commissioner and did not succeed in the endeavour until 1950 with the appointment of Mr. Harris, a senior valuer from the Inland Revenue Department in London. He faced a difficult situation including the lack of suitably qualified staff, unavailability of maps to form the basis of the revaluation task and the complacency of government to whom the revaluation was perceived as just another name for higher taxation.

Mr. C.C.H. Hipgrave, M.B.E., arrived in 1951 to deal with the problem of revaluation and to put the necessary framework in place for this exercise. His report gave an invaluable appreciation of the difficulties involved in undertaking a revaluation exercise. His suggestions formed the basis of the report by the Mission of the International Bank for Reconstruction and Development in 1952 following a hurricane that devastated the island in 1951. It was recommended that large-scale planimetric maps be produced from aerial photographs for the city of Kingston and the other principal towns of the island as well as cadastral maps, delineating boundaries for title purposes.

In 1954, Professor J.R. and Mrs. Hicks were invited to visit Jamaica to investigate and report on the revenue system of the island and to make recommendations to enable government to more efficiently use its revenue sources. The issue of property taxes was addressed under the section of the report dealing with local finance. They recommended the retaining of capital value as the basis for property tax and further suggested that the progressive rates applied to property tax should be reconsidered in favour of a flat rate.

In 1955, the government sought through the United Nations, the services of a qualified advisor practised in the unimproved value system. This yielded the services of Mr J.F.N. Murray, from Australia whose report of findings and recommendations was presented in June 1956. This essentially served as the blue-print for the development of the system of land taxation based on unimproved values. The report also contained the draft of a Valuation Law that was substantially the Bill that was presented to Parliament. This comprehensive report dealt with several key aspects including, the incidence of land tax, tax rates, an appreciation of the valuation problems, the valuation of improvements, sales analyses, the collation of sales evidence, revaluation preparation, staff requirements and the legislation necessary to give legal effect to the recommendations.

Mr. J.M. Copes (also an Australian), was appointed the first Commissioner of Valuation with the responsibility for implementing Mr. Murray's recommendations. He piloted, organized and established the Land Valuation Division, under the Ministry of Agriculture, and directed the programme of revaluation from 1956 to 1961 (based on the Land Valuation Act, 73 of 1956).

The legal framework of property valuation

The Land Valuation Act 1957

The Land Valuation Act (as amended) remains the primary legislation under which property values are determined. From a study of the proceedings of the House of Representative as recorded in the Jamaica Hansard (Session 1956 – 57 No.3), the following were the two major objectives in introducing the Land Valuation Bill (Lyons and McCluskey, 1999). Firstly, it was considered desirable to introduce a tax base which:

- did not tax a person in the efforts he put into the land;
- provided a means of taxing values created by the community at large; and
- discouraged the withholding of land from use.

Secondly, the current system of valuation was unsatisfactory for the following reasons:

- it placed too great a reliance on the voluntary declaration of value by the owner as a basis for preparing the valuation rolls;
- it was pointed out that, by and large, individual inspections of land were not made under the present system;
- it was not difficult to see that the present system would lead to competitive under assessment on the part of landowners with the inevitable result that the rolls would lack uniformity – a feature which is generally regarded as a *sine qua non* for a rational system of land taxation;
- anomalies and inequalities were wide spread due not only to the basic defects on the system but also to the failure to undertake a general revaluation.

The Land Valuation Act of 1956 made provision for the administration of the Act by the Commissioner of Valuation, under the direction of the Minister. The Commissioner was required to make a valuation of the unimproved and improved value of every parcel of land in each district. The parishes formed district boundaries for the purpose of the Act. The Commissioner was required to set the date at which each parcel of land was to be valued, however, it was under the authority of the Minister to bring the valuation roll into effect. The Act made provision for a process of appeal for persons not agreeing with the valuation of the Commissioner. This was initially to a Valuation Board, today the appeal is to the Revenue Court, with further appeal to the Court of Appeal.

Although the Act provided for the determination of two bases of value, the unimproved and improved value, the rolls were published with only one set of values i.e. unimproved values. The following extract from Ministry Paper No.4 (1959) – Revaluation of Land: Proposed System of Taxation, explains why only one base was provided:

> The house will recall that is was intended that property tax and parish rates, the two principal forms of land tax, should be based on unimproved values as defined in the Land Valuation Law, that is to say, on the actual market value of the land exclusive of the values of any buildings, cultivation's, or other improvements on/or attached to the land. On the other hand, it was intended that charges for particular services, such as water and fire, should be based on improved values.

> It was found, however, that to attempt to compile two sets of valuation rolls would take so long that it might well have taken more than ten years to complete the valuations of the whole island. Moreover, it was thought that there was no important reason for insisting that special rates should be charged on improved values. The availability of special services in a given area in itself enhances the unimproved value of the land and the removal of all elements that discourage improvement of the land was though to be better secured by having a simple uninformed system applicable to every type of rate. It was therefore decided that only one valuation roll should be prepared, that is to say, a roll based on unimproved values and the property tax, parish rates and service charges would all be based on that roll. It will be necessary to amend the Land Valuation Law, 1956 to provide for this matter.

The Law was subsequently amended by deleting the improved value of the land as one of the particulars required to be set out in the valuation roll in respect of each parcel. If, however, at some future time, it is decided to revert to the two bases, the Act provided for the Minister to prescribe by regulation that the improved value of the land is an additional particular to be shown on the valuation roll.

Development of the property cadastre

It was to take Jamaica approximately 18 years from the passing of the 1956
legislation to complete the first revaluation of the entire island. This meant
that some parishes were being revalued for the first time since the 1937
revaluation. The programme commenced in 1956 under the direction of the
Valuation Department, a Division, under the then Ministry of Agriculture and
Lands. The office was structured with a small nucleus of trained professional
valuers who directed operations together with a work force of 'para valuers'
who were trained locally to carry out certain mass valuation functions and to
be responsible for the bulk of the valuations which were mainly rural and
comprised of relatively low value parcels (Lyons and McCluskey, 1999).
They were also responsible for the referencing and identification of parcels
and would sketch these on a map to allow for the ascribing of the unique geo-
code map based reference numbers. This exercise was based on the
development of an eleven digit reference number comprising a map, grid,
enclosure and parcel number called the 'Valuation Number' which uniquely
identifies parcels by virtue of ownership and use.

It had been widely held prior to 1956 that a cadastral survey was a prerequisite for the establishment of a fiscal cadastre. However, in his report Mr
Murray not only disagreed with this view but offered an alternative to the
matter of valuation and the cadastre. He wrote:

> A detailed cadastral survey is not essential for the valuation purposes but its
> existence would make the task of approval easier and would ensure, with
> certainty, the identification of each parcel and the location of its boundaries.

> The cost of production of such a map would not, in my opinion, be justified,
> and the additional information obtained from precise surveys would not
> warrant the huge cost involved, because most of the difficulties of location
> and identification are referable to small properties which yield little in
> revenue, further, a detailed survey would take many years to complete while
> the valuation is urgently needed.

> There is available, in Jamaica, a considerable volume of information which
> might be used for or adapted to valuation purposes and, as the valuation
> proceeds, a sketch map, with admitted imperfections, might be compiled and
> would show the mosaic of ownerships. The preparation of the valuation map
> would proceed, *pari passu*, with the work of appraisal and the new valuations
> might be applied to parishes without waiting for the completion of the whole
> survey.

However, in undertaking the revaluation programme which commenced in 1957 after the establishment of the Land Valuation Division it was necessary to have some sort of map based identification of the parcels forming the valuation roll. The change in the methodology of preparing the new valuation roll was fundamental. At the time of establishing the Land Valuation Division the maps, plane and aerial photographs available included:

- topographical sheets covering the whole island at a scale of 1:50.000;
- general map of Jamaica at a scale of 1:250,000;
- aerial photographs taken in 1941 covering the whole island, at a scale of 1:50,000;
- aerial photographs taken between 1951 and 1953 covering the whole island to a scale of 1:12,5000;
- aerial photographs of urban areas taken in 1954 to a scale of 1:6,000;
- cadastral sheets to a scale of 1:15,840 covering several parishes;
- plans at Titles Office; and
- estate plans and maps.

The number of holdings to be valued at this time was estimated to be approximately 350,000, with over 60 per cent estimated to be small, low value rural holdings with no precisely defined boundaries which were expected to yield low tax revenues. Additionally, registered titles existed for approximately 45 per cent of the total number of parcels island-wide. The majority of these registrations existed in the urban centres where, the requirements of loan financing, mortgages, and so on, made such registration a pre-requisite. In many of the rugged rural areas of Jamaica this was not possible. It was against this background that the revaluation programme was executed. The mapping and valuation strategies were then developed to produce a fiscal cadastre capable of justifying the revenue yield.

The valuation base maps were produced at a scale of 1:12,500 using the various aerial photographs. This produced 248 maps with grid lines extending 30,000 feet in easting and 20,000 in northings. All available survey plans and estate maps in respect of properties in excess of 8 hectares (20 acres) were plotted on the base map to produce field sheets showing the mosaic of ownership. The blank spaces were completed by site investigations and surveys in the field. These surveys were not very precise though adequate enough to establish ownership and values of these 'missing holdings'. The field work led to an increase in the number of parcels in St. Catherine from 39,481 on the old roll to 41,404 on the new roll. Ownership for unregistered parcels were established by the field exercise using 'owners return forms', similar to ingivings previously used in the preparation of the 1901 valuation roll.

Larger properties had to be inspected in detail and inventories of soil type, slope categories and land use capabilities documented. This record is still available and utilized in more recent revaluation and valuation exercises. The smaller parcels were grouped in classes, with each class inspected and sales analyzed. Valuations were then made on the basis of value standards arrived at after careful analysis of recent transactions, topography, land use and so forth.

The data gathered on parcel characteristics and environmental factors in addition to those on ownership and values during this and subsequent programmes are an essential ingredient of a Land Information System and form the basis of the development of the Geographic Information System and a digital cadastre which is in the final stages of development.

The National Land Agency

The National Land Agency (NLA) was created as a result of the need for Jamaica to deliver an integrated, efficient approach to providing a transparent land information system and to meet the objectives of the 1996 National Land Policy. The NLA is principally a merger of the Office of Titles, Surveys Division and Land Valuation and Estates Department. The rationale for this merger was expressed in terms of promoting tenure security, sustainable taxation and a decision support structure for the citizens of Jamaica. It is absolutely clear that these structural changes will have a significant and positive effect on the primary functions of the Land Valuation Division in terms of future revaluations. Principally, the integrating of the various disparate databases (Titles, Surveys and Land Valuation) into one main NLA controlled database will have major benefits. Linked to this, the development of a spatial referencing system will create an environment that will provide the base data for all subsequent revaluations.

Among the Agency's objectives is an efficient approach to streamlining the administration and management of land, in particular government owned lands. The Agency is undertaking progammes to:

- establish an efficient and transparent land divestment and land titling system;
- create modern cadastral and other maps for Jamaica; and
- develop modern information systems to support the sustainable development of Jamaica's resources.

Land Valuation Division

The current Land Valuation Division (LVD) of the National Land Agency has its origins in 1957 with the passing of the Land Valuation Act 1957. Since its inception the Land Valuation Division under the powers of the Land Valuation Act has responsibility to undertake a revaluation of every parcel of land. Given that land valuation is now a division within an Executive Agency, the statutory role of the Commissioner of Land Valuations (appointed under Section 16(a) of the Revenue Administration Act) would appear to be subsumed within the role of Director of Land Valuation. The structure of the LVD is based around four regions and given the geographic nature of Jamaica this regional structure provides for an important local presence in terms of the implementing and maintaining valuation rolls.

Land ownership and tenure

The issue of land ownership, use and rights is a particularly sensitive issue, and more so since the 1830s when the mass of the population first earned the right to hold landed property. One of the major problems facing Jamaica, and most developing countries, is the inaccessibility and unaffordability of land to large groups of the population, particularly low-income households. The unavailability of legally accessible and affordable land has contributed to the chronic problems of squatting and other illegal development on both government and private lands. Given the importance that each Jamaican attaches to land it is not surprising that Jamaica has had a land registration system for some considerable time. Until 1889, The Island Records Office was the sole recorder of land registration. In the same year the Registration of Titles Act was passed which institutionalised land registration under a modified Torrens Registration System. This system provides:

- the state guarantee of title;
- boundary identification;
- precise survey of parcel; and
- an assurance fund.

The registration system unfortunately does not provide for mandatory registration. Property owners who recognise the benefits of the system seek to register their land holdings, whilst others hold property at common law and private conveyancing. This creates a rather fragmented picture with a mosaic of land held with and without title registration. It is estimated that Jamaica contains approximately 680,000 land parcels of varying sizes of which less than 55 per cent have a registered title. There is a reluctance on the part of land owners to register their lands due primarily to high survey fees, advertising charges and legal fees. To facilitate the implementation of the tenure regularization and cadastral mapping programme, the government has agreed to provide incentives for voluntary title registration within certain geographic areas. These incentives will take the form of waivers of transfer tax and stamp duties for property registration regularization, waiver of sub-division approval fees, and the waiver of Natural Resources and Conservation Authority permit fees where necessary.

There are also other problems related to other forms of traditional land ownership such as 'family lands'. Although having no legal status, family land can be defined as land that passes undivided to a group of relatives, with each person having customary rights. 'Family lands' as a term means, that the number of persons entitled to make a legal claim is so great that no identifiable group can be deemed to be the owner. However, the primary form of land ownership is freehold and leasehold. Freehold ownership is proved through the registered title, which is superior to the common law title and is considered to be conclusive evidence of ownership. Financing is often inaccessible to persons who lack a registered title as proof of land ownership.

In view of the social and economic benefits which flow from possessing registered titles the government is hoping that the newly established mechanisms to make the process simpler, quicker and less costly will result in more widespread registration. The development of a National Land Policy in 1996 has sought to establish the framework needed for Jamaica to become more progressive and modern in its approaches to land administration, geographic information management systems and land development planning. At present the Torrens system is being underpinned with the development of a digital cadastre of parcels under the Land Titling Project. At present the National Land Agency manages certificates of title for around 390,000 land parcels which are held in manual files. The scale of the problem becomes more evident when one considers that this system has to store some 4.3 million documents. The solution is to electronically archive titles and supporting documents such as caveats and plans. The application will provide a repository for all land parcels and be available for government departments. In addition, the public will be able to avail of the system for the purchase of maps. A number of initiatives in support of e-government have been launched. In January 2003 the National Land Agency introduced *eLandjamaica*. It is an internet based service that provides selected title, valuation and digital map information to the agencies customers.

Spatial mapping

The country's geographic data management polices and objectives were enunciated in the National Land Policy (1996). They included the development and implementation of land information systems and practices for proper planning, development and management of land and to ensure that land and land related data information is readily available as a tool for a variety of other activities.

Fundamental to the optimal use of geographic information systems, is the availability of current, complete and accurate textual and graphic data. It is critical that common interest data such as topographic maps, parcel maps, socio-economic and land use data are collected and structured in a database to be readily accessed to be used for decision making. The country's maps are severely out-of-date, the most recent maps are the 1:50,000 metric series that was done twenty years ago, and are based on photographs taken in the late 1970s. The last comprehensive large scale mapping of the capital city is over 40 years old and was based on 1950s photographs. Sectoral consultations revealed that priority data sets were critical to the national GIS infrastructure. These are base maps, parcels, administrative, environmental, utility networks and transportation data sets and related meta-databases.

The Government is spearheading initiatives to create a comprehensive digital base map and a digital parcel index map of the island. Through an integrated government initiative the National Land Agency is coordinating the preparation of a digital cadastral index map for the island (DaCosta, 2003). The NLA in collaboration with the Forestry Department and the National Works Agency are currently creating the cadastral index for the parishes of Trelawny, St. Ann and Manchester. The World Bank under the Public Sector Modernization Programme has provided funds to outsource the preparation of the cadastral index for Kinston and St. Andrew and St. James. It is estimated that the cadastral index mapping exercise for the island will be completed in two years, at an approximate cost of J$51 million, provided that fund and staff are available.

Local government reform and current structure

The institution of local government has existed in Jamaica for over 300 years, having been established in about 1662 (Miller, 1996). The original system was essentially imported from England and was based on local authorities, which had jurisdiction within their parishes for the relief of the poor and maintenance of roads. This 'vestry' based system remained relatively unchanged for some 200 years, until 1865 when the main changes that were effected was the creation of 14 parishes councils (from 22). In addition, there was an expansion of the role of local government to include public markets, abattoirs, public health, water supplies, fire protection, street lighting and the operation of gas works. In Jamaica the 'Parish' is the name given to the unit local government administration. In addition to the metropolitan area of Kingston and St. Andrew which, although comprising two parishes, is a single local government unit, the island is divided into twelve parishes, viz., St. Thomas, Portland, St. Mary, St. Ann, Trelawny, St. James, Hanover, Westmoreland, St. Elizabeth, Manchester, Clarendon and St. Catherine.

In 1985 the then government transferred almost all of the major functions of the parish councils to central government agencies, for example, public health went to the Ministry of Health, roads to the Ministry of Construction, and public cleansing and public markets went to agencies of the Ministry of Local Government. Local government has essentially deteriorated since the mid 1980s both in respect of financing and local autonomy.

The Local Government Reform Process was launched in 1994. The present government of Jamaica firmly believes that there is no substitute for the direct involvement of the public and their comments in the decision making process. A strong and vibrant system of decentralized administration is essential to the achievement of good governance. The government therefore seeks to create modern local authorities with the capacity, vision and resource base necessary to deliver the range of services for which they are responsible, as well as appropriate mechanisms for accountability and transparency. The Local Government Reform Programme had as its aim:

> ...to establish a strong, viable and vibrant system of decentralized administration through which citizens in their communities and within their parishes can become more involved and have greater control over local affairs.

The specific objectives of the Reform Programme are:

- restoration of functions and responsibilities, which were removed from local government, and rehabilitation of the councils;
- establishment of new arrangements for the financing of local government which will allocate to them adequate and independent sources of revenue, and will give local authorities effective control over these sources of revenue;
- to up-grade the institutional capability of local authorities to ensure that they are able to perform their functions in an efficient and cost-effective manner;
- to effect a comprehensive revision of all out-dated legislation which presently constitute a major constraint to the effective performance of the councils; and
- to examine the present distribution of service responsibilities between central and local.

To meet the aim and objectives it was considered imperative that a process of financial reform was required which would seek to provide parish councils with adequate and independent sources of revenue. Up to 1973, local rates provided the means of financing major property related services delivered at the local level. The local rates included:

- sanitation rate which was intended to cover the costs of public cleansing services;
- lighting rate which generated revenues to meet the cost of street lights;
- fire rate which covered the costs of fire services;
- parish or corporate rate which contributed to meeting the administrative costs and general expenditure of parish councils;
- water rate to pay for water consumption and to meet debt servicing charges in respect of loans, which had been borrowed to construct water schemes; and
- municipal improvement rate was imposed on communities/schemes which were beneficiaries of special improvement works.

Then in 1974 these separate rates were merged with the property tax and all revenue collected was paid into the Consolidated Fund. This served to disconnect the revenue and expenditure functions leading to an excessive and growing dependence upon central government funds. Parishes were then given a grant in lieu of the property tax and up until 1996, 90 per cent of the revenue required to fund local services came in the form of a deficit grant from central government. On the 1 April 1996 the situation altered, to where parishes are now in receipt of land tax revenue. Parishes will continue to receive grants or contributions from central government, however, this will be generally confined to:

- grants in lieu of taxes for government owned property. Under the present legislation this type of property is exempt;
- specific grants in respect of social/welfare services such as poor relief, minor water supplies and local housing;
- support for traditional central government functions such as, emergency relief and disaster mitigation.

The land tax is specifically aligned to meet the cost of property related services including;

- expansion and maintenance of street lighting;
- collection and disposal of refuse;
- repairs to fire stations;
- community infrastructure and civic improvements; and
- rehabilitation of parochial and farm roads.

The re-introduction of local rates to parish councils was seen as an important step in building the link between the taxpayer who is the direct beneficiary of the service provided by the tax. They provide far greater flexibility in future adjustments to reflect increases in costs of delivering services. In addition, local rates provide dedicated financing for the various services, and facilitates greater citizen choice and responsibility in demanding services.

The main sources of revenue to be transferred to the parish councils included the land tax, motor vehicle license fees, spirit and trade licences and the power to set fees and user charges for services under their jurisdiction.

Importance of the land tax

Prior to April 1996 revenue raised from the land tax was paid directly into the Consolidated Fund. Parish councils had extremely limited sources of own revenue amounting to only 10 per cent of their total revenue. More importance is however now being attached to land tax as it will represent an important and growing source of independent revenue. Figure 2.1 illustrates the breakdown of the various sources of revenue available to councils. It is clear that specific grants and general grants dominate the revenue with approximately 52 per cent. However, property tax is still a significant revenue earner representing some 27 per cent of total revenue and 55 per cent of own revenue (excluding grants).

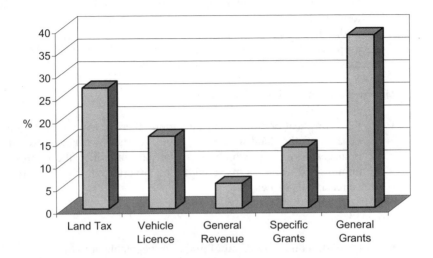

Figure 2.1   Sources of revenue available to Parish Councils

Valuation definitions

All land in Jamaica is valued in accordance with unimproved value as defined in the Land Valuation Act 1956. Valuations are based on the market value of the land, that is, the price you would expect to receive if you were selling the land alone. This disregards the value of any improvements on the land, such as buildings or crops. Within the valuation exercise the following factors are taken into account, area of parcel, location, use, land prices in the area, zoning, development potential, topography and land capabilities. The following statutory definitions prescribe the nature of the interest to be valued. The various definitions relating to the value base are contained in the Land Valuation Act 1956 (Law 73 of 1956, came into force on 18 January 1957).

Unimproved value means:

•   in relation to unimproved land the capital sum which the fee simple of the land together with any licence or other right or privilege (if any) for the time being affecting the land, might be expected to realise if offered for sale on such reasonable terms and conditions as a *bona fide* seller would require;

- in relation to improved land the capital sum which the fee simple of the land might be expected to realise if offered for sale on such reasonable terms and conditions as a *bona fide* seller would require, assuming that at the time as at which the value is required to be ascertained for the purposes of this Act the improvements as defined in this Act do not exist. (Section 2, Land Valuation Act 1957).

Improvements in relation to land means:

- those physical additions and alterations thereto and all works for the benefit of the land made or done by the owner or any of his predecessors in title which, as at the date on which the improved or unimproved value is required to be ascertained, has the effect of increasing its value:

Provided that;

- the destruction or removal of timber or vegetable growth;
- the draining, filling, excavation or reclamation of land;
- the making of retaining walls or other similar works necessary designed to arrest or prevent erosion or flooding of land; or
- the grading or levelling of the land.

shall not be regarded as improvements

The law distinguishes between unimproved and improved land.

Improved land means:

- land on which improvements as defined in the act have been effected.

Improved value means:

- in relation to land the capital sum which the fee simple of the land together with any licence or other right or privilege (if any) for the time being affecting the land, might be expected to realise if offered for sale on such reasonable terms and conditions as a *bona fide* seller would require.

Unimproved land means:

- land on which no improvements as defined in the act have been effected.

The importance of the proviso that 'clearing' of land is not an improvement, is an important one, since in the valuing of land it is not necessary to investigate the actual state of the land before it was cleared, thus avoiding possible areas of dispute as to the original state of the land. These 'invisible' improvements are said to have merged with the land, and for the purpose of the valuation law are not to be regarded as improvements.

Of some significance is the definition of the unimproved value of improved land. It can be observed that two methods are prescribed and that the figure to be adopted as the assessed value is the higher of the values produced by the methods. The first may be termed as one of abstraction, where the improvements are deemed to be non-existent. The second, is a method of subtraction whereby the unimproved value is essentially the residual figure after deducting the value of improvements from the improved value. In determining the unimproved value, the Commissioner may assume that:

- the land may be used, or continue to be used, for any purpose for which it was being used or could have been used at the time as at which the value is required to be ascertained;
- such improvements as may be required in order to enable the land to be so used or continue to be so used, will be made or continue to be made.

Therefore, unimproved value does not mean strict adherence to current use, but rather all the advantages that the land possesses, present or future, may be taken into consideration. The unimproved value shall be less than the sum obtained by deducting the value of the improvements from the improved value. Where the value of the improvements in relation to land, is defined as that added value which the improvements give to the land, irrespective of the cost of the improvements.

As the definition of land is not exclusive of mineral deposits, it follows that the unimproved value of the land would include such deposits. In relation to the large bauxite deposits found in Jamaica, the bauxite companies reached an agreement with the government of Jamaica that in lieu of taxing the capital value of the deposits, public revenue from bauxite would be raised on a royalty basis. As a result of these agreements, the lands owned by the bauxite companies are valued for the purpose of property tax on the basis of their surface use, which for the most part would be agricultural.

Value of improvement means:

in relation to land the added value which improvements give to the land at the time as at which the value is required to be ascertained for the purpose of the act irrespective of the cost of the improvements (added value).

Provided that the added value shall in no case exceed the amount that should reasonably be involved in effecting, at that time as at which the value is required to be ascertained for the purposes of the act, improvements of a nature and efficiency equivalent to the existing improvements (replacement cost).

Owner means:

The person who, whether jointly or severally is seized or possessed of or entitled to any estate or interest in the land and shall include any person who, whether severally or jointly, claims that there is vested in him, and any person in whom the Commissioner believes there is vested, in possession, remainder or reversion, any estate or interest at law or in equity in the parcel of land.

Administration of property tax

The responsibility for the valuation of all land parcels for land tax is vested in the Land Valuation Division (LVD) (a Department within the National Land Agency) which is organised into four geographical regions with sub-offices. The LVD has within its mission statement an obligation to ensure that every parcel of land in Jamaica is valued for property tax purposes. Such valuations are undertaken in accordance with internationally recognised professional standards and that the valuation roll is maintained to the highest possible standard. The valuation of each parcel of land requires a detailed measurement and classification of the following; soil rating, slope category, land class (agricultural, commercial, residential, industrial, institutional, and recreational), land use type, neighbourhood characteristics, availability of services and coding of physical characteristics.

Valuation roll

Within the Land Valuation Act (Section 11) revaluations should be prepared for each district on a quinquennial basis. However, the Minister may by order require that a revaluation be undertaken at intervals of less than five years. When a revaluation has taken place a valuation roll is prepared for each district and contained prescribed particulars to include the following:

- the name, nationality and postal address of the owner;
- the situation, description and measurement or area of the land;
- the unimproved value of the land;
- such additional particulars, including the improved value of the land, as may be prescribed.

Notwithstanding the statutory requirement to implement quinquennial revaluations, general island wide revaluations have taken place in 1974, 1984, 1993 and 2002 all based on the unimproved value system.

Alteration of the roll

The valuation roll may be amended between revaluations, as necessary to reflect the following:

- subdivision of the land;
- two or more parcels of unoccupied land adjoining each other are valued as one parcel, and one or more parcels has been sold or is occupied;
- the value of the land has been altered due to the effect of public works or services;
- the land has been permanently damaged by adverse natural causes, for example, flooding;
- the unimproved value has been altered either by the loss or acquisition of a licence or other rights or privileges, that form part of the value of the land;
- land used exclusively for residential purposes when valued, changes to industrial or other purposes which, in the opinion of the Commissioner, alters its value;
- in the opinion of the Commissioner, circumstances affecting the valuation of the land render an alteration necessary or desirable for preserving or attaining uniformity in values between the subject valuation and those subsisting valuations of other comparable parcels of land.

Objection to assessments

If on receipt of a Notice of Valuation the landowner is dissatisfied, he/she may within a period of 60 days of service of the notice, serve a Notice of Objection on the Commissioner. The grounds for an objection are restricted to one or more of the following:

- the assessed values are either too high or too low;
- that lands which should be included in one valuation have been valued separately, or vice versa;
- that the person named in the Notice is not the owner.

In considering the objection, the Commissioner may either disallow it, or allow it either wholly or in part. On receipt of the Notice of Decision of the Commissioner, if the landowner is still dissatisfied, he may within 60 days of that decision, or such longer period as may be permitted by rules of court, appeal to the Revenue Court. The Revenue Court has the power to confirm, reduce or indeed increase the assessment. If either the Commissioner or any person affected by the decision of the Revenue Court is dissatisfied with the decision of the Revenue Court may within 60 days of the decision appeal to the Court of Appeal.

Size of the tax base

The growth in the tax base is an important indicator of the dynamic nature of the property tax system. Static or declining tax bases are indicative of systems which are failing to maintain the currency of the valuation roll and neglecting the essential requirement of capturing physical changes to property. There is also a direct link between the coverage of the tax base and the potential tax capacity generated by the roll. The ultimate aim is to ensure that whatever services are funded by the property tax the cost is equitably spread amongst the taxpayers on the valuation roll. Therefore, ensuring that the valuation roll is current and continually updated is a key function.

By analysing the growth of the tax base in Jamaica it is possible to draw conclusions as to the relative buoyancy of the property tax in terms of the number of taxable parcels. As the supply of land is fixed, the growth in the number of parcels is an indication of the taxable spread of costs among the various communities.

The size of the tax base has been increasing gradually since 1974. In fact the overall increase since 1954 is some 108 per cent (from 324,911 parcels). The size of the tax base has been increasing gradually since 1974 with a 38 per cent increase in the total number of parcels to date (2002). This represents an increase of around 1 per cent per annum, which, from an international perspective is considered an acceptable growth in the tax base. It is interesting to note however, that the growth in the number of parcels for Kingston is the lowest of all the parishes. In fact the number of parcels from 1991 has fallen by around 2 per cent. This figure seems unlikely and one must question the accuracy of the parcel numbers for Kingston. Several parishes have however seen a significant increase in the number of parcels, for example Manchester, Clarendon, St. James and St. Catherine. This was due to several reasons, but primarily the increase in residential sub-divisions and the diligent efforts of the valuation department in ensuring the capture of assessable units (see Table 2.1).

Table 2.1   Parcel statistics by parish

Parish	Number of parcels				% change from 1974
	1974	1986	1991	2002	
Kingston	11,163	12,371	12,398	12,137	9
St. Andrew	66,272	77,726	79,083	86,954	31
St. Thomas	26,768	31,746	32,821	34,895	30
Portland	24,176	28,824	29,470	30,931	28
St. Mary	34,707	36,840	38,325	43,139	24
St. Ann	41,952	46,987	48,855	54,110	29
Trelawny	21,961	23,343	23,682	25,654	17
St. James	24,114	29,172	30,043	34,384	43
Hanover	14,676	16,441	16,690	19,597	33
Westmoreland	25,860	28,285	29,129	32,189	24
St. Elizabeth	40,223	43,983	46,013	52,514	31
Manchester	38,922	44,863	46,903	53,833	38
Clarendon	59,334	70,268	73,059	79,480	34
St. Catherine	61,727	86,177	89,039	116,767	89
Totals	491,855	577,026	595,510	676,584	38

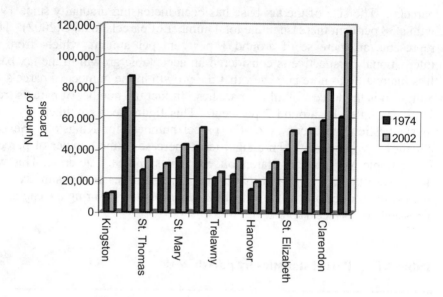

Figure 2.2   Total parcel numbers 1974 and 2002

Figures 2.2 and 2.3 illustrate the growth in the total number of parcels since the 1974 revaluation.   The growth whilst not dramatic has maintained a steady increase in the number of separately valued parcels.   The tax base coverage would appear to be quite comprehensive including both registered and unregistered parcels.   However, a major problem within the present land tenure system relates to the fact that in the region of only one half of the total parcels are registered.   There is a considerable numbers of parcels which are traded without government knowledge.   As the owner is the taxable entity it becomes a significant problem in maintaining an up-to-date register of landowners.

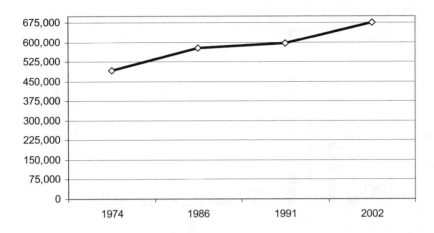

Figure 2.3   Increase in total parcel numbers from 1974-2002

Land use categories

Figure 2.4 provides an overview of the land use categories maintained by the Land Valuation Division. Agriculture (25 per cent) and residential (41 per cent) represent the main land uses, however, there are in excess of 180,000 parcels which have not been ascribed a land use code. Of the total number of parcels some 93 per cent are in private ownership, the remaining 7 per cent, approximating to 44,000 parcels are owned by various government departments and agencies.

The urban rural split illustrates the dominance of the rural sector to Jamaica with approximately 62 per cent of parcels being categorised as being rural.

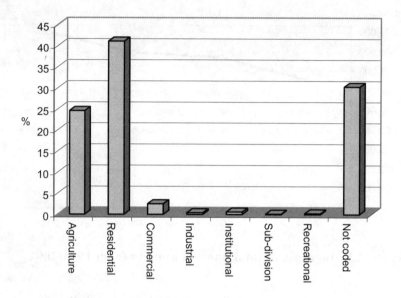

Figure 2.4   Land use categories

Revaluations

The revaluation cycle in Jamaica whilst prescribed by law as being quinquennial (Land Valuation Act) has yet to achieve this standard. Revaluations were undertaken in 1901, 1911, 1929 and 1937; these latter reassessments could in the purist from not be termed as revaluations but more as attempts to 'update' values.   Subsequent revaluations based on unimproved value were effected in 1957, 1974, 1984, 1993 and 2002.   The shift in values occasioned by the 2002 revaluation has resulted in an average 6-fold increase in assessed values.   Figure 2.5 illustrates the increase in the value of real property measured at the revaluation years.   This clearly indicates the need to have regular and frequent revaluations particularly to reflect volatile market conditions.

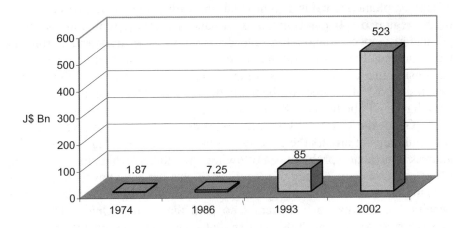

Figure 2.5   Total value of parcels at revaluation years

Collection

The Commissioner of Inland Revenue assess a property tax payable by every person in possession of property liable to the property tax. A Notice of Assessment specifies the amount of property tax properly to be paid. The tax is payable by the owner, which means the person who, whether jointly or severally is in possession or entitled to any estate or interest in land. The due date for payment is on the 1 April in each year, however, payment can be made at any time during this month, made payable at any of the 28 Collectorates.

Where the tax has not been paid within the month of April a penalty of 10 per cent on the full amount of the tax is added to the debt. Interest of 15 per cent (or such other rate as the Minister may prescribe) per annum is levied on property tax unpaid for a period of 30 days after the collection date. The tax may be payable by four equal quarterly instalments (April, July, October and January). If an instalment is not paid in the due month then all property tax becomes due, this in effect removes any future right to pay the debt by instalment. The Property Tax Act 1903 (amended) provides for the forfeiture of property for non-payment of property taxes.

The collection of the property tax is seen as one of the weaknesses of the system. Tax arrears have historically been a problem. Risden (1977) estimates that in fiscal year 1977, the tax collected was only 61 per cent of the collectable amount. Holland and Follain (1990) for financial year 1984 estimated that collections levels were in the region of 50 per cent. A problem of tax compliance remains a significant one with compliance levels currently in the region of 60 per cent. Tax arrears is a more significant problem, particularly since property tax revenue has now been transferred from the Consolidated Fund to the parish councils. Given their own service responsibilities parishes will become increasingly conscious of the need to match the cost of services to the available revenue, therefore arrears and tax compliance will be high on the parish agenda.

Given the historically low levels of compliance and the year-on-year accumulations of arrears the government has been considering taking steps to address this acute problem. Following the 2002 revaluation the Prime Minister announced a range of incentives to encourage taxpayers to pay their property tax arrears. Essentially the government would grant a full waiver of penalties or interest to taxpayers who paid their outstanding debt for the period up to 31 March 2002. After that date payments up to April 2002 would attract a discount of 75 per cent; those payments up to May 2002 would attract a 50 per cent discount and payments up to June 2002 would receive a 25 per cent discount. Given the fact that local government is to finance the cost of property related services administrative and legal procedures for the collection of the property tax need to be strengthened. The government has set a particularly high compliance rate of 70 per cent following the recent revaluation. In this regard the following changes are considered as imperative:

- the Collector of Taxes to issue a certificate confirming that all outstanding property taxes have been paid as at the date of transfer and mortgage documents are submitted for stamping and registration;
- legislation to provide for the sale of a property for non-payment of property taxes after two years have expired. This is considered as a remedy of last resort, but should have a positive effect of preventing delinquency by absentee owners;
- the need to be able to collect arrears beyond the present six year limit;
- all businesses seeking the renewal of licences will be required to submit evidence that property tax payments are up-to-date; and
- an integrated computerisation system which would make it possible to pay property taxes at any collectorate throughout the island.

Exemptions

The Property Tax Act specifies a number of properties that are exempt from the property tax, including the following:

- all buildings held in trust exclusively for public religious worship including contiguous churchyards and burial grounds;
- all buildings and lands used solely for charitable or educational purposes;
- all buildings and lands belonging to and used by the University of the West Indies;
- all buildings and lands belonging to primary schools, secondary schools;
- all unoccupied property belonging to, and all property in the occupation of the Crown, the Government of the Island, or any parish council or the Kingston and St. Andrew Corporation;
- all freehold property vested in the Commissioner of Lands and in the actual occupation of the Crown, the Government of the Island, or any Parish Council or the Kingston and St. Andrew Corporation;
- all buildings belonging to any church including, rectories, halls and all land provided it does not exceed one acre;
- all buildings and lands belonging to and used solely for the purposes of a private hospital.

Land Taxation Relief

The Land Taxation Relief Act 1960 (Law 4 of 1960) allows landowners to enjoy derating or relief from tax liability in the following cases:

- agricultural land; and
- specified lands for which potential has been taken into account.

The Act is administered by the Land Taxation Relief Board (appointed by the Minister) comprising six members including the Commissioners of Land Valuation and Inland Revenue. The Board does not have the jurisdiction to change assessments, but simply adjudicate on the request for relief. Relief is granted to the current owner and ceases on the sale of the parcel or if he/she dies, relief is therefore personal and not transferable and must be reapplied for.

Agricultural land

Derating is provided for specified land uses, essentially agricultural land. A derating Certificate if approved is effective for periods ranging from one to three years, as specified by the Board. The derating certificate ceases to have effect as soon as the land to which it relates or part thereof is subdivided or used for any purposes other than that purpose for which the certificate was granted. It must however be demonstrated that the land at the time of the valuation was being used bona fide as agricultural land and the valuation takes into account the potentialities of the land for use other than agricultural land. The derating relief is currently 50 per cent of the tax assessment. Prior to 1993 the level of relief was 75 per cent. Agricultural land is defined in The Land Taxation (Relief) Act 1960 as being:

> land which for the time being is used exclusively or principally for agricultural, horticultural or pastoral purposes or for the keeping of bees, poultry or livestock

In determining whether a derating certificate ought to be granted, the Board may take into account whether the land in respect of which the application is made is in substantial production. In determining this, the Board may take the following into account:

- whether the whole of the land is used exclusively for agricultural purposes;
- the extent to which and the manner in which;

  - arable land is being cropped (where the land has not been cropped for more than two or more years the land shall not be regarded as being in substantial agricultural production);
  - the land is stocked;
  - pasture land is being maintained;
  - the capacity of the land;
  - any other factor which affects the development of the land.

Potential uses for dwellings

Statutory relief is granted in those cases where the valuation takes into account a potential use of the subject land which would give a higher assessed value than the current use. An example would be where the owner (occupier) of a dwelling is in a location where the character of the location has changed from predominately residential to commercial. In this case the valuation of the parcel will reflect commercial values of the potential uses. In this case the owner must show that the house is being used as a bona fide dwelling house and the valuation of the land takes into account the potentialities of that land as suitable for any of the following types of development:

- hotel or guest house; or
- shop, office or other commercial building; or
- an industrial building; or
- a block or residential flats; or
- a type of residence which would necessitate redevelopment of the land and involve substantial capital expenditure. In this case the state of repair of the dwelling will be an important factor.

The Board in determining whether or not a relief certificate ought to be granted will have regard to all the circumstances and may take the following into account:

- whether it is reasonable that the land should continue to be used for its existing purpose; and
- whether the payment of the whole amount of land tax would because of circumstances peculiar to the applicant cause hardship.

In relation to the level of relief, it is at the discretion of the Board to determine by how much the tax assessment should be reduced.

Potential uses for approved purposes

Relief is also provided where land is in bona fide use at the time of valuation, for an approved purpose, and the valuation took into account the potential of that land being used as a suitable site for a subdivision or for any of the types of development noted above. Approved Purpose covers the provision of playing fields for cricket, football and other out-door games. An Approved Organisation refers to Member's Club registered as such under the Registration of Clubs Act. Under the Property Tax Act the Minister of Finance is empowered to give approval for relief to any purpose or organisation if he is satisfied that either the purpose or the organisation is mainly of a social, cultural or educational nature. Therefore schools, churches, hospitals and certain charitable organisations may qualify for relief.

Hardship relief

Relief from property tax on the grounds of hardship may also be granted at the discretion of the Minister of Finance. In this case the Special Discretionary Relief is granted in genuine cases of hardship where the taxpayer finds it burdensome to pay the property tax. Those typically entitled to relief have been those on low fixed incomes, including the elderly and pensioners. If in spite of the level of relief a taxpayer is still suffering hardship a case may be made to the Minister of Finance for the remission of the tax.

Tax rate structure

The property tax in Jamaica, certainly in recent times is a national tax. The valuation, collection, enforcement and tax rate setting are central government functions. Local government have no control over the levels of property tax. Property tax rates in Jamaica have traditionally been based on the principal of progressivity and established at the same level across the whole country. For the 1974, 1986 and 1993 revaluations Tables 2.2a, b and c show the tax rate structure adopted. One of the largest issues concerning these rates is related to the fact that the figures shown remained fixed until the next revaluation. Revenue in real terms therefore declined significantly whilst costs of services increased.

1974 tax structure

Table 2.2a   Property tax rate schedule (1974)

For first $2,000 of value	$5
For every $1 of the next £2,000 of value	0.10c
For every $1 of the next £6,000 of value	1.75c
For every $1 of the next £6,000 of value	2.50c
For every $1 of the next £9,000 of value	3.25c
For every $1 of the next £25,000 of value	4.00c
For every $1 of remainder	4.50c

1986 tax structure

Table 2.2b   Property tax rate schedule (1986)

For first $4,000 of value	$5
For every $1 of the next £6,000 of value	0.10c
For every $1 of the next £6,000 of value	1.50c
For every $1 of the next £9,000 of value	1.75c
For every $1 of the next £25,000 of value	2.00c
For every $1 of the next £50,000 of value	2.25c
For every $1 of remainder	3.00c

1993 tax structure

Table 2.2c   Property tax rate schedule (1993)

For first $20,000 of value	$50
For every $1 of the next £30,000 of value	0.10c
For every $1 of the next £50,000 of value	0.30c
For every $1 of the next £400,000 of value	0.75c
For every $1 of the next £500,000 of value	1.50c
For every $1 of the next £1,500,000 of value	2.00c
For every $1 of the next £2,500,000 of value	2.50c
For every $1 of remainder	3.00c

2002 tax structure

Following the 2002 revaluation the government's intention was to introduce 11 value bands and average tax amounts were specified for each band according to Table 2.3.

Table 2.3   Property value bands

Band	Property value	($)	Tax ($)
1	Less than	200,000	600
2	200,001 –	300,000	800
3	300,001 –	400,000	1,100
4	400,001 –	500,000	1,500
5	500,001 –	1 million	1,700
6	1 million –	2.5 million	4,000
7	2.5 million –	5 million	11,000
8	5 million –	10 million	87,000
9	10 million –	50 million	320,000
10	50 million –	200 million	1.5 million
11	Greater than	200 million	4 million

The government then subsequently introduced specific tax rates in a similar format to those applied after previous revaluations (see Tables 2.2a, b and c). These are shown in Table 2.4.

Table 2.4   Property tax rate schedule (2002)

For first $200,000 of value		$600
For every $1 of the next	£100,000 of value	0.30c
For every $1 of the next	£100,000 of value	0.30c
For every $1 of the next	£100,000 of value	0.30c
For every $1 of the next	£500,000 of value	0.30c
For every $1 of the next	£1,500,000 of value	0.50c
For every $1 of the next	£2,500,000 of value	1.75c
For every $1 of the next	£5,000,000 of value	1.75c
For every $1 of the next	£40,000,000 of value	1.75c
For every $1 of the next	£150,000,000 of value	1.75c

The problem in having property classified into 11 value bands with average tax amounts associated with each band led to significant confusion with taxpayers, as the actual tax bill often was different to the average amount. For example, a property having an assessed value of $1.2 million, is in the band 1m to 2.5m and has an average bill of $4,000; the actual bill is $4,000 calculated as follows:

First 200,000	600
Next 800,000	2,400
Next 1,000,000	1,000

| | Total tax | $4,000 |

In addition, a property having a value of $11 million should have an average tax bill of $320,000. The actual bill is however;

First 200,000	600
Next 800,000	2,400
Next 1,500,000	7,500
Next 8,500,000	148,750

| | Total tax | $159,250 |

One of the important issues relating to the tax structure is the lack of buoyancy within the system. This is principally due to the inherent fixed nature of the progressive rates, which remain fixed between revaluations, therefore the only opportunity to change the rates is at a forthcoming general revaluation. As all land parcels is or should be included within the valuation roll, the amount of revenue raised each year is relatively speaking fixed. This has the obvious disadvantage of being inflation prone in relation to escalating costs of service provision to be funded by a static revenue source. Clearly, this represents as aspect of future property tax reform which should address this lack of revenue buoyancy, by even increasing the tax rates by the annual rate of inflation as an intra-revaluation measure.

The annual gross collectable revenue under the 1983 revaluation was in the region of $88 million, for the 1993 revaluation the gross collectable revenue increased to around $450 million and it is estimated that for the 2002 revaluation the figure is around $2.3 billion. After adjustments for reliefs the government have stated that the tax raised should be in the region of $1.7 billion based on a compliance rate of 66 per cent. In relation to Table 2.5 after the 2002 revaluation some 84 per cent of parcels (574,732) have an assessed value of up to $1,000,000 and contribute some 28 per cent of the gross tax burden. At the other end of the scale parcels with assessed values of greater than 2.5 million contribute in the region of 65 per cent.

Table 2.5   Distribution of parcels by value category

Number of parcels	Value band	Average tax bill (J$)	Potential gross tax (J$)	% of parcels
181,422	1	600	108,853,200	26.67
87,553	2	800	70,042,400	12.87
79,965	3	1,100	87,961,500	11.75
66,288	4	1,500	99,432,000	9.74
159, 504	5	1,700	271,156,800	23.45
75,047	6	4,000	300,188,000	11.03
22,907	7	11,000	251,977,000	3.37
5,031	8	87,000	437,697,000	0.74
2,425	9	320,000	776,000,000	0.36
154	10	1,500,000	231,000,000	0.02
7	11	3,000,000	21,000,000	0.00
680,303			2,662,307,900	100.00

Note: *The figures are exclusive of any form of relief*

Kingston case study

The capital of Jamaica, Kingston represents a metropolitan area comprising two parishes, Kingston and St. Andrew (KSAC). It is one of the most densely populated areas on the island supporting a population of around one million. Figure 2.6 shows the growth in the number of parcels since 1974.

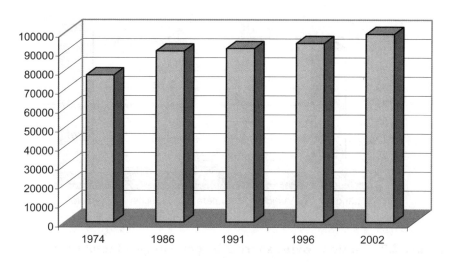

Figure 2.6   Increase in the number of parcels for KSAC

There has been a steady growth in the number of taxable parcels within the metropolitan area since 1974, representing an increase of 28 per cent over the period to 2002.

The revenue for the KSAC is derived from the following main sources property tax, motor vehicle licences, general revenue (trade licences, building and sub-division fees, market fees, water rates, cemeteries fees, shop licences, income from investments parking fees and fines), specific grants (poor relief services, minor water supplies, public water) and general assistance grants (direction and administration, street lighting, parks and market administration).   Figure 2.7 illustrates the relative breakdown between the main sources.

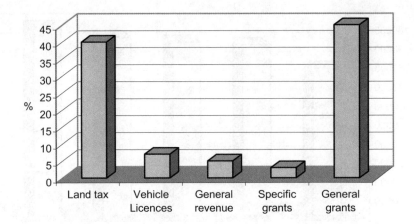

Figure 2.7   Main revenue sources by percentage of total revenue

Intergovernmental grants from the centre dominate the revenue source. However, as the land tax has now been returned to the sole control of the parishes it is likely that its importance will increase and reliance from the centre will decrease.

Critical review

In relation to resources the unimproved value system is much more cost effective in comparison to improved value systems. Given the diversity in terms of improvements to land and the need to have a system that would continuously monitor changes and cause reassessments creates an incredible pressure on monetary and human resources. Having a tax basis that excludes improvements should provide for a more cost effective and efficient allocation of scarce resources.

It satisfies the canons of horizontal equity to the extent that market values are determined on the basis of highest and best use, and concerning vertical equity, this can be achieved by structuring the rate of tax on a progressive rather than a proportional basis, so as to more effectively capture the taxable capacity of real property.

The system discourages speculation in land to the extent that the real cost of holding unproductive land is made prohibitive. In other words the level of tax would be the same notwithstanding that an actual income is being derived thus, in effect 'forcing' the holders of idle land into either developing it or selling it. The converse argument is also true in that the system does not discourage development as improvements to the land are part of the tax base.

It is generally accepted that a site value approach should in theory, at least, result in the implementation of frequent and regular revaluations. In practice however, other factors adversely affect the implementing of regular revaluations such as political will and taxpayer lobbying. The quality of the valuation roll is therefore adversely affected by the infrequent revaluations. Since the implementation of site value in 1956, there have been four revaluations, the first in 1974, then in 1984, 1993 and the last being in 2002.

There are a number of disadvantages of the site value system including that it penalises the holding of accommodation land particularly when a change of use is not yet economic. In addition it is also argued that it is insensitive to the taxpayer's ability to pay, for example where the present use is not the most valuable and where the tax is assessed on the latter value.

A considerable degree of wealth is tied up in buildings and other improvements to land that is effectively exempt for taxation. This does create a fairly restricted or narrow tax base with the result that tax rates on land need to higher than they would normally be.

The property tax system is to some extent affected by the rather liberal exemptions particularly for agricultural land (Risden, 1980). Clearly, within most property tax systems there are the 'common' exemptions and reliefs which one would expect however when the tax base is effectively narrowed by other less rationalistic exemptions questions pertaining to vertical equity arise. This fact has in part been recognised by government as the rate of relief has been reduced from 75 per cent to 50 per cent. In addition, the previous relief granted to hotel land has been removed as from the 1993 general revaluation.

The level of collection efficiency has already been mentioned however, it is worth noting that the Collector of Taxes should have the power to seek the payment of arrears notwithstanding the time bar of 6 years imposed by the Statute of Limitations. Clearly, if action is taken prior to the six years there should be no legal impediment in pursuing the claim for arrears. The problem would seem to occur in seeking to impose payment on arrears which have been outstanding for more than 6 years before collection action has been taken. To remedy this latter aspect legislation would need to be enacted to empower the Collector of Taxes.

Advantages and disadvantages of the property tax

One of the main advantages of the land tax pertains to the assessment process where a valuation is required of only the unimproved land. This means that once the land characteristics have been recorded there is no need to regularly re-inspect the property. Alterations to the buildings or other improvements on the parcel are effectively ignored. In terms of resources, this represents a considerable saving over improved value systems. In theory and indeed in practice the land value approach should lend itself to mass appraisal more readily than other forms of property taxation, however, in Jamaica this has yet to be fully implemented.

The land tax should induce a more economical and rational use of land. As the basis of the tax is highest and best use this in association with an appropriate rate structure should create the environment for maximising the use of land. In turn, this should reduce the holding of land for speculative purposes. The disadvantage of this is that it penalizes the holding of accommodation land when a change of use is not yet viable or economic.

An unimproved value system is often criticised as being insensitive to the taxpayer's ability to pay, particularly where a property is not earning an economic income. Whilst all cases cannot be legislated for, the tax system can provide the necessary hardship protection for those in most need. The current provisions in Jamaica provide for the protection and relief for established needy cases. The existing practice of granting agricultural derating at 50 per cent (reduced from 75 per cent in 1993) is aimed at protecting the agricultural community. This can have a number of revenue based effects such as reducing the level of tax for predominantly rural parishes, unless some form of central government equalisation is used to provide for the shortfall. Rather than giving relief on this basis an alternative approach might be to establish a differentiated rate for agricultural land.

For any category of land use, a pattern of normal development can usually be established. A recognised ratio of unimproved value to full market value (reflecting improvements) can fall within 'accepted' ranges such as 3:1 or 4:1. However, cases can arise when the value of the improvements cause a significant increase in this ratio. These unique properties are taxed only on the unimproved land value with the value of improvements being exempt. To capture this excess development value it could be argued that the value of improvements should be reflected in the tax base. Properties having an unimproved value in excess of a prescribed amount and a ratio greater than a 'normal' ratio would be valued on an improved value basis.

Valuation issues

All parcels are valued to the highest and best use as determined by the town and country planning regulations and zoning. There are still sufficient bare land sales to ensure that the roll values in most areas including the major cities and urban areas can be objectively determined. However, there is a declining trend in the availability of such direct evidence consequently there is a need to place greater reliance on indirect evidence such as improved sales. In the latter case residual valuations are undertaken to extract the value of the site. Within the definition of unimproved value two methods are prescribed for the assessment of the unimproved value from improved value, with the higher figure being the one adopted for tax purposes. The first assumes that the improvements are non-existent and the second is where the unimproved value is obtained as a residual by deducting the value of the improvements from the improved value. Many of the currently vacant parcels are owned by either the State or by absentee landowners. It has been suggested that government owned land should make a contribution in lieu of the land tax. The problem of absentee landowners is more difficult as the owners have not been identified. The proposed change in the law in terms of extending the period of unpaid taxes in excess of the current six years should address this current loophole.

The system of valuing to unimproved values is relatively simple and straightforward and well understood by the taxpayers.

Buoyancy

A major reason for the real decline in the property tax revenues is directly related to the failure in keeping the base up to date. The period of time between revaluations is unduly long and has created an imbalance between the current value of properties and the level of the property tax paid. It is becoming increasingly important to ensure that land value changes are regularly reflected in the tax base.

Another feature of the land tax relates to the fact that the rate schedule determined at a revaluation year remains fixed until the next revaluation, which can be for as much as ten years. The revenue collected in the years following the revaluation is therefore prone to inflation. Whilst the revenue is fixed in nominal terms the real revenue is declining. This lack of liquidity results in the land tax being unable to keep pace with the cost of service provision. This particular point will become increasingly important as the land tax revenue becomes the main revenue source for the parish councils.

Exemptions and reliefs

As presently structured the property tax in Jamaica is classified according to land use. Different rate schedules apply according to the use the land is put to for example, agricultural land is entitled to, on application, to 50 per cent relief. Land owned by government is at present exempt, however, it is likely that government will make a contribution in lieu of property tax to local government. At present given the system of agricultural relief there would be a greater incentive to develop land for agriculture than for residential. If the tax is capitalised the differential rates will result in differential changes in the market value of land according to its use. Because of the tax, parcels of land that can be used for agricultural purposes will sell for higher prices than for land which can be used for residential or commercial uses.

The derating of agricultural land is not totally clear, it might be as a means to protect this industry from competition or to reflect the fact that this industry requires substantial areas of this factor of production. To obtain relief the land must be used exclusively or principally for agriculture. The agricultural industry is an important export sector within the Jamaican economy. However, does it follow from this that agriculture should be partially derated. A land value tax should leave unchanged the structure of incentives for farmers who have been employing their land optimally, and would encourage those who have not to make better use of their land or to sell it. On equity grounds, land value taxation is not as appropriate on commercial farms as it is on large commercial or industrial enterprises. This preferential treatment of a specific category needs to be analysed in terms of the revenue foregone and the effect on the other land use sectors.

Progressive tax rates

The property tax in Jamaica is progressive (see Table 2.4) and is progressive with respect to each parcel rather than the aggregate of the parcels owned by each taxpayer. The progressive rate structure enables a lighter taxation on a large number of holdings and raises a significantly higher percentage of the total collected revenue from a small number of properties, usually the most expensive ones. It therefore tends to concentrate the revenue yield into classes where collection is perceived to be easier. Hence, a progressive rate structure is likely to me more acceptable than a proportional one. An additional reason for progressive rates in Jamaica was the need to force large idle land holdings into active use.

GIS and Land Information System

The Land Administration and Management Project (LAMP) was established in 1997 to promote the efficient administration and management of land resources in Jamaica in an integrated and sustainable manner. This would facilitate easier access to land for low-income individuals and develop an efficient and transparent land market. The project will facilitate the modernisation of all facets of land administration including the establishment of a national GIS network, the creation of digital maps, the development of a national cadastre to create the platform for a systematic programme of land titling. The creation of island-wide digital maps will result in increased efficiencies with the administration of the land tax.

Alternative system

It must be demonstrated that if the unimproved value system is to be maintained it must be sustainable in comparison with the alternative approaches. As outlined by St. Clare Risden (1977) it has to be shown conclusively that:

•   the unimproved value system can capture the full taxable capacity of real property and is therefore capable of yielding the optimum revenue level;
•   the system is less expensive to administer in relation to potential tax yield than any alternative system;
•   the system satisfies the fiscal canon of equity, since the tax base is not distorted, nor is the tax incidence skewed; and
•   the system provides for a strategy for the discouraging of holding vacant or under-utilised land.

From a fiscal point of view, one of the most significant aspects to be considered is the cost of administration in relation to the potential tax yield. In addition, the costs associated with being able to maintain the currency of the assessed values particularly in times of rapidly changing values. In view of this it is important to consider the constraints such as the time taken to prepare the valuation roll and the availability of professional and technical personnel.

The relatively high cost of recording improved property, has to be measured against more economical means in determining the taxable base. It is accepted that a capital improved system is considerably more expensive and requires greater resources to ensure the tax base is maintained. One of the attractions of a capital improved system is that, in theory, the improvements to land (i.e. buildings, extensions etc) is supposed to be reflected into the value of the tax base on an annual basis so that the taxable base is buoyant or elastic. But where there are resource constraints in terms of trained, experienced personnel the gain in moving to capital improved might be more illusionary than real. There is the associated problem of being able to maintain an accurate register of improvements to land particularly in an environment where such improvements are undertaken without the necessary approvals having been obtained. In relation to the situation in Jamaica the costs of effectively administering an improved value system could not be justified on the grounds of tax sustainability. It would be extremely difficult to envisage how Jamaica could now move to improved values given the costs involved in capturing the improvements to land.

References

Bahl, R. (1997), 'The Jamaican Tax Reform: Its Design and Performance', in W. Thirsk (ed.), *Tax Reform in Developing Countries*, World Bank, Washington DC, pp. 167-231.

Chang, W.S. (1966), 'Recent Experiences of Establishing Land Value Taxation in Jamaica', in A. Woodruff, J.R. Brown and L. Sein (eds), *Land Taxation, Land Tenure and Land Reform in Developing Countries*, University of Hartford.

Da Costa, J. (2003), 'Land Policy Administration and Management: A Jamaica Case Study', in A. Williams, A. (ed.), *Land in the Caribbean: Issues of Land Policy, Administration and Management in the English Speaking Caribbean*, University of Wisconsin-Madison, US, pp. 229-279.

Government of Jamaica (1994), '*Towards a Land Policy for Jamaica: A Synopsis*', Green Paper, 4/94, Kingston.

Hicks, J.R. and Hicks, U.K. (1954), '*Report on Finance and Taxation in Jamaica*', Government of Jamaica, Kingston.

Holland, D.M. (1968), 'A Study of Land Taxation in Jamaica', in A.P. Becker (ed.), *Land and Building Taxes: Their Effect on Economic Development*, University of Wisconsin Press, Maddison, United States, pp. 239-286.

Holland, D. and Follain, J. (1990), 'The Property Tax in Jamaica', in R. Bahl (ed.), *The Jamaican Tax Reform*, Lincoln Institute of Land Policy, Cambridge, United States, pp. 605-639.

Land Valuation Department (1997), '*Technical Staff Manual*', Kingston.

Local Government Reform Unit (1997), '*Status Report on the Local Government Reform Programme and the Parish Infrastructure Development Project*', Kingston.

Lyons, S. and McCluskey, W.J. (1999), 'Unimproved Land Value Taxation in Jamaica', in W.J. McCluskey (ed.), *Property Tax: An International Comparative Review*, Ashgate Publishing Limited, UK, pp. 385-410.

Miller, K.L. (1996), '*Historical and Contemporary Perspectives on Local Government Reform in Jamaica*', Ministry of Local Government and Works, Kingston, pp. 1-7.

Ministry of Local Government and Works (1996), '*Historical and Contemporary Perspectives on Local Government in Jamaica*', Government of Jamaica, Kingston.

Ministry of Local Government, Youth and Community Development (1993), '*Reform of Local Government, Ministry Paper No. 8/93*', Government of Jamaica, Kingston.

Morgan, D.J. (1957), 'Land Valuation and Land Taxation in Jamaica', *Public Finance*, vol. 12 no. 3, pp. 232-238.

Murray, J.F.N. (1956), 'Valuation, Land Taxation and Rating', Report to the Government of Jamaica, Kingston, Jamaica, pp. 1-27.

National Land Policy of Jamaica (1996), Government of Jamaica, Kingston.

Risden, O. St. Clare (1976), 'A History of Jamaica's Experience with Site Value Taxation', in R. Bahl (ed.), *The Taxation of Urban Property in Less Developed Countries*, TRED-10, University of Wisconsin Press, United States, pp. 247-261.

Risden, O. St. Clare (1977), '*An Analysis of Alternative Strategies for the Period 1977 to the Decade of the 1980s*', Land Valuation Office, Kingston.

Risden, O. St. Clare (1980), '*Site Value Taxation in Developing Countries*', paper presented at Caribbean Association of Tax Administrators, St. Kitts.

Simpson, P. St. A. (1987), '*Mapping for Land Valuation Purposes in Jamaica*', Land Valuation Department, Kingston.

Smith, A. (1776), '*Wealth of Nations*', University of Chicago Press, Illinois, United States.

Legislation referred to:

The Land Valuation Act 1957 (Law 73 of 1956).
The Land Taxation (Relief) Act 1959 (Law 4 of 1960).
The Property Tax Act 1903.
The Tax Collection Act 1867.
The Hotel Incentives Act 1968 (Law 16 of 1968).

Chapter 3

The Local Government Rating System in Fiji

Guest Author Abdul Hassan

Introduction

Fiji lies in the Pacific Ocean midway between the Equator and the South Pole, and between longitudes 175 and 178 west and latitude 15 and 22 south. The 180th meridian cuts through Fiji, but the International Dateline is towards the east and thus the entire group shares the same day. The national territory contains some 330 islands, however, only about 100 of these are inhabited. The total land area is approximately 18,000 square kilometres. The two largest islands, Viti Levu and Vanua Levu, account for about 87 per cent of the total land area and contain most of the population and economic activities. The islands of the Fiji Group are volcanic in origin and generally mountainous with only 16 percent of the land being suitable for agriculture. In 1996, the population amounted to 772,655 with a multi-ethnic composition: Fijians 51 per cent; Indians 43 per cent and others 6 per cent. The category others comprises people of Chinese, European, partly European, Rotuman and other origins.

Land tenure in Fiji

Land tenure defines the way in which people 'own' an interest in land and how they use it (Boydell and Reddy, 2000). It is the system in any society for holding land, which is governed by statute, local custom or a combination of both. To gain an appreciation of the current land tenure system in Fiji it is important to recognize the impact that history has had on the holding and ownership of land. The Deed of Cession in 1874 laid the foundation for Fiji's land tenure system by recognizing the native Fijians as the first inhabitants of Fiji thereby guaranteeing them the lion share of the national acreage. After 1874 when the British colonial rule began land tenure patterns were fixed; the rights of Fijians in the land were guaranteed and rights of Europeans and other foreigners who had acquired land in a *bona fide* manner prior to 1874 were also recognized. The land problem in Fiji is complex in nature primarily because unlike in many other countries beyond the South Pacific region, most of it is under communal ownership. Of the total land area, 3.91 per cent is held by the government, 8.15 per cent is held as freehold, the Fijian landowning units (native land) hold 87.94 per cent and Rotuman land 0.25 per cent (see Table 3.1). Since the small portion of state and freehold land was not sufficient for the demands for agricultural, leasehold land, native land, which is inalienable, was opened up for agricultural development. This land was leased out to tenants under the provision of the 1880 Native Land Ordinance, then through the Native Land Trust Board and the Native Land Trust Act of 1940, and later under the Agricultural Land Ordinance of 1966 and the Agricultural Landlord and Tenant Act (ALTA) of 1976.

Table 3.1   Fijian land tenure statistics

Type	%	Owner	Area
Native land	83.29	Community owned land	1,615,940
Crown land	8.41	Crown freehold	67,068
Freehold	8.06	General public	147,448
Rotuma	0.24	Rotuman People	4,452
	100.00		1,829,908

Source: Ministry of Lands and Mineral Resources

The land tenure system in Fiji comprises of three main types of land:

* native land;
* crown / state land; and
* freehold land.

Native land

Approximately 7,000 square miles of Fiji's total land area, representing some 87.94 per cent is classified as native land and is owned by individual land-owning units and administered through the Native Lands Trust Board on behalf of the owners. Native lands may be leased or occupancy granted under licence for different urban uses but cannot be sold unlike freehold land. Rents on native leasehold land is regulated at 6 per cent of the unimproved capital vale of the land and is reassessed every 5 years. Native land is classified as being either Native Reserve and Non-Reserve land. The essential differences between these two types of land are:

- that Native reserve can only be used by Fijians;
- that the majority of the land owning unit must approve the granting of a license/lease on Native Reserve; and
- that Native Reserves are not be subject to the Agricultural Landlordand Tenants Act.

Crown or State land

Crown or State land that is administered by Government's Lands Department and is governed by Crowns Lands Act, Chap. 113 and 132, Laws of Fiji and Crowns Lands (leases and licenses) Regulation 1980. This is described as:

> ... all lands in Fiji including foreshore and the soils under the water of Fiji and all lands which have been/may be thereafter acquired on behalf of the Government for any public purpose.

There are several different types of state land (Boydell and Reddy, 2000):

- Schedule A land; is former native land, which has fallen to the state by virtue of the extinction of the members of the owning *mataqali* and now reverted to native land;
- Schedule B land; land that was not occupied nor claimed by Fijians when the Native Land Commission determined areas of native land and now reverted to native land;
- State freehold; land bought over the years either from holders of Crown Grants issued in consequences of the findings at Lands Claim Commission or directly from the Fijians during the period 1905-1908;
- Crown land without title;
- Crown Tiri;
- Crown foreshore; and
- Native land acquired by the Crown.

Freehold land

Land held under freehold title constitutes approximately 8.15 per cent of the total land area of Fiji and is normally referred to as Native Grant, Crown Grant and Certificate of Title on the Standard Sheets. It is generally owned absolutely by individuals or corporations and represents the most secure form of tenure.

Provincial and local government

Fiji is divided into 14 provinces, which represent administrative units each governed by a Provincial Council. The functions of Provincial Councils are: 'to promote the health, welfare and good government of Fijians resident in the province and to carry out such other duties and functions which the Minister or the Fijian Affairs Board may see fit to delegate to such council'. The Provincial Councils have similar powers to municipal councils, including the making of by-laws, levying of rates and control of building construction in Fijian villages.

Local government was first established in Fiji under the Towns Ordinance of 1877. The Town of Levuka was proclaimed under this legislation. As a result of the changing economic geography of Fiji after the introduction of indentured labour from India and the need for a deep-water harbour, an urban centre was established at Suva, the present capital. Suva was proclaimed a Town in 1881 and Capital in 1953. Townships were proclaimed under the Municipal Institutions Ordinance of 1909 that was succeeded by the Townships Ordinance. Town Boards that comprised mainly nominated members and a number of civil servants serving in their ex-officio capacities administered townships.

Municipal government

The major urban centres are proclaimed as City or Town under the Local Government Act (Cap. 125) with the Ministry of Local Government, Housing and the Environment having overall responsibility over municipal government. The Local Government Act makes provision for two classes of municipalities, i.e. cities and towns and districts. As of 2004, there were two Cities (Suva and Lautoka) and ten Towns (Ba, Labasa, Lami, Levuka, Nadi, Nausori, Nasinu, Savusavu, Sigatoka and Tavua). All areas outside the jurisdiction of proclaimed cities, towns and Fijian villages come under the control of the rural local authorities, which are public health authorities constituted under the Public Health Act (Cap. 111). Their primary responsibility is to control public health, building construction and other matters governed by The Public Health Act. Many of them have considerable peri-urban housing development powers but they have no power to raise rates.

Function of local councils

Each council is required under the Local Government Act to undertake all such activities that are lawful and expedient to promote the health, welfare and convenience of the inhabitants of the municipality and to preserve amenities. Specific functions of municipalities elaborated in the Act include public utility services, roading provision, public health, control and licensing of market stalls, maintenance of parks and gardens, recreational facilities, waste management, river maintenance, land and building development, town planning and land sub-division, building control, housing schemes to provide dwellings for persons of small means, streets and drainage. Under the above broad provisions councils undertake a large variety of developmental works and services.

Rural local authorities cover large areas outside of towns and have to deal with varying amounts of urban development within their boundaries. In addition to their main function as public health authorities, they undertake a variety of functions usually undertaken by urban local authorities such as building control, town planning and garbage disposal, emptying of septic tanks and issuing business licences.

Municipal government has important responsibilities to discharge in the overall development of the nation. With increasing population density and urban development their responsibilities are expanding continuously and councils are placing an increased emphasis on their role in environmental management at local level. This increase in responsibilities has tended not to be matched by new initiatives of municipalities to mobilize more revenue. Furthermore, although an increasing portion of the national tax revenue is collected in municipalities, there is very limited financial assistance from the government to municipalities. Some of the smaller town councils appear to have very limited revenue to be able to provide the full range of local government services.

Local government revenue

Municipalities are self-financing authorities funding a significant part of their operations from revenues generated from the property tax (generally known as the town rate) and other local incomes such as rents, fees and charges. Councils base the town rates on the unimproved capital value of land (UCV); the income from this source usually accounts for some 50per cent of the total income. State land within a municipality is legally exempt from the payment of rates but the Director of Lands pays a grant-in-lieu approximately equal to the rate calculated for the UCV. The remaining income is generated from rents of commercial premises, fees from the markets and the bus stations, business licence fees, building fees and parking fees. Financial grants from central government are uncommon and where granted are typically earmarked for specific development projects. Additionally, councils have the power to raise loans from the local capital market to finance capital development works. The Local Government Act empowers councils to levy rates up to 10 per cent per dollar of the UCV for the general rate and up to an additional five per cent for loan purposes. However, most councils levy a total rate of 1.0 to 2.5 dollar cents. In some councils there have been considerable political objections to raising the level of rates beyond current levels. Consequently, in many cases the level of rates levied has not kept up with the rate of inflation and there has been at least one case of deficit budgeting in recent years. Agricultural lands within municipal boundaries are rated at a lower level compared to land under urban use.

The UCV is based on the value of land in its original state, disregarding the nature or value of buildings and other structural improvements on the land. A town-planning scheme is a prerequisite for the valuation process. Reassessment of the UCV is undertaken every six years and is usually undertaken by the Valuation Section of the Lands Department. In the past the city councils use government valuers for this exercise. There is growing concern among some councils that the UCV system of valuation does not result in an equitable sharing of the financial burden since sites with considerable building development and with land uses benefiting from various types of municipal services, are levied at the same rate as vacant or underdeveloped lands. There is a consensus that instead of switching entirely to a new system, possibly based on the improved capital value (ICV) or on the assessed annual value based on rental, councils should choose between the different valuation systems, possibly one which would value properties in accordance with the level of use of the municipal services.

Origins of the property tax in Fiji

Before independence Fiji was under British rule (1874-1970) and shared in some significant aspects of a common colonial heritage with its neighbouring countries Australia and New Zealand. Being part of the former British Empire, the three countries were administered through a similar legal, political, economic and institutional structure. Thus the basis for assessing local government rates in Fiji on the unimproved capital value System (UCV) was inherited from these two countries. Meeking (1994) reports that UCV was popularised in Australia in the late nineteenth century by Henry George. George believed in the notion of rating on land values, as a means of encouraging development. It is a part of the unearned increment on the value of the land returned to a community.

In recent years, many alterations have been made to the form and substance of the rating systems in Australia and New Zealand. In the case of Fiji, with the exception of one preliminary government review (Narayan, 1999), no empirical research has been undertaken on the rating system. As Herps (2001) observed, defects in the local government rating systems are very serious distortions of a revenue scheme that had originally promised equitable treatment of all. Property is still being used as a medium to generate rate for local councils for the reasons given below.

Numerous enquiries into rating and taxing have been conducted throughout the world and the constant outcome has been for the sustaining of a rate based on the property value (Meeking, 1994). There is strong support for rating on property value on the grounds that the form of tax is simple, visible and easily identifiable (McCluskey, 1999). The property cannot shift geographically in response to a change in a rate. The yield of tax is predictable and collection is difficult to evade. The cost of maintaining the rate is not high and the rate is a perceptible tax (IRRV, 1999). A deliberate decision is taken to raise the rate in the dollar to meet increased costs.

There are two primary principles of taxation; the ability to pay and the benefits received (White, 2000). A good property tax should be equitable, neutral, visible, simple and competitive. It should be administratively efficient and provide adequate and stable sources of revenue to a local council. A tax that is fair or equitable should have horizontal and vertical equity. A local council tax (rate) needs to be easily understood, by the taxpayers. It should be difficult to evade and avoid. Most importantly, a local rate should be impartial between one person and another. Property tax should provide stable and adequate revenue to support ongoing local council responsibilities and services.

The International Association of Assessing Officers (IAAO, 1992) maintains that a common objective of taxation is neutrality, which should be designed so that it does not distort economic decisions. A uniform broad-based tax is supposed to be neutral and serves to improve economic efficiency. It encourages development, which according to economic theory increases general welfare. High tax on one property shifts investment to others with lower tax. For example, a tax charged on an owner of an apartment building will be passed along to a tenant in the form of higher rents.

A property tax that fully meets all the above criteria is yet to be discovered. The competitiveness is becoming an important tax criterion and many multinational companies and even individual's move to other states and countries in search of a tax climate, which is most favourable to them. Does the local government tax system in Fiji have this characteristic? Under the local council tax structure, do property owners with rental incomes of $25,000 per annum and $50,000 per annum pay different amounts of tax (rate) on their properties? Not at this stage. Thus it is quite apparent that Fiji has a problem with vertical equity in the property tax. Under the present system of provision in rates, low-income earners end up paying a higher rate on their properties as a proportion of their income. In cases where low-income families are renting a house, the property owner can pass property tax through the rent charged to a tenant. Consequently, a low-income family who rent housing can end up paying proportionately even more property tax as a percentage of their income than their wealthier home-owning counterpart. Despite several shortcomings the property tax is still considered to be the most reliable method of raising tax by local councils

Advantages of property tax

In spite of its unpopularity with both taxpayers and scholars of tax policy, the property tax remains the most important source of income for local governments all over the world (White, 2000). Local governments continue to rely on property tax because of its dependability and stability as a source of income when compared to an income or sales tax. It is relatively difficult to avoid at the local government level. Property tax provides local governments with an opportunity to exercise independence over the quantity and quality of services offered to the taxpayers. If administered correctly it provides ratepayers with a greater voice than other forms of taxation in determining the amount of taxes to be paid. Since efficient local government services add an increment to the value of property, it is both fair and appropriate that the property owner should share in paying for providing it.

The International Assessing Officers Association (1997) claims that a property tax assessment exercise has other benefits. It provides useful information on the land and building. If the information is well maintained, updated and publicly available, it has many public uses. The immovability of the tax base gives taxpayers an opportunity to receive and challenge not only their assessment but also the assessment on similar or surrounding properties. A property tax system is more transparent than other tax systems. Along with advantages the property tax has several disadvantages as described in the next section.

Disadvantages of property tax

Despite the local control of the property tax system and its accessibility, the property tax is considered by the public to be the most unpopular local tax (IAAO, 1997). Property tax is based on unrealised market values and is poorly related to cash flow. This makes it difficult for the poor retired persons and others who own several properties as they may lack cash to meet tax payment. As a large sum payment, property tax makes the magnitude of the tax more apparent and even more unpopular. In many cases property owners do not understand the relationship between assessed value and tax, and therefore misunderstand how changes in the property value relate to the change in tax. Assessment is perceived as inequitable. Lack of adequate state oversight and lack of uniformity are indicators of actual inequitable treatment.

Taxation

In Fiji Income Tax and Value Added Tax (VAT) is levied by the central government under the Income Tax Act of 1974 and the VAT Decree of 1991 respectively. The Commissioner of Inland Revenue administers the Act and Decree. The major sources of revenue for the government are income tax, comprising normal and withholding tax on individual and companies and VAT.

The major source of income for the local governments is rates collected from individual property owners. Taxation is the first fiscal expression of the relationship between local government and the individual taxpayer. The fundamental principles of taxation are that it should bear as lightly as possible upon production so as least to check the increase in the general fund from which tax must be paid and the community maintained. Taxes should be borne equitably, so as to give no citizen an advantage or put any at a disadvantage as compared to others.

The case for local government revenue collection and spending for the public service is founded on the premise that each ratepayer cannot make provision on its own in all cases and that those services are most suitably delivered by the local councils. To provide such services a council can use taxation as a means of redistributing wealth within the community. Having said that, the rationale why tax is unjustly distributed in the first place is rarely explained to the property owners.

Local government rating systems

McCluskey *et al* (1997) states that globally three rating systems exist, based on unimproved capital value of land, capital value and assessed annual market rental value. The first two systems may be viewed as partial wealth taxes whereas assessed annual value may be seen as an attempt to tax the current yearly income from properties. Each country should evolve its own system appropriate to its cultural values, historical background and political situation. The choice of tax system should be linked directly with the land tenure system and the most common form of land holding.

Researchers in the field (Elliot and Zulu, 2000) believe that the property rating system is an intervention in the urban land market and affects land use. Different property rating systems have been offered to encourage different outcomes with respect to property development. For example, the site value basis encourages a quicker development response and minimises holding cost. In addition, this system discourages land speculation i.e. the holding back of unimproved or under-improved property from use. This would bring the highest current returns in order to reap the advantages of a higher sale price or higher annual returns without any substantial capital investment. It discourages urban decline resulting from neglect and under utilisation of buildings and other resources by property owners through lack of capital investment. Since in Fiji local council rating is based on UCV, it is important to investigate the merits and demerits of the system.

Unimproved capital value rating system

Studying a local council rating system of a country is an important subject and it is highly desirable to examine whatever empirical information is available locally and abroad. Relevant information does not often provide institutions that conform to ideal types. The reasons are that the property tax is a product of natural, cultural and historical circumstances, which vary in time and place. Consequently property tax systems differ among states and countries at a given time and vary for each state and country with the passage of time.

Australia and New Zealand provide an unusual opportunity for observing and studying different methods of property taxes in operation, often side by side. In both countries the tax is levied on land value alone as well as on land and building. State governments in Australia administer most of the assessment of property tax while in New Zealand this power is retained by local government.

It is of interest to note that several countries have changed their rating system from a capital value to an UCV (Becker *et al*, 1969). One such country is Jamaica that adopted the UCV system. It is a poor developing island nation similar to Fiji in many ways and achieved independence in 1962. For a poor developing country, to improve the existing economic situation the best option is to introduce the UCV rating system (Becker *et al*, 1969). The advantages of an UCV system are that it encourages development of land and stimulates construction work. Under an UCV system, property owners will get the benefits but they would not undertake expenditure or expend effort to account for the enhancement in values.

Becker *et al* (1969) further supports the UCV method because it is an unearned increment. Revenue in the form of raised income redistributed and economic decisions are not affected. Commenting on the UCV system, Becker *et al* maintains that in several under-developed countries a large number of unimproved, or vacant site sales are still available and could easily be used to establish UCV for developed sites. In many developing countries, decisions on land use show several values but not that which is reflected in the market. For instance, the sentimental attachment to a large subsistence holding may lead the owner to withhold the land from subdivision or sale. Taxing such a holding on the unimproved capital value system may force such a landowner to make a more rational decision on holding back the land. Of course it may just cause him to be filled with bitter resentment against the local authority.

Certain sales evidence may be treated as vacant because of the poor condition of structural improvements on the site or the fact that the improvements may have become obsolete, adding little value to the property (Becker *et al*, 1969). Analysis of these types of sales will provide a basis to establish land values. The difficulty in generating suitable revenue from land was commented on by George (1992):

> Separate the value of the clearly distinguishable improvements made within a moderate period, from the value of land, should they be destroyed. This manifestly is all that justice or policy requires. Absolute accuracy is impossible in any system and to attempt to separate all that the human race has done from what nature originally provided would be as absurd as impracticable.

> The fact is that each generation builds and improves for itself and not for the remote future. In addition, the further fact is that each generation is heir not only to the natural powers of the earth, but to all that remains of the work of past generations.

McCluskey *et al* (1997) describes the land value basis of taxation as favourable because of its potential for improving the efficiency of urban land use. They argued that this form of taxation is straightforward if land alone is taxed; the owner will have an incentive to develop the land to its most effective use. They further support Becker's argument that the site value system is most suitable for developing countries. McCluskey *et al* (1997) report that Hector Wilks, who studied the practicalities of land value taxation in the urban centres of Whitstable in the United Kingdom in the years 1964 and 1974, arrived at the following conclusion:

> Comparability with the orthodox (UK) annual value the total rateable value is of the same order as the orthodox rateable value list, because of the extra land and so on that one brings in and the extra values that accrue, so that the rate can be of the same order of figure.

> It is clear and incisive to operate and from the valuer's point of view, the number of problems seems to be far less than those, which we have to meet on the orthodox system.

> The only problem that I can see in the United Kingdom on bringing in such a method is the interim period or changeover. It is bound into the system in this country that the occupier pays the rates. All leases of, and transactions in, land are based on this premise. Is it worth upsetting all this; is it worth having to review by statute every transaction in land, every lease for this other system of taxation? Now that I have done my two reports, my answer is an uncompromising "Yes". It is all worthwhile.

Tricket (1982) stated that the concept of UCV is the product of an unsophisticated economy. Such a view would support its adoption in developing countries. He pointed out that this was the reason why the UCV system was adopted in most of the Australian States in the early stages of their development. The belief is that this system has a particular philosophical attraction to those responsible for the development of a largely undeveloped state. The UCV rating system is seen as a positive step in encouraging development and settlement on land.

The UCV system (Mander, 1982) is a system that encourages development because it exempts improvements and taxes the 'community' created unearned increment. However, the system disregards the owner's ability to pay and penalises properties tied to their older use in changing use situations. The UCV system does not have any degree of vertical equity. Vertical equity refers to any difference in tax burden borne by taxpayers who are not similarly situated.

Becker *et al* (1969) list four incentives for the UCV system of rating. First, the most important consequence of unimproved or land value tax in an urban area will be a sizeable stimulus in economic development and the use of land. Secondly, these incentives can help bring about such increased development because structures are exempted from tax. Thirdly, investment funds, which may be required to acquire land, can be used to purchase larger sites or can be invested in improvements on a large scale. It has been established that the high cost of purchasing land for development or redevelopment has become a serious problem in developed countries even where credit is readily available. Fourthly, the unburdening effect gives an incentive for increased economic development and eliminates property tax obligation from the value of improvements.

The UCV system adopted in Fiji relates to the rates charged on the open market value of the land, excluding improvements. Property owners and registered lessees are required to pay an annual rate based on the percentage of the UCV of the land. Section 62 of the Local Government Act 1972 (Fiji) and Local Government Amendment Act 1980 (Fiji) defines Unimproved Capital Value as:

> The capital sum which the land, if it were held for an estate in fee simple unencumbered by any mortgage or charge thereon, might be expected to realise at the time of valuation or revaluation if offered for sale on such reasonable terms and conditions as a bona fide seller expected to require and assuming that the improvements, if any, thereon or appertaining thereto had not been made.
>
> Provided that in any valuation of land on which structures have been erected such valuation shall not take into account the actual use of the

land, but the use for which the land is zoned under any existing planning scheme.

An issue of concern in Fiji relates to how well ratepayers understand the basis and principles upon which the tax is levied. The government has never sought ratepayer's views on the UCV system. Experience with ratepayers would suggest that they do not understand the basis and principles on which the tax is levied. Empirical analysis of the current system in Fiji demonstrates that ratepayers are not paying rates in direct proportion to the capital value of their properties and the services they need from the local councils. Due to the lack of knowledge by ratepayers the public perceives the existing rating system as generally fair.

It appears that since the introduction of the local government rating system in Fiji in the early twentieth century it has been widely accepted with little criticism. The UCV system appears straightforward, efficient and easy to administer. The government is focusing on operational efficiency rather than on equity considerations.   The striving for administrative efficiency in terms of the ease of collection of the rates seems to take clear precedence over any issues of inequity in operation or unfairness to ratepayers.

Rating valuation

Approximately 500,000 properties are rateable in the urban areas in Fiji with landowners and lessees of land being required to pay a yearly rate based on a percentage of the unimproved value of their land. Properties situated outside of local government boundaries are not rated.

Improvements

In relation to land means all work done or materials used at any time on or for the benefit of land by the expenditure of capital or labour or both by any owner or occupier thereof or any predecessor in title in so far as the effect of the work done or material used is to increase the value of the land and the benefit thereof is unexhausted at the time of valuation; but except in the case of land owned and occupied by the Crown or by a statutory public body, does not include work done or material used on or for the benefit of the land by the Crown or by any statutory public body, except to the extent that the same has been paid for or contributed to by the person who is the owner or occupier of the land at the time of the valuation.

Provided that:

- the reclamation of the land from the sea shall not in any case be deemed to be improvements either of the land reclaimed or of any other land; and
- work done or material used at any time on or for the benefit of any land by the expenditure of capital or labour or both by any owner or occupier thereof or any predecessor in title (whether required by any written law or not) by the provision of streets, roads or drains, or the carrying out of any subdivision, reclamation, leveling, cutting or filling or any other work to make such land suitable or more suitable for building purposes, shall not be deemed to be improvements.

Section 64(1) of the Local Government Act 1972 provides that for the purpose of ascertaining and determining the unimproved value of rateable land, every council shall undertake a general valuation of all land at least once every six years.

Section 64(2) goes on to provide that, a general valuation shall not be invalid by reason of the fact that any rateable land has been erroneously omitted from a valuation roll.

Section 64(3) states that a council may at any time cause a valuation to be made of any rateable land where:

- such land has been erroneously omitted from the most recent general valuation; or
- such land was not rateable at the date of the most recent general valuation; or
- the unimproved value of the land has increased since the last general valuation by reason of;

  - the existence of any street which has since the time of such valuation been declared to be a street by the council; or
  - the scaling by the council of an official survey plan of subdivision; or
  - the scale or letting since the time of such valuation of any land on which work has been done to bring it into condition suitable for building; or
  - there has been any change in the use of such land.

Section 64(4) provides that the council may at any time cause a valuation to be made of any rateable land where the unimproved value of the land has decreased since the most recent general valuation by reason of the destruction, damage or demolition of improvements previously made and standing upon the land.

In addition, any valuation made between general valuations shall be made on the basis of values subsisting as at the date of the last preceding general valuation to ensure that the new valuation will preserve uniformity with existing assessed values of comparable parcels of land.

Under the definition of unimproved value as defined in the 1972 Local Government Act care must be taken to value property according to its current zoning. Some difficulty will obviously be experienced when assessing valuations under this Act.

Basis of rating

The local council determines each year the rate in the dollar at a meeting of the members of the local council. A general rate is usually determined by taking the total unimproved value of the local authority area, excluding non-rateable lands usually government owned and occupied, and dividing it into the budget determined for the year. For example, if the total rateable unimproved value of the area was $1,000,000 and the council assessed its annual budget (or outgoings) at $50,000, the general rate would then be 5 cents in the dollar. In addition to the general rate, service charges for the collection of garbage are determined.

Valuation authority

In undertaking rating valuations section 65 of 1972 Local Government Act provides that a council shall appoint a valuer approved by the Minister and if necessary, an assistant valuer. In Fiji it is normal for local councils to appoint valuers from the Department of Lands and Mineral Resources.

Valuations and assessments

Under section 66 (1) of the Local Government Act 1972 all valuations made under the provisions of this Part of this act shall be entered in a rate book to be kept for the purpose together with such particulars of the rateable land as the council may determine. Subject to the other provisions of this act, a valuation when entered in the rate book shall be the value of the land upon which all rates made by the council shall be assessed and shall remain in force until the land is again valued under the provisions of section 64 of the Local Government Act. The rate book shall be open to the inspection of the public at all reasonable times and the owner-occupier of rateable land and or his agent may take copies of the entries relating to such land without fee. Such information includes the legal description, parcel size, owners or lessee's name and assessed value.

Rateable land

All land including Crown Land, within a municipality is considered as rateable land for the purpose of the Local Government Act. Section 60 also states the lands within a municipality, which are not subject to rating.

Publication of notice of valuation

The council is obliged to publish twice in a newspaper published in Fiji and circulating in the municipality a notice informing all persons interested in the fact that a general valuation has been made and entered in the rate book. In addition, the notice will stipulate a date not being less than one month after the last of such publications before which appeals may be brought against the valuation of any rateable land (section 67).

Objections to valuation

The council or any person aggrieved by a valuation may appeal against such valuation in the Magistrates Court. Filing shall make any appeal with the court before the date declared by the notice published in accordance with the provisions of section 67 a written memorandum of appeal stating the grounds upon which the appeal is made. The Local Government Act 1972 does not specifically state the grounds for an appeal against a valuation. However, the normal grounds for such an appeal would include:

- that the values determined are too high or too low;
- that the description of the land not included in the valuation has not been so included;
- that the areas of land that should have been included in the valuation have not been included;
- that area of land that has been included in the valuation should not have been included.

Case study of Suva City

Suva City Council has a responsibility to ensure that the welfare of the ratepayers is maintained. Rates charged should be fair and property owners should pay in proportion to the services they require from the city council. Under the broad provisions the council undertakes a large variety of developmental works and services. The Suva City Council is a self-financing authority, funding a large part of operations from the revenues generated from the land tax (generally known as the city rate) and other local incomes. Council rates are based on the UCV of land with income from this source usually accounting for some two-thirds or more of the total income (see Figure 3.1).

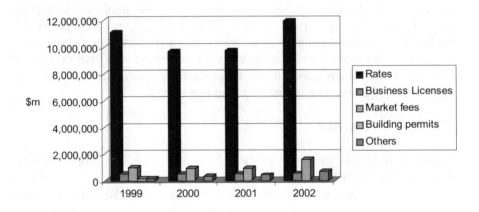

Figure 3.1   Study of Suva City Council revenue, 1999-2002

The city council determines the rate in the dollar annually as part of the annual budget. The Local Government Act (1972) empowers the council to levy rates up to 10 per cent per dollar of the UCV for the general rate and up to an additional five per cent for loan purposes however, the council levies a total rate of 1.0 to 2.5 cents in a dollar. Figure 3.2 shows the rates levied by the Suva City Council from 1999 to 2003.

In some cases there has been a considerable political objection to raising the level of rates beyond current levels. The UCV is based on the value of land in its original state, disregarding the nature or value of buildings and other improvements on the land. A town-planning scheme is a prerequisite for the valuation process. The Valuation Section of the Lands Department undertakes reassessment of the UCV every six years. There is a growing concern in the council that the UCV system of valuation does not result in an equitable sharing of the financial burden since sites with considerable building development and with land uses benefiting from various types of municipal services are levied at the same rate as vacant or underdeveloped lands.

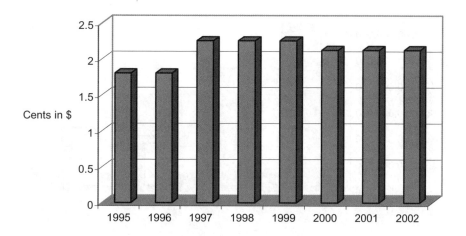

Figure 3.2   Rates levied in $ of UCV

Figure 3.3 shows the number of rateable properties by class. The residential class being overwhelmingly the largest having almost 84 per cent by number of the total rateable properties. Commercial property accounts for 8 per cent and industrial and others are 4 per cent respectively.

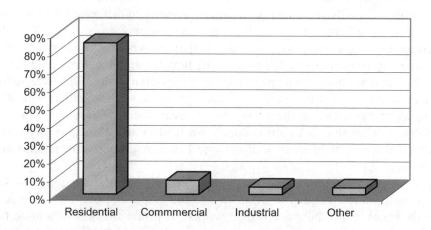

Figure 3.3   Property types in Suva

During the revaluation of the Suva City in 2004 the total Unimproved Capital Value of the City was $688 million of which the residential properties represented $297m of the total UCV, commercial $212m, industrial $82m and other properties $97m (see Figure 3.4).

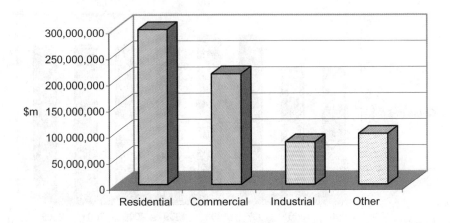

Figure 3.4   Distribution of unimproved capital values by property type: Suva City

The Importance of rate equity

It is a widely accepted criterion that equity in tax structure is important. It takes two forms, firstly, horizontal equity where all ratepayers are rated the same and secondly, vertical equity where property in different situations are assessed at different rates. These are the major factors that affect the perception of the ratepayers. Many taxpayers wish to know what other people pay or do not pay irrespective of how the rate has been calculated. In the vertical equity concept properties of different values are assessed at different levels. For example, low and high value single-family residential properties are valued at the same level of assessment. There may not be a precise relationship between property ownership and ability to pay rates, though there is at least an indirect one between property ownership and wealth.

A property tax should be judged according to the adequacy of the revenue produced, equity and fairness to the taxpayers, and understanding by the taxpayers of how the system works. A prime attribute of a good tax system is its ability to produce adequate funds for the services that a local council is expected to provide. It is to be noted that the purpose of the property tax system is to recoup the expenditure for the services provided to individual property owners. The requirement is an equitable distribution of the rate between property owners. Failing to achieve a just distribution of rates raises the question of social justice.

The conditions in which all countries are seeking to improve their property tax systems differ in many ways from the past. The promotion of social justice and an equitable distribution of the tax burden are very much to the fore. In particular, underdeveloped countries are entering the development process in a climate of worldwide concern for social justice and the consideration of equity in the formulation of its property tax. There are two reasons why governments are concerned with equity and social justice. The first is that today's moral climate requires that a government should be responsive to public opinion and be able to demonstrate that social justice is one of the central concerns. The second reason for concern is a pragmatic one. In all countries aspiration for tax improvement should be spread across all property owners. Unless this issue is taken seriously during any reform there may be serious frustration and social unrest resulting in the minimum degree of success.

Current trends in property tax reform

In many countries one common priority has been the rationalisation of government to improve service delivery and the provision of physical infrastructure (White, 2000). The basic goal is to strengthen central government decision-making and oversight functions, while transferring increased responsibility for service delivery and infrastructure maintenance to local councils. To achieve this countries are adopting a variety of local government reform efforts aimed at improving local-level service delivery and economic governance. Attention is drawn to improving local level finance and the area for enhanced revenue mobilisation is the property tax.

The greatest single force changing and expanding the role of local governments is the push for equality and social justice. The fear of social justice as representing equality opens many discussions to address issues including taxation. Justice is referred to as the process by which the arbitrary distributions are ignored and a correct balance is established between competing claims in relation to the distribution of benefits and burdens that form part of, or result from, social institutions (Meier, 1993). Each person is to have a fair right to the most extensive basic liberty compatible with a similar liberty for others.

The liability of real estate to rating levies and the basis of assessing the value of land where liability depended on value was seen as a matter of only local significance in several countries including Fiji. In recent times, however, most noticeable changes have been seen in this position. An example is the increased tendency for ownership of large properties in the hands of corporations, whether they are public or private companies. The changes in the lending policies made the investment dollar very mobile. The development in many local council areas is a simple proof of this mobility. This is one important element as to why local governments should be thinking about a fair system so that all ratepayers pay rates on an equitable basis. As pointed out earlier, property tax revenue is a significant item in the council budget. The relative revenue yield from the tax assumes an important position in a council's budget.

Critical review

It has been observed that the unimproved capital value basis for rating provides much more incentive for urban development. This may be relevant in some local council areas in Fiji where development is still in progress and old structures require upgrading. It encourages landowners to remove obsolete and dilapidated structures from their land. It also provides incentives to undertake redevelopment, refurbishment and upgrading of existing structures. As a result of redevelopment, values of the properties in the neighbourhood will tend to rise, benefiting the owner and the community at large and expanding the non-property tax base. It has been noted that unimproved capital value systems provide incentive for the full utilisation of land, as there is no penalty in the form of higher taxes for the making of improvements. UCV assessment can be done more cheaply and uniformly. The value of land fits more easily into the general pattern of values and assessment can be done using mass appraisal techniques.

The UCV system is seen as being cheap to administer. In Fiji, only government valuers who are familiar with UCV system undertake rating valuation work. The exercise is to determine the benchmark values and interpolate them to determine a land value for each parcel within a rating area. The system is seen as more straightforward compared to the valuation of improvements as required under an improved capital value system.

A major disadvantage of the UCV system is that of obtaining accurate transaction data for vacant plots, particularly in highly developed areas. In the absence of unimproved sales, the sites may be valued by reference to a residual approach or by isolating land value from sales of both land and buildings. The two cities in Fiji, namely Suva and Lautoka, are almost completely developed within the metropolitan area and as a consequence it is very difficult to obtain vacant sales information.

Another disadvantage associated with the UCV method is that it provides a limited tax base and therefore produces sufficient revenue only at high nominal rates. Excluding the value of improvements results in a significant proportion of the value of property being effectively exempted from the property tax. Two similar lots may have the same UCV but in terms of the development, they may be producing significantly different levels of income/profit for the property owners. It can therefore be argued that the UCV system is insensitive to vertical and horizontal equities as well as to the taxpayer's ability to pay.

An important issue is that under the present UCV system properties situated in better locations pay higher rates in comparison to those located on lower valued sections, notwithstanding that both enjoy the same services. In addition, an owner of a vacant lot pays the same rates as an adjoining improved section.

It is important to maintain fairness in the system, so that property owners pay rates in proportion to the development of their property and the services they enjoy from local councils. The International Association of Assessing Officers (IAAO, 1997) suggests that the property rate can be a stable and economically efficient revenue base for local councils if the rate structure provides the highest possible degree of equity among the ratepayers. The other disadvantage of the present system is that the majority of land in urban centres of Fiji is leasehold, notwithstanding that the rating value is based on freehold title.

The United Nations (1968) pointed out that sales are considered the best evidence of value if enough reliable data is available. The present difficulty stems in Fiji from the nature of land tenure in local council areas, which is predominantly leasehold. It is therefore difficult to arrive at fee simple values (UCV) of rateable properties. Thus the requirement under the section 63 of the Local Government Act is not fulfilled.

Other difficulties and anomalies are associated with the definition of UCV. For example, improvements such as levelling, clearing and filling carried out many years in the past are virtually impossible to identify. A further important issue relates to the ability to pay. Generally speaking any rating system that lacks the fairness factor will not command widespread ratepayers' support.

Fiji could also consider the introduction of differential rating. In New Zealand the rating legislation has been amended to provide for special rateable values for areas where zoning has resulted in rating anomalies.

Furthermore, the rating authorities have designated differential rating areas where they have been considered necessary to attain equity between separate groups of ratepayers.

In New Zealand and Australia legislation makes provision for using different rates in the dollar within the rating area of an authority. It is based on the use and location of the land. For example, if agricultural land falls within a local council area a deduction is normally given in the rates when compared with rates on land for other uses. A different rate in the dollar for different uses can be specified in order to ameliorate any perceived equity problems. In all cases the rating authority makes the decision after seeking the approval of the ratepayers.

A further advantage of differential rating is that a greater flexibility can be exercised to distribute the rate burden among different classes of property. This would clearly be of benefit if capital value rating is to be considered in place of the existing rate structure. Adopting this approach a local council can encourage or discourage certain classes of development within its jurisdiction. In addition, it is possible to promote certain types of development or commercial operations by charging a reduced rate in the dollar for that particular development.

The purpose of the tax assessment or valuation is to provide an equitable basis for distributing the burden of the property tax. A system that delivers fair and defensible valuations at reasonable costs is likely to be widely accepted. What is important in the tax system is that of objectivity which in turn reduces disputes or collusion. It needs a methodology appropriate to a country as well as a system where the market information is readily available in the local jurisdiction.

References

Anderson, M. and Kelly, B. (2000), '*Assessing Minnesota's Property Tax: Improving Affordability for Homeowners*', Property Tax Study Committee, Minnesota.

Balsley, H.L. (1970), '*Qualitative Research Methods for Business and Economics*', Random House, New York.

Becker, P.A., Woodruff, A.M., Racz, L.L., Strasma, J. and Holland, H.D. (1969), '*Land and Building Taxes: Their effect on Economic Development*', University of Wisconsin Press, Wisconsin.

Bird, R.M. and Oldman, O. (1975), '*Reading on Taxation in Developing Countries*', Johns Hopkins, Baltimore, United States.

Boydell, S. and Reddy, W. (2000), '*Contemporary Land Tenure Issues in the Republic of Fiji*', paper presented at Pacific Rim Real Estate Society conference, Sydney, Australia.

Cesare, C.M.D. (1999), 'Vertical Assessment Equity: A Fair analysis' (http://www.surveying.salford.ac.uk/buhu/biztruit/papers/cesare.htm) (cited 2/6/01 2001).

Connellan, O. and Lichfield, N. (1997), '*Land Value Taxation in Britain for the Benefit of the Community: History, Achievements and Prospects*', Lincoln Institute of Land Policy, Working Paper, Cambridge, MA, United States.

Connellan, O. (2004), '*Land Value Taxation in Britain: Experience and Opportunities*', Lincoln Institute of Land Policy, Cambridge, MA, United States.

Connellan, O. and Plimmer, F. (1996), '*Is Market Value a Desirable Basis for Property Taxation?*', paper presented at European Real Estate Society Conference, Belfast, Northern Ireland.

Cooke, S.C. (1998), 'Lessons from the Property Tax Initiatives in Idaho', *Northwest Journal of Business and Economics,* vol. 6 no. 4, pp. 63-76.

Dillinger, W. (1988), '*Urban Property Tax Reform: a case of the Philippines*', Infrastructure and Urban Development Department, World Bank, New York.

Dillinger, W. (1991), '*Urban Property Tax Reform: Infrastructure and Urban Development Department*', World Bank, New York.

Elliot, P. and Zulu, M. (2000), '*The Incentive Effect of Property Taxation on the Property Developer as Landowner: A Conceptual Framework*', paper presented at Pacific Rim Real Estate Society Conference, Sydney, Australia.

Ellis, L. (1994), '*Research Methods in the Social Sciences*', Wm C. Brown Communication, United States.

George, H. (1992), '*Progress and Poverty*', John S. Swift, New York.

Gillespie, L. (1956), 'Annual Value System of Rating', *The New Zealand Valuer,* vol. 14 no. 4, pp. 11-14.

Guise, J.W.B. (1959), 'Some Thoughts on Unimproved Value', *The New Zealand Valuer,* vol. 17 no. 4, pp.125-132.

Harvey, D. (1976), '*Social Justice and the City*', Edward Arnold, London.

Herps, M.D. (2001), '*Land Value Taxation in Australia and its Potential for Reforming our Chaotic Tax System*', Macquarie University, School of Economics.

Inglis, E.R. (1960), 'Unimproved Capital Value: The need for Clarification of the Definition', *The New Zealand Valuer,* vol. 17 no. 7, pp. 245-268.

Finance', Institute of Revenues and Rating Valuation, London.

IAAO (1992), '*Communication: Understanding Your Assessment*', International Association of Assessing Officers, Chicago, United States.

IAAO (1997), '*Standards on Property Tax Policy*', International Association of Assessing Officers, Chicago, United States.

IRRV (1999), '*Principles for Local Government* Mander, M.R. (1982), 'New Zealand Rating Valuation System', *The Valuer,* vol. 16 no. 3, pp. 239-241.

McCluskey,W.J., Connellan, O. and Plimmer, F. (1997), '*Landed Property Tax: The Best of All Possible Worlds*', paper presented at RICS Cutting Edge Conference, Dublin, Ireland.

Meeking, P.S. (1994), '*Overview of the Australian Property Tax System*', paper presented at the Congress International Federation of Surveyors, Melbourne, Australia.

Meier, R. (1993), '*Social Justice and Local Development Policy*', Sage Publications, Beverly Hills, California. .

Narayan, V. (1999), '*Review of Unimproved Value Basis of Land Valuation in Municipal Councils of Fiji*', paper presented to the Fiji Government, Suva.

Tricket, J. (1982), 'Unimproved Value in Queensland', *The Valuer*, pp. 237-238.

United Nations (1968), '*Manual of Land Tax Administration*', Department of Economic and Social Affairs United Nations, New York.

Walpole, R.E. (1974), '*Introduction to Statistics*', Macmillan Publishing, New York.

Waugh, B. (2001), 'Local Government Rating', Valuer-General, New Zealand.

Legislation referred to:

Local Government Act (1972), Fiji.
Counter Inflation Act (1973), Fiji.
Local Government Act (1974), New Zealand.
Rating Valuation Act (1998), New Zealand.
Valuation of Land Act (1971), South Australia.
Local Government Act (1999), South Australia.
Valuation of Land Act (1916), No. 2 New South Wales.
Valuation of Land Act (1944), Queensland.

Chapter 4

Land Value Taxation in Kenya

Guest Author Washington H.A. Olima

Introduction

Kenya has a total area of 580,367 square kilometres, about the size of Texas or one-quarter the size of the Democratic Republic of Congo. Only about 20 per cent of Kenya's land is considered to have high or medium potential for farming or intensive livestock production. Another 10 per cent of the land is categorized as marginal for agriculture, while the remaining 70 per cent is used for extensive grazing or taken up by national parks and forests (Migot-Adholla et al, 1994). According to the 1999 population census estimates, Kenya had a total population of 28.8 million and has one of the highest agricultural population densities in the world when it's agroclimatic potential is taken into consideration (Republic of Kenya, 2000).

Kenya, bordered by Tanzania, Uganda, Sudan, Ethiopia and Somali is divided into eight administrative units known as provinces: Nairobi, Central, Nyanza, Western, Eastern, Rift Valley, Coast and North Eastern. When Kenya was founded as a settler colony, large tracts of the most fertile agricultural land were set aside for exclusive occupation of white settlers under freehold tenure or leasehold. Africans were confined to specific 'native reserves', where land pressure was soon aggravated by rapid population growth, restriction of movement, prohibition of production of high-value commodities, and price discrimination.

The establishment of a settler colonial economy in Kenya led to demands of ideas of land ownership that were to dominate the entire span of both the colonial and post-colonial land policy in Kenya (Kiamba, 1989). Okoth-Ogendo (1978) observed that 'the settler concern was that the property system should provide an environment in which private enterprise would have the fullest expression and protection'. The individualization of land ownership did not take place in a vacuum, but in a total historical context where the introduction and dominance of the capitalist mode of production had the sanctity and inviolability of private property as its central principle (Ley, 1975).

Landed property in Kenya is owned by an individual, group of individuals, company, or public authority and is subject to a local charge levied by the local authorities. This local charge, commonly referred to as property tax is levied for the purposes of collecting revenue to finance local government services. In Kenya, under the Local Government Act of 1963 (Chapter 265 of the Laws of Kenya), local authorities were created and charged with the responsibility of providing and maintaining a wide range of public services such as primary education and public health (Syagga, 1994). Local authorities like Nairobi, Mombasa, Kisumu and Nakuru are, however, charged with the responsibility of providing a range of services such as:

- establishment and maintenance of hospitals, clinics and health centres within the local authority area of jurisdiction;
- provision of environmental health services by ensuring that there are good sanitary, garbage collection, and sewerage services;
- provision of clean and treated water to its residents. For this purpose there should be maintenance of waterworks and water mains and protection of water against pollution. This is aimed at ensuring that people within its area of jurisdiction stay healthy so as to engage in productive activities for the development of the area;
- establishment and maintenance of primary and nursery schools within the respective areas of jurisdiction;
- provision and maintenance of public roads, footpaths and bridges within its boundaries;
- establishment and maintenance of such offices and buildings for the purpose of council and public meetings and assemblies and also provision of low cost housing for the residents;
- establishment and maintenance of cultural and social facilities such as art galleries, museums, zoos, parks and recreational facilities for entertainment within its boundaries;
- provision and maintenance of cemeteries, crematoria and mortuaries and control the burial for the dead within its area;
- establishment, maintenance, letting and management of public markets and market buildings;
- monitoring and control of building development and planning. To achieve this function, for example, the Nairobi City Council (NCC) through Planning and Architecture department have to ensure that all plans for new buildings and extensions conform to the building by

laws and planning regulations. This function is aimed at ensuring that buildings erected are fit for human habitation; and

• provision and maintenance of street lights.

Local authorities undertake these functions through committees, which are usually constituted under Part VI of the Local Government Act, Cap 265 of the Laws of Kenya. Such committees include among others: finance, health, town planning and staff committees. The decisions of these committees are, however, subject to confirmation of the full council meetings of the relevant authority.

Historical background to property taxation

Property taxation practice traces its origin to the feudal era in England when the Anglo-Saxon Kings delegated to the villages and towns the duties of watching over their local affairs instead of the state (Emery and Wilks, 1984). Thus a number of institutions developed including one that grew amid church vesting where citizens, chaired by a priest, organized the execution of works such as road and bridge construction and church repairs. In order to meet the costs of these activities a levy was put on the occupiers of land. The other form of institution grew around the town corporations, which were given charters to exercise some local autonomy. The Poor Relief Act, often referred to as the State of Elizabeth enacted in 1601, is arguably seen to be the foundation of modern property taxation in Britain. It has, however, undergone several amendments both in United Kingdom and her former colonies.

The introduction of property taxation, commonly referred to as rating in Kenya is a relatively recent phenomenon. It was not until the beginning of the last century that it was introduced by the British colonial rule when local governments were created. In an attempt to enable the created local authorities to meet the challenges, the British colonial administration tried any policy on land management that had worked elsewhere. According to Hicks (1961), the campaign for taxing land spread from South Africa into Rhodesia and later to the three British East African territories of Kenya, Uganda and Tanganyika (Tanzania).

Land taxation was introduced in Kenya in 1900, when the first system was applied in Mombasa on an annual rental value basis under street cleaning and regulations. The following year, the same was applied in Nairobi. In 1923, annual value rating was, however, found wanting as only a few properties had been developed. The desire was thus to widen the base of the tax and it was not until 1928 that the recommendations of the District Committee to apply unimproved site value rating was introduced. In Nairobi, however, this had been introduced in 1920 in conformity with the systems then existing in Australia, New Zealand and West Canada. This was a departure from the English system that was found unsuitable in new growing townships. The introduction of site value was to a great extent influenced by Henry George's ideas of a single land tax system.

Revenue sources for local authorities in Kenya

Local authorities in Kenya are empowered by the Local Government Act Cap 265 of the Laws of Kenya to raise their revenue from a variety of sources including indirect taxes, income from property, sales of goods and services, and loans (Olima, 1999: 359). Local authorities therefore raise revenue to meet their expenditure and provide public services such as street lighting, maintenance of the streets, refuse collection and disposal, sewerage disposal and fire-fighting services through the following:

- charging of fees in form of service charge for the services rendered;
- letting of residential housing estates at a rent to the members of the public;
- levying of fees for the supply of treated piped water for domestic use. This fee is levied on the users of water;
- levying of fees for the purpose of collection and disposal of garbage;
- temporary borrowing from financial institutions;
- grants in form of Local Authorities Transfer Fund (LATF) from the Central Government. According to the Local Government Act, such grants are given in order to improve the financial position of those local authorities with below average revenue and above average needs; and
- levying of fees in form of rates on all ratable property owners within the jurisdiction of a local authority for the purpose of providing and maintaining essential services such as roads and sewer.

Fees and charges include payments to local authorities for certain services, which directly benefit only a certain class of the community or individuals who use them. These include house rents paid for council houses, school fees, water and sewerage charges among others. Licences, on the other hand, are fees paid for permits issued by a local authority for the purposes of carrying out certain trades, businesses and occupations as provided for under the local government regulations (1963). These include market fees, slaughter fees and bus park fees among others. The service charge which was introduced in 1992 and later withdrawn in 2000 generated a substantial amount of revenue. But local authorities could only spend 50 per cent of the collected service charge without seeking approval from the Minister of Local Authorities.

Revenue from water and sewerage is basically borrowed and has to be refunded. The account is used to repay loans and for capital expenditures especially for the provision of water and sewerage services. The other tax forms can be increased only to a limited extent because of their interaction with state taxes. Currently, there is a general move in Kenya to privatize the provision of water and sewerage services through the formation of water and sewerage companies in major urban centers.

The land rate is considered as an instrument to close the deficit between other revenues and estimated expenditure. The percentage rate is adjusted according to this deficit, and the rating authority apportions the total rate liability among ratepayers accordingly, in line with statutory requirements. The requirements empower rating authorities to levy a rate on the unimproved site value of the land appearing in the valuation roll provided such a rate will not, without consent of the Minister, exceed four per cent of the unimproved site value (Valuation for Rating Act, Cap. 267 Laws of Kenya).

The financial structure of local government is characterized by both current and capital accounts. Current revenue falling under the General Fund Vote, is derived from direct sales of goods and services, fees and charges, but the main source of finance stems from fiscal measures imposed on private property (Gachuru and Olima, 1998).

The legal framework of property valuation and taxation

There are basically two pieces of legislation and legal framework that govern the operations of local authorities in respect to property valuation and taxation. These include:

- the Valuation for Rating Act (1984) Cap 266, Laws of Kenya; and
- the Rating Act (1986), Cap 267, Laws of Kenya.

Basically, the laws relating to administration and forms of rating in Kenya are contained in two Acts of Parliament which were passed to enable local authorities throughout the country to rate land and buildings.

The Valuation for Rating Act (1984) Cap. 266, Laws of Kenya

This Act provides for valuation of land for the purposes of levying rates. Essentially it deals with methods of valuation for purposes of rating and the procedures to be followed in the preparation of valuation rolls.

The Valuation for Rating Act provides for three systems of rating namely: area rating, unimproved site value rating and improvement rating. Unimproved site value rating and improvement rating apply to urban areas whereas area rating was to be applied to agricultural land. Urban authorities are allowed by law to use either unimproved site rating or improvement rating or both methods. However, unimproved site value rating has proved to be more attractive to local authorities because of its amenability to mass appraisal and simplicity in comparison to other methods. In applying site value rating, rates are based on the market value of the unimproved bare land, and where the land is developed, the improvements are ignored.

Improvement rating, however, was only tried in Mombasa but was abandoned after a short period of time due to defects in the law (Aritho-Gitonga, 1980). The system never succeeded due to its influence on development and also to the fact that by then, many Kenyan towns had low levels of development, for instance, buildings which could not be valued with any certainty as they were constructed of mud, tin and paper, and the local authority by laws regarded such developments as illegal.

Value definitions

The basis of assessment of land for purposes of levying rates are provided in Section 8 of the Valuation for Rating Act as the value of land and the value of unimproved land.

Value of land

Section 8(1) provides the definition of the value of land as:

> ...the value of land shall, for the purposes of a valuation roll or supplementary valuation roll, be the sum which the freehold in possession free from encumbrances therein might be expected to realize at the time of

valuation if offered for sale on such reasonable terms and conditions as a bona fide seller might be expected to impose, due regard being had, not only to that particular land, but also to other land of similar class, character or position, and to other comparative factors, and to any restrictions imposed on the land, and on the use of the land, by the local authority or a town planning authority by or under any by-laws or town planning powers or the Eviction of Tenants (Control) (Mombasa) Act, being restrictions which either increase or decrease the value of the land.

Value of unimproved land

Section 8(2) provides the definition of the value of unimproved land as:

> ...the value of unimproved land shall, for the purposes of a valuation roll or supplementary valuation roll, be the sum which the freehold in possession free from encumbrances therein might be expected to realize at the time of valuation if offered for sale on such reasonable terms and conditions as a bona fide seller might be expected to impose, and if the improvements, if any, thereon, therein or thereunder had not been made, due regard being had, not only to that particular land, but also to other land of similar class, character or position, and to other comparative factors, and to any restrictions imposed on the land, and on the use of the land, by the local authority or a town planning authority by or under any by-laws or town planning powers, being restrictions which either increase or decrease the value of the land.

In arriving at the value of land under this section, the valuer may adopt any suitable method of valuation. When a valuation roll or supplementary valuation roll includes the value of the unimproved land, the value of any improvements and the value of the land, then the value of improvements shall in no case exceed the amount found by deducting the value of the unimproved land from the value of the land.

Improvement, in relation to land, means all work done or material used on, in or under such land by the expenditure of money or labour in so far as the effect of such work done or material used is to increase the value of the land, but does not include machinery, whether fixed to the soil or not.

Sections 25(1) and 26(1) for the Valuation of Rating Act 1984 stipulate that both public land and community land should be for the purposes of assessing the contribution in lieu of rates payable be valued in accordance with the principles laid down in this act. In arriving at the value of land, the valuer is empowered to use any suitable method of valuation since the act does not specify methods of valuation to be used. This has, however, given rise to several conflicting interpretations in valuation methods which in turn introduces uncertainty and complexity in valuations (Olima, 1999). For instance, a petrol service station with ancillary buildings is for purposes of rating based on the throughput method of valuation, while adjacent plots are based on general area zoning and plot sizes. It is a contention that although the valuation courts in Kenya have upheld the use of the throughput method, it is essentially a measure of annual value and not capital value. The Kenyan experience is that these uncertainties in valuations introduce unnecessary disputes and costly litigation between rateable owners and rating authorities.

The Rating Act of 1986, Chapter 267 of the Laws of Kenya

The Rating Act 1986 is supplementary to the Valuation for Rating Act, and simply empowers urban and rural authorities to be rating authorities under the Valuation for Rating Act (Olima, 1999). Local authorities derive the power to levy rates from Section 3 of the Rating Act which states that 'Rates shall be levied by the rating authority to meet all liabilities falling to be discharged out of the general rates fund'.

Section 4(1) of the Rating Act stipulates the forms of rating that the rating authority may adopt for the purposes of levying rates. They include:

• an area rate in urban areas in accordance with Section 5;
• an agricultural rental value rate in rural areas;
• a site value rate or a site value rate in combination with an improvement rate in accordance with Section 6.

The form of rating and the area to which it is to be applied is subject to approval by the Minister of Local Government. For instance, Section 5 provides that the rating authority may, with the approval of the Minister, adopt one or more of the following methods of area rating:

• a flat rate upon the area of land;
• a graduated rate upon the area of land;
• a differential flat rate or a differential graduated rate upon the area of land according to the use to which the land is put, or capable or being put, or for which it is reserved;
• an industrial rate upon the area of land used for other than agricultural or residential purposes;
• a residential rate upon the area of land used for residential purposes; and

- such other method of rating upon the area of land or buildings or other immovable property as the rating authority may resolve.

The rating authority may adopt different methods of area rating for different parts of a rating authority area and may from time to time vary the method or methods adopted. The percentage rate charged using the various forms of rating as mentioned above should not exceed 4 per cent of the unimproved value of land unless consented to by the Minister of Local Government.

Land tenure

The land delivery system in Kenya has no doubt had immense effects on the land tenure, ownership patterns, allocation procedures, and other land transactions. A survey carried out within the Ministry of Lands and Settlement revealed that various activities are performed. These land transactions include seeking consent to transfer, approval of part development plans, new land allocations, approval of sub-divisions, extensions of leases, and change of users.

Land tenure touches deep emotions. It often plays a critical role in the individual's sense of participation in a society, as well as in the investment of labour and capital likely to be made on any parcel of land. The form of land tenure in any area has a profound effect on physical urban land patterns.

Access to land, through either regulation of tenure in existing unauthorized areas or supplying of new land, is generally determined by tenure, the distribution of ownership patterns, cost in relation to household income, and aspects of land administration system such as responsibility for subdivision, land allocation and systems for regulating use. In Kenyan urban areas, the public land allocation and tenure system was introduced by the colonial administration. It entailed a strong administrative control over the supply of land, and has turned out to be cumbersome and bureaucratic. The state bureaucracy is still responsible for the overall management of land, determining who gets what, where and how in respect to public land. This is particularly important since land registration and taxation are at the same time state controlled. However, recent years have witnessed a decreasing capability of the state to manage urban land. The exponential growth in bureaucracy is evident in procedures of legal transactions in, and legal development of, land. Little attention seems to be given to real costs

to landowners and land developers. Politics normally triumphs over law.
Table 4.1 shows the basic categories of land in Kenya.

Table 4.1   Basic categories of land in Kenya

Land category	Ownership	Type	User	Governing Legislation
Government Land	Kenya Government on behalf of the public	Utilized. Unutilized. Unalienated (reserved)	Government own use. General public uses	Government Lands Act, Cap. 280. Administered by the Commissioner of Lands
Trust Land (Communal land)	Under trusteeship by local authorities under customary laws and rights	Utilized. Unutilized	Local residents. Various uses including agriculture	Trust Lands Act, Cap. 288. The Commissioner of Lands is the administering agent.
Private Land	Private individuals	Freehold and leasehold tenure	Registered individuals organizations Various uses	Registered Land Act, Cap. 300.

Source: Republic of Kenya (1991)

Importance of land/property tax

Local authorities in Kenya have continued with their endeavor to provide
services to the growing population. However, the growth in expenditure
has always surpassed that of revenue resulting in budget deficits over the
years. Tables 4.2 and 4.3 provide for the sources of recurrent revenue for
both Municipal Councils and the County or Town Councils, respectively.
Out of this revenue, property rates have made a significant contribution.
For all the municipal councils put together, the rates have been contributing
an average of 27 per cent of the revenue over the years, depending on the
efficiency of recovery. The figures have fluctuated from a very low rate of
18 per cent in 1995 to a rate of 38.1 per cent in 1997 but which again
dropped to 27 per cent in 1999. In case of Town and Country Councils, the

contribution of rates to revenue has averaged 12.15 per cent, and varying from a low of 6.01 per cent in 1997 to a reasonably good rate of 30 per cent in 1995. In both cases, however, apart from the sale of goods and services, which provides the highest revenue base, rates are the next highest source of revenue.

Table 4.2   Municipal councils: economic analysis of current revenue in million KShs, 1993-1999

Current Revenue	1993	1994	1995	1996	1997	1998	1999
Property Rates	58.96	60.24	36.23	87.12	87.12	107.23	86.16
Indirect Taxes (Licences & Cesses)	18.00	7.47	21.86	28.15	17.99	27.22	16.81
Property Rents	16.01	23.08	10.40	20.98	15.46	25.95	18.81
Current Transfers	0.03	0.03	2.32	1.12	0.50	8.18	0.04
Sale of Good and Services	139.16	152.23	130.52	112.72	107.35	179.16	201.74
Total	232.16	243.16	201.33	250.09	228.42	347.74	323.56
Rates as % of Total	25.40	25.4	18.00	35.00	38.10	31.00	27.00

Source: Kenya Economic Survey, 2000

Table 4.3   Town, urban and county councils: economic analysis of recurrent revenue in million KShs, 1993-1999

Current Revenue	1993	1994	1995	1996	1997	1998	1999
Property Rates	3.95	5.12	24.55	13.22	3.97	23.00	10.42
Indirect Taxes (Licences & Cesses)	10.72	15.20	20.11	16.27	13.37	18.79	22.58
Property Rents	0.63	2.22	8.05	1.88	0.75	3.03	1.91
Current Transfers	0.11	0.18	0.21	0.02	0.06	0.02	0.18
Sale of Good and Services	38.90	37.41	29.99	29.58	47.87	50.76	76.93
Total	54.13	243.05	82.91	60.97	66.02	95.60	112.02
Rates as % of Total	7.30	8.50	30.00	22.00	6.01	24.05	9.30

Source: Kenya Economic Survey, 2000

With improved collection, rates can be a major source of revenue to reduce the levels of deficits currently experienced by local authorities. Tables 4.4a and 4.4b which are derived from the Economic Survey 2000 provide for analysis of total expenditures against the total revenues by the local authorities over periods between 1995 and 1999. Expenditures have been increasing at a faster rate than revenues. This is mainly due to a lack of diversification in the sources or revenue, and stagnating current sources, against increasing demand for them. The low revenue for town, urban, and county councils is mainly due to the low level of development since most of the councils are predominantly rural in nature. Furthermore, land values are low, most properties are not rateable since they are unsurveyed, and the tax is not well developed in the councils. What is evident is that deficits are growing and therefore there is urgent need to arrest the situation.

Table 4.4a   Revenue and expenditure for municipal councils in millions KShs: 1995-1999

Year	1995	1996	1997	1998	1999
Revenue (R)	240.00	253.67	269.74	358.73	338.64
Expenditure (E)	373.36	325.00	348.32	450.36	409.47
R/E as %	64.28	78.05	77.44	79.65	82.70

Source: Kenya Economic Survey, 2000

Table 4.4b   Revenue and expenditure for town and county councils in millions KShs: 1995-1999

Year	1995	1996	1997	1998	1999
Revenue (R)	82.91	61.05	66.04	95.96	112.32
Expenditure (E)	87.76	86.22	97.51	121.17	133.49
R/E as %	94.47	70.81	67.73	79.19	84.14

Source: Kenya Economic Survey, 2000

The financial situation of most other local authorities is extremely serious. Technically, most of them are insolvent with a deficit in the General Revenue Fund considerably exceeding its debtor's accounts, i.e. supported by unpaid rates, and charges rather than liquid assets (Gachuru and Olima, 1998). By 1990, the real expenditures of municipal councils were declining overall by more than 12 per cent while urban populations were rising at an estimated 7 per cent per annum. The result is, chronic delinquency on the part of the local authorities and overdue debt service liability. The financial distress of the majority of local authorities has reached crisis proportions.

Increases in local government expenditure entails increased borrowing from central government and more dependence on government grants. Central government controls the revenue raising capacity of local authorities as well as setting limits on the level of borrowing from the Local Government Loans Authority (LGLA). Currently, there is a grant system in the form of LATF (Local Authority Transfer Fund) to facilitate the flow of budgetary resources from central government to cover any deficits that may arise. However, because of the limitations inherent in the government grants and local sources of revenue for local authorities, there is a need to fully utilize existing sources, which are not controlled by central government.

Administration of property tax

It is the responsibility of the respective local authority to coordinate the valuation of their properties for rating purposes, preparation of valuation rolls, and collection of the approved rates. The assessment departments are locally based within the jurisdiction of a given local authority. The practice however, varies from one local authority to another. For instance, in the case of Nairobi City Council and other large municipalities including Mombasa, Kisumu and Nakuru, the assessment departments are within the authorities. For example, in the case of Nairobi City Council the assessment of rateable properties is carried out by their own in-house valuers with the assistance of technicians in the Department of Valuation.

In 1996, for instance, the number of staff involved in the assessment of rateable properties and preparation of the valuation roll within Nairobi City Council was twenty three of which ten were valuers, twelve were technicians and one was a valuation assistant (Kich, 1996). On the other hand, local authorities with no valuers in their direct employment have to rely on either the services of valuers employed by the central government or valuers employed by private valuation firms. For instance, Nyeri County Council initially relied on government valuers but have since stopped and currently hire private valuation firms (Githinji, 1990). Valuers in Kenya, however, whether or not working in public or private sectors are at least graduates in Land Economics from either the University of Nairobi or other recognized universities. In addition, they must be members of the Institution of Surveyors of Kenya and registered by the Valuers Registration Board.

Procedure for preparing the valuation roll

It is the obligation of the rating authority to ensure that a valuation roll is prepared at least once in every ten years or such longer period as the Minister of Local Government may approve, in accordance with section 3 of the Valuation for Rating Act 1984. Before the beginning of the work, the rating authority is required to pass a number of resolutions and obtain the Minister's approval. The resolutions to be passed include the appointment of the valuer, adoption of the form of rating to be applied (whether improvement, site value or area rating) and declaration of an area within the council boundary to be rateable area. It is stipulated that only one form of rating can be adopted by a rating authority at any time.

The preparation of the valuation roll by valuers begins with the collection of all relevant development plans from the planning department. The sales figures available are marked on a map to give the valuer a picture of the land values in the town. Section 5 of the Valuation for Rating Act 1984 gives the valuers power to enter and inspect properties or call for any data that they may require to enable them to carry out thorough analysis so as to arrive at the appropriate site values. The valuation roll when completed will show all the rateable properties in terms of:

- the description, situation and area of the land valued;
- name and address of rateable owner;
- the value of the land;
- the value of the unimproved land; and
- the assessment for improvement rate.

Many local authorities still do not prepare valuation rolls every ten years as statutorily required. Apart from the lack of adequate valuers, the absence of recent registered property sales has also led to the application of outdated valuation roll. In many cases the life of a valuation roll is fifteen years or more. For instance, the last valuation for rating in Nairobi was carried out in 1980. Since 1980 valuers have been preparing supplementary valuation rolls based on changes in ownership, user and possible cases of subdivision. The problem is not peculiar to the city of Nairobi only. The Municipal Council of Mombasa which is the second largest urban authority in Kenya sent out rate demands for 1995 based on values of all land appearing in the 1981 valuation rolls. Other towns which rely on government valuers for assessment of rates are in more difficult situations.

Section 4 of the Valuation for Rating Act gives a local authority the power to amend the valuation roll and to cause supplementary valuation rolls to be prepared at least once in each of the years following the year of valuation. The reasons for such action may include the following situations:

- any rateable property omitted from the valuation roll;
- any new ratable property;
- any rateable property which is subdivided or consolidated with other rateable property; or
- any rateable property which, from any cause particular to such rateable property arising since the time of valuation, has materially increased or decreased in value.

A supplementary valuation roll shall include only those alterations and additions to the valuation roll that are permitted by subsection (1) or subsection (2) of section 4.

Before the adoption of the main or supplementary valuation roll, the valuer is expected to sign the roll and date its completion, and then transmit it to the town clerk in compliance with section 9(1) of the Act. The town clerk shall then present the roll before a meeting of the local authority, after which it shall be available for public inspection at the local authority offices. A percentage rate to be applied to the value of unimproved land is determined by the resolution of the council and approved, by the Minister for Local Government if it exceeds 4 per cent. For instance, the highest rate of 13 per cent is levied by Mombasa Municipal Council, albeit on 1981 values. Nairobi city Council from 1996 levied a rate of 12 per cent on residential land and 13 per cent on commercial/industrial land, although again, on 1982 site values. Any person may during ordinary business hours inspect the draft main or supplementary roll and take copies or extracts from it.

The objection process

Once the draft valuation roll or the draft supplementary valuation roll is completed, it is gazetted for public information to enable rateable owners not satisfied with the assessment to lodge their objections. The objections may arise either from inclusion of any rateable property in, or omission of any rateable property from the valuation roll, and value ascribed in any valuation roll to any rateable property. As in many countries, this is a critical part of the tax system where property owners are given the opportunity to examine whether or not the assessment is fair and reasonable. The statutory period for lodging objections with the town clerk is 28 days from the date of publication of notice in the Kenya Gazette.

The town clerk shall, within 21 days after the date on which a notice of objection is lodged with him, send a copy to the rateable owner of the rateable property to which the objection relates, if such person is not the maker of the objection. If, on the expiration of the period of 28 days no objections have been received, or, if all objections duly received have been withdrawn before the day fixed for the first sitting of the valuation court, the town clerk shall endorse the draft valuation roll or draft supplementary valuation roll and sign a certificate to that effect. Section 12 of the Valuation for Rating Act, establishes a valuation court, consisting of a chairman who may be a magistrate having power to hold a subordinate court of the first class, or an advocate of not less than five years experience, and not less than two additional members appointed with the approval of the Minister for local Government. The valuation court is appointed for the purposes of hearing objections and determining appropriate values.

The town clerk or any other person appointed by the local authority acts as clerk to the valuation court. At every sitting of a valuation court three members present constitute a quorum, and all the decisions are arrived at by a majority decision. After hearing all the objections, the valuation court confirms or amends the draft valuation roll or draft supplementary roll by way of reduction, increase, addition or omission. The chairman of the valuation court then endorses and signs a certificate confirming the completion of the exercise. The town clerk will then publish a notice that the draft valuation or draft supplementary valuation roll has been signed and certified. Section 18(2) of the Valuation for Rating Act provides that a valuation roll duly signed by either the chairman of a valuation court or the town clerk shall remain in force until it is wholly superseded by a new valuation roll.

Any person who has appeared before a valuation court, and is aggrieved by the decision of the valuation court on the determination of objection, may appeal against the decision of the valuation court within one month from the date of the notice to:

- the High Court, if such valuation court was appointed under section 12 of this Act;
- a subordinate court held by a Senior Resident Magistrate or a Resident Magistrate, if such valuation court was appointed under section 13 of the Act.

The appeal to the High Court after the valuation court is final in the determination of rateable values.

Exemptions, reliefs and concessions

There are certain properties, which are exempted from valuation for rating purposes. The types of properties exempted are provided under section 27(1) of the Valuation for Rating Act, and include:

- places for public religious worship;
- cemeteries, crematoria and burial or burning grounds;
- hospitals or other institutions for the treatment of the sick;
- educational institutions (including public schools within the meaning of the Education Act), and including the residence of students provided directly by educational institutions or forming part of, or being ancillary to, educational institutions;
- charitable institutions and libraries;
- outdoor sports; and
- National Parks within the meaning of the National Park of Kenya Act.

However, the listed properties are exempted from rating in as much as they are not used for profit making or for residential purposes other than for the residence of students. Section 22(1) of the Rating Act points out that no area rate or agricultural rental value rate shall be imposed on any land which would be land in respect of which no valuation for the purposes of any rate may be made under the Valuation for Rating Act. The rating authority, however, can provide reliefs and concessions in the determination of rates payable by the prospective rateable owners. For instance, Nairobi City Council from 1996 levies a general rate of 13 per cent of the unimproved site value of land as appearing in the 1982 valuation roll. In accordance with section 22(2) of the Rating Act, Nairobi City Council effected a reduction or remission of payment of the rates levied as follows:

- rates equivalent to 1 per cent of the unimproved site value on land designated for residential purposes; and
- rates equivalent to 3 per cent of the unimproved site value on land designated for agricultural purposes.

In addition, section 16(2) of the Rating Act empowers the rating authority with the approval of the Minister to allow a discount of not more than 5 per cent or such other discount on any rate paid on or before the day in which such rate becomes payable. Subsequently, the Nairobi City Council in 1996 resolved that the discounts ranging between 1 per cent and 5 per cent be applied on full payments of rates in 1996 as follows: full payments received by January – 5 per cent; February – 4 per cent; March – 3 per cent; April – 2 per cent; and May – 1 per cent. However, rate accounts with outstanding balances as at 31st December, 1995 do not qualify for the discount. If any rates remained unpaid after the 31st May 1996 interest at the rate of 2 per cent monthly or part thereof to be paid to the Nairobi City council on the amount unpaid. The concessions rarely benefit the ratepayers. Due to the bureaucratic procedures within the local authorities, the demand notices often reach the ratepayers late.

The law is very explicit on the collection procedures. Section 15(1) of the Rating Act, Chapter 267 provides that every rate levied by the rating authority shall become due on the first day of January in the financial year for which it is levied and shall become payable on such day in the same financial year as shall be fixed by the rating authority. The payment day and the amount of rate are to be made public by the rating authority by giving at least 30 days' notice.

Section 16(1) of the same Act provides that when the rating authority has given notice under Section 15 of the day on which any rate levied will become payable, it shall be the duty of every person liable for such rate to pay the amount of such rate at the offices of the rating authority or at any place. The Nairobi City Council and all other rating authorities in Kenya have accounts offices that deal with collection of all forms of rates.

Section 17 deals with procedures for enforcing rate payment by defaulters. When a rateable owner fails to pay rates due within the stipulated time period, plus any interest on any such unpaid rate, the rating authority may make a written demand notice on the rateable owner requiring him or her to make rate payment plus any interest that has accrued thereto within 14 days after service of the written demand notice. Failure to comply means the rating authority is empowered to take proceedings in a subordinate court of the first class to secure the payment of such rate and interest. A decree granted by a subordinate court in favour of the rating authority may be enforced by any rules made under the Civil Procedure Act, Chapter 22 of the Laws of Kenya. In those situations where the sum due from the rateable owner is secured by a charge over the landed property by virtue of section 19, the degree holder may apply to the High Court by originating summons to order the sale of such land to recover the amount of rate plus any interest due. The proceedings to recover unpaid rates may be commenced at any time within 12 years of the day upon which the rates become due and payable. In addition, section 18 of the Rating Act empowers the rating authority to recover unpaid rates from tenants or occupiers of the rateable property by issuing a notice requiring them to make all future payments of the rent directly to the rating authority until such a time that all the unpaid rates plus any accrued interest have been paid.

The actual collection of rates in the local authorities have experienced several problems. The methods adopted are themselves inefficient and ineffective. Frequently local authorities place advertisements in local newspapers appealing to ratepayers to remit their payments. This is an indication that local authorities are unable to collect all the rates due. The ineffective administration has resulted in a high rate of defaulting. For example, in the period between 1976 and 1979 the Kenya Railways Corporation owed the Nairobi City Council about KShs. 1.8 million in rates (Ogero, 1981). In the year 2003, at least 59 per cent of rates due in Mombasa Municipal Council remained unpaid (Otunga, 2004).

Inspite of the legal framework, the lack of specific machinery to enforce rate collection has been identified as a problem in the administration of rating system in Kenya (Olima and Syagga, 1996). According to Olima and Syagga (1996), the problem may be attributed to tax collection methods as aggravated by the administrative bureaucracy in local government. In addition, there is poor response by the ratepayers and long legal process involved when dealing with defaulters (Kich, 1996). For instance, in the case of Nairobi City Council there have been about 2,000 cases filed in court since the middle of 1990 against defaulters, out of which only 500 cases had been determined by the end of 1991. The situation is further complicated because, unlike water or electricity where services are denied as soon as a consumer defaults, rate defaulting has no immediate remedies, except where the owner decided to transfer the property.

Critical review

Rating is viewed with mixed feelings, both from a policy objective and from its implementation. As a tax system, rating has both advantages and disadvantages which have been the subject of debate. This section of the chapter will however, be devoted to the discussion of the merits and problems of the unimproved site value rating as practised in Kenya.

Advantages of unimproved site value rating

- the unimproved site value rating system is certain in terms of revenue generation because all the parcels of land are rated whether or not they are developed. Rates are certain both to the taxpayer and the tax collector and hence can be planned for well in advance. This is because a rate is a predetermined form of taxation and is always fixed with the aim of a given time frame;

- rating is flexible in the sense that exemptions and reliefs can readily be granted by a rating authority to certain categories of property;

- the unimproved site value rating system discourages land speculation because it increases the cost of holding such land. Anybody buying land for speculative purposes finds it a disadvantage to hold such land;

- it may encourage land development by speeding up the development process for residential, commercial, and industrial purposes. This is because unimproved site value rating ignores income receivable from property, and hence reduces the tax burden on the developed property;

- rates are difficult to avoid or evade. This is because landed property is fixed in location and thus can neither be hidden from the rating authority nor be moved away from rate assessors; and

- rates are relatively easy to collect. Should a rateable owner delay in paying or refuse to pay, the rating authority in question is empowered under section 17 of the Rating Act to distrain upon the personal goods and chattels of rateable owner to the value of the rates owed. The same section empowers the rating authority to occupy the landed property in question and take profits accruing until such a time when all the rates owed to them plus any interest thereto has been recovered.

Disadvantages of unimproved site value rating

- Rating does not totally conform to the principles of ability to pay and benefits received. This is because rating, especially, the unimproved site value rating system is regressive in terms of the rateable owner's income from the rateable property. It may be considered unjust because it fails to tax the ability to pay by placing equal burdens on landowners who may have unequal income structures. Even where rating is based on the income received from landed property, it still falls short of meeting the characteristics of equity since income is not a perfect indicator of the ability of the rateable owner to pay. This is because however much income is received from a landed property, the expenditure pattern may reduce the rateable owner's ability to pay (Kich, 1996; Ndeleki, 1991);

- the unimproved site value rating system provides for a minimal tax base because in areas where developments are substantial, for example, in Nairobi's Central Business District the unimproved site value rating system applied on its own cannot provide sufficient revenue, which is required to service the numerous facilities and amenities provided. In addition, it is difficult to assess, quantify and apportion benefits received by individual rateable owners and to charge them appropriately. This has largely contributed to the inequality in rating.

Conclusions

With better management of property administration, it is possible that the contribution of this tax to local authorities can be enhanced. The current practice is for local authorities to strike different rates of tax on the assessed site values. Assuming the rates are reasonable, since they must be approved by the Minister of Local Government in the case of each local authority, if the site values had been current, the taxes levied could be equally substantial. What is then required to be improved is the methods of collection. This, however, assumes that Kenya does not wish to change the rating system from the unimproved site value. Other countries in the region, notably Tanzania, Uganda and Zambia have adopted different systems of rating.

Local authorities in Kenya have experienced several difficulties and problems in the administration of property tax. In practice, the problems which hamper the optimization of rating as one of the major sources of revenue for local authorities may be described as technical, social and administrative as well as legal problems relating to the Valuation for Rating Act and the Rating Act. The property tax issues revolve around appraisal, rating, billing, collection, and other administrative functions including policy and institutional issues (Olima, 2001). The procedural issues include taxable properties, identifying tax liability, valuation and billing and collection. There is often an inability to administer property rolls adequately compounded by widespread payment evasion, under-assessment of valuations far below market prices, and lack of proper coordination between rates assessment and collection process.

The policy issues that impede the efficiency of administering the property tax revolve around central government control over local authorities, inequalities and ambiguous assessments, inadequate assessment practices, and recruitment and retention of professionally qualified valuers by local authorities (Olima, 2001).

The current low yield from urban property taxes reflects failures in the administration of the tax. In Kenya, a large proportion of properties are missing from the valuation rolls, properties on valuation rolls are inaccurately valued and collection efficiency is extremely poor. These administrative failures can be adequately addressed through procedural reforms including adaptation of a different system of rating, valuation accuracy, and improved collection efficiency. Adopting a different system of rating could involve using unimproved site value rating for undeveloped land and improvement rating for developed properties.

Inefficient administration and low rates, however, are political liabilities inherent in the property tax. Inappropriate policy and poor tax administration affect the attainment of a sustained increase in yields (Olima and Syagga, 1996). Any reform therefore needs to be targeted at the two aspects identified. A suitable rating tax must be evaluated using the following general criteria, i.e. yield, equity, economic efficiency and ability to implement. An equitable way of collecting socially created land values must be devised. While rate increases offer the prospect of quick revenue increases, taken individually they exaggerate the inequities in the incidence of the tax. An increase in the effective tax rate places the burden of the increase on those few individuals whose properties are on the tax rolls, accurately valued, and from whom taxes are actually collected. For instance, the current Nairobi City Council revenue base from the 1982 roll is KShs. 40 billion which at a 15 per cent rate struck by the Council should collect KShs. 2.7 billion per annum. The collection rate is currently approximately 47 per cent. If the roll is revised, the revenue base should rise to KShs. 385 billion, which even at a 1 per cent rate the revenue, will rise to KShs. 38.5 billion. This is the current potential.

There is therefore an urgent need for improvements in administration to institute efficient machinery for appropriate land inventory, including geographical information systems (GIS). Jica has completed a mapping and preparation of ʻproperty management model for Nairobi for approximately 15 square kilometres as a pilot study on spatial infrastructure study for Nairobi. This should be followed with a more appropriate rating system and efficient collection system.

References

Aritho-Gitonga, G.M. (1980), 'Rating: Local Property Taxation in Kenya', *Tropical Environmental Journal*, University of Nigeria.

Emery, R. and Wilks, H.M. (1984), *'Principles and Practice of Rating Valuation'*, Estates Gazette Limited, London.

Gachuru, M.W. and Olima, W.H.A. (1998), 'Real Property Taxation: A Dwindling Revenue Source for Local Authorities in Kenya', *Journal of Property Tax Assessment and Administration*, vol. 3 no. 2, pp. 5-23.

Githinji, L.G.W. (1990), *'The Rating System in Kenya and the Need to Improve on It'*, Final Year Project, Department of Land Development, University of Nairobi.

Hicks, V.K. (1961), *'Development from Below'*, Oxford University Press, London.

Kelly, R. (2004), 'Property Taxation in Kenya', in R.M. Bird and E. Slack (eds), *International Handbook of Land and Property Taxation*, Edward Elgar Publishing Limited, UK, pp. 177-188.

Kiamba, M. (1989), 'The Introduction and Evolution of Private Landed Property in Kenya', in *Development and Change*, vol. 20, Sage Publications, London.

Kich, J.A. (1996), *'An Evaluation of Rating System in Kenya: A Case Study of Nairobi City Council'*, Department of Land Development, University of Nairobi.

Ley, C. (1975), *'Underdevelopment in Kenya: The Political Economy of Neocolonialism'*, Heinemann, London.

Migot-Adholla, S.E., Place, F. and Oluoch-Kosura, W. (1994), 'Security of Tenure and Land Productivity in Kenya', in Bruce, J.W. and Migot-Adholla, S.E. (eds), *Searching For Land Tenure Security in Africa*, Kendall/Hunt Publishing Company.

Ndeleki, D. (1991), *'Rating in Zambia'*, Diploma Project, Ardhi Institute, Dar-es-Salaam, Tanzania.

Ogero, B.B. (1981), *'Financial Problems of Urban Authorities: A Case Study of Nairobi City Council'*, M.A. Thesis, University of Nairobi.

Okoth-Ogendo, H.W.O. (1978), *'The Political Economy of Land Law: An Essay in the Legal Organization of Underdevelopment in Kenya, 1895-1974'*, unpublished PhD dissertation, Yale University.

Olima, W.H.A. (1999), 'Real Property Taxation in Kenya', in W.J. McCluskey (ed.), *Property Tax; An International Comparative Review,* Ashgate Publishing Limited, UK, pp. 358-374.

Olima, W.H.A. and Syagga, P.M. (1996), 'Rating System in Kenya: Evolution, Constraints and Potentials', *Journal of Property Tax Assessment and Administration*, vol. 2 no. 1, pp. 21-31.

Otunga, M.O. (2004), *'The Current Rating System and Practice in Kenya: A Case Study of the Mombasa Municipal Council with Special Reference to the 1991 Main Draft Valuation Roll'*, paper submitted for the award of professional Diploma of the Institution of Surveyors of Kenya.

Republic of Kenya (2000), *'Population Census Report 1999'*, Government Printers, Nairobi.
Republic of Kenya (1995), *'Kenya Economic Survey'*, Government Printers, Nairobi.
Syagga, P.M. (1994), *'Real Estate Valuation Handbook: With Special Reference to Kenya'*, Nairobi University Press, Kenya.

Legislation referred to:

Republic of Kenya (1965); *Local Government Act* Chapter 265, Laws of Kenya.
Republic of Kenya (1986), The Rating Act Chapter 267, Laws of Kenya.
Republic of Kenya (1986), *The Valuation for Rating Act* Chapter 266, Laws of Kenya.

Chapter 5

Property Tax Systems and Rating in New Zealand

William J. McCluskey

Introduction

The British colony of New Zealand became an independent dominion in 1907. It occupies approximately 27.1 million hectares and in terms of land area is similar in size to Japan and the United Kingdom of Great Britain. New Zealand lies in the southwest Pacific, about 1,600 kilometres southeast of Australia. It is made up of two main islands (North and South Island), Stewart Island and several small outlying islands. The landscape is a mixture of flat country, rolling hill country and mountains. The South Island in particular has numerous peaks, fiords and glaciers, lakes and fast flowing rivers. New Zealand has a mild climate with few extremes due to it being located in an ocean environment. This climate means that New Zealand is well suited to agriculture and horticulture that are still vitally important to the economy.

Traditionally a predominantly rural economy, New Zealand's economic base has diversified significantly across all sectors (manufacturing, services and tourism) over the last 30 years. This has been reflected in progressive urbanization. Since 1984, New Zealand has undergone considerable economic restructuring. These changes have involved dismantling the extensive tariffs and protection that sheltered New Zealand's productive sector from overseas competition and made locally produced goods and services less competitive than those produced overseas.

Historical developments in property taxation

At present in New Zealand local authorities have the choice of three alternative systems on which the real property tax or rates may be levied.

These systems are firstly, the total value of land, buildings and other improvements (capital improved value); secondly, the site value only (unimproved value); and thirdly, the annual rental value. However, local authorities have not always enjoyed a choice between these three rating systems. During the first decade of British colonization in the 1840s, annual value was the most extensively used basis for rating, which was in effect an adoption of the 'English system' of rates. By the mid-1850s all the main rating systems employed today had been adopted in one form or another by various local authorities under the then provincial system of regional government.

With the abolition of the provincial system in 1876 the central government in the same year passed the Rating Act which was designed to achieve a uniform system of rating throughout the country. This act provided for annual value rating only. However, it became obvious that most properties were being bought and sold rather than rented and in just six years in 1882, the tide of opinion had changed and the annual value system was displaced by compulsory capital value rating with only a few exceptions. The effect of this statute was that almost all counties (rural areas) adopted capital value rating with the boroughs (urban areas) adopting an annual value system. The reasons given for the 1882 change were; (i) undeveloped land and land held for speculative purposes had no rental value but a definite market or capital value; (ii) farm improvements usually added more to the annual rental value than to the capital value; and (iii) the introduction of an national property tax based on capital justified the introduction of a common valuation and tax basis (Dowse and Hargreaves, 1999).

The first major step towards the present day position was made in 1893 with the Rating Acts Amendment Act which provided for any local authority to choose by resolution either capital value or annual value as the basis for setting its rates. The unimproved value system interestingly was rejected by central government in 1893, however, its popularity had been on the increase since the depression of the 1880s. It was against this background that that the works of two liberal thinkers, the English philosopher, John Stuart Mill, and the American writer, Henry George, found ready support among the reformists (Keall, 2000). The ideas of the two philosophers had special relevance for the field of land taxation. Mill argued that since landowners received a gratuitous reward as the value of their landholdings increased with the progress of the community, there should be a special tax imposed on land to allow the community to share in the values it had created. George reasoned along similar lines that this unearned increment should be the only form of taxation since it did not penalise landowner's efforts to improve their property.

The early 1890s saw public opinion ready to accept the principle of a tax based on the unimproved value of the land. Then in 1891 the national property tax was modified to give partial exemption to improvements and then the following year full exemption was granted. These developments in general taxation were followed by similar changes in local taxation, and in 1896 the Rating on Unimproved Value Act was passed which made the unimproved value system the third option open to local authorities. However, the local authority could only change to unimproved value if the proposal was first approved by a poll of ratepayers. Similarly, once unimproved value had been adopted as the basis for rating it could only be abandoned with the support of ratepayers.

After 1896, with the advent of three recognised systems of rating available to local authorities, there was a steady move away from annual value and capital value rating to unimproved value rating. The proportion of territorial local authorities using unimproved values increased from 64.2 per cent in 1956 to 76.1 per cent in 1966, while the proportion rating on capital and annual value, declined from 29.5 per cent to 19.3 per cent and 6.3 per cent to 4.6 per cent respectively. Clearly, over the last fifty years land value based rating has been the dominant system. However, since 1985 there has been a noticeable swing back towards the use of capital improved value. This is more evident within the larger urban areas. Figure 5.1 illustrates the movement in the usage of the three main tax bases since 1942.

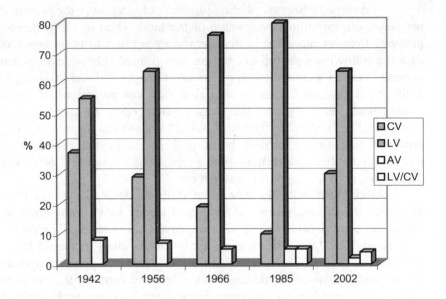

Figure 5.1   Systems used by local authorities in percentage terms

Up until 1976 local authorities could switch from capital values to annual values rating systems without reference to ratepayers, but any change in adopting or abandoning land value required a majority poll of ratepayers. At present local authorities can now change the rating system without recourse to a taxpayer poll however, public consultations would normally take place. Since 1989 a number of territorial authorities (TAs) have switched to capital value rating, they include Dunedin (1989), Tasman (1991), Banks Peninsula (1992), South Waikato (1993), Invercargill (1994), South Taranaki (1994), Otorohanga (1996), Lower Hutt (1997) and Franklin (1999).

The function and organisation of local government

Central and local government are independent of one another politically, administratively and financially. Although local government is a creation of parliament, it remains autonomous financially. The pattern and structure of local government were largely shaped by the growth and distribution of population and by the needs of the economy and people for improved communications, especially roads. The provincial governments, abolished in 1875, progressively gave way to a fragmented system of territorial and single purpose local authorities. One historical dominant feature of local government in New Zealand has been the degree of fragmentation despite the need to consolidate local communities. There has been a proliferation of ad hoc authorities, each with its separate area of influence, which has resulted in a diffusion of responsibility for developments in the local and regional setting (Scott, 1979). Figure 5.2 illustrates the significant decrease in the number of local authorities since 1876.

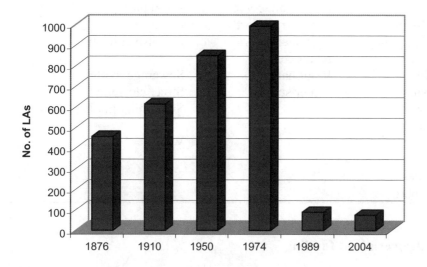

Figure 5.2   Number of local authorities 1876-2004

Recognition of the need for adjustments to the structure of local government goes well into the past; however, progress on local government reorganisation and the formation of regional government was slow. Various commissions were instructed to investigate local government including the Local Government Commission 1974 and the 1989 Local Government Commission. Following this last review of local government the current structure incorporates 12 regional councils, 74 territorial authorities including four unitary authorities (i.e. authorities encompassing the duties and powers of both territorial authorities and regional councils), 15 cities, 58 districts and the Chatham Islands.

Regional councils and TAs have traditionally worked as two spheres of local government with different functions and little overlap. The key principle underpinning the division has been the separation of service delivery functions. Table 5.1 illustrates the various functions under the responsibility of each tier of government.

Table 5.1   Functions of the tiers of government

Central	Regional	Local
Currency	Environmental management	Building and environmental consents
Defence	Flood protection	Libraries
Education	Land management	Local parks
Employment	Public transport	Local roads
Foreign policy	Regional natural resources	Rubbish collection
Health	Regional parks	Sewerage treatment
Housing	Water supply	Street cleaning
Law and Order		Swimming pools
Postal		Water
Social Services		
Transport		

Local government funding

Overall local government has six main categories of revenue sources, with rates representing the pre-eminent source of funds. The others include the sale of goods and services, grants and subsidies, fees and fines, petroleum tax and interest and dividends. Table 5.2 shows the magnitude of each of the sources or revenue available to territorial authorities.

Table 5.2   Local government finances: 2003

Source	%
Rates	56
Sale of goods and services	19
Grants	10.5
Interest	10
Fees and fines	3.5
Petroleum tax	0.75

Source: Local Government Association, Wellington, New Zealand

Table 5.3 provides data on the principle revenue sources available to local authorities. It is clearly evident the importance of rates within a local authority revenue budget.

Table 5.3   Local authority revenue statistics ($ million)

	1999	2000	2001	2002	2003
Sales Income	687	712	730	769	812
Rates, fees, petrol tax	2,176	2,304	2,416	2,518	2,646
Grants	391	399	400	440	471
Investment income	372	334	293	420	301

Source: Statistics New Zealand, 2002

In July 1996, the government introduced legislation supporting new financial management provisions for local authorities that came into force in July 1998. The government was also conscious that there was a need to redesign local government's funding tools in line with the new provisions. It was felt that the previous legislation, The Rating Powers Act 1988 (RPA) was overly prescriptive and lacked clarity and consistency. To address these concerns a Review of Local Government Funding Powers was initiated to develop a comprehensive, coherent, and flexible legislative framework of funding powers for councils.

Following on from the Review and the consultation process legislation was put before parliament and has recently been given Royal assent. The Local Government (Rating) Act 2002 (effective from July 2003) replaces the Rating Powers Act 1988, and relates to powers to set, assess and collect rates to fund local government activities. The primary intention of this legislation was to update and simplify existing rating powers to meet the needs of modern local authorities. The Act provides greater flexibility for local authorities as they determine how to raise revenue through rates. Essentially the Act has three main purposes:

* to provide local authorities with flexible powers to set, assess, and collect rates;
* to ensure rates reflect decisions made in a transparent and consultative manner; and
* to provide for processes and information to ensure ratepayers can identify and understand their liability for rates.

The revenue funding toolbox

The funding toolbox available to local authorities is effectively a range of
revenue raising mechanisms designed to create a transparent and
accountable decision making process distinguishing:

- functions it wishes to fund by spreading the cost across the
  community as a whole (public good expenditures); and
- those functions which it wishes to fund in a more targeted way from
  particular groups benefiting from those functions (private good
  expenditures).

A toolbox consistent with the aims of this process requires:

- a set of tools for raising revenue across the community in general –
  in effect, powers to tax; and
- one or more sets of tools for the funding of particular functions by
  those benefiting from particular services – involving a range of
  possible fees, charges and prices.

Different principles are normally applied to the design of taxes, fees,
charges and prices within the arena of local government finance. The
design of a taxing power needs to have specific regard to generally
accepted principles of taxation, such as efficiency, fairness and equity,
while powers to impose fees, charges and prices are more appropriately
designed by reference to principles of efficient pricing.

It is recognised that it is not always practicable or efficient for all
functions which give rise to private benefits to be funded by pricing (that is,
where individuals pay directly for the quantity of a good or service which
they purchase). There is an additional range of tools that allows the
funding of expenditures to be borne by the identified groups who benefit
from these functions. These tools are generally referred to as 'targeted
funding tools'. In some circumstances these may be both a fairer and more
efficient option for funding functions that give rise to private benefits, than
reverting back to use of a general taxing power. Familiar local authority
funding tools such as separate rates and uniform annual charges for
particular functions fall within this group, as does the current charge for
sewerage on a per pan basis.

Property rates are the principle revenue sources used to fund the cost of council services in proportion to the total community based cost. The rating component incorporates the general rates as well as differential rates. However, councils have been empowered to apply direct user charges for services. In addition, where direct charging or pricing of the service is not appropriate councils have the option to apply targeted funding tools.

Rating basis and legal definitions

During the early days of local government, there was a reasonable volume of market evidence which enabled a proper valuation of property based on a true unimproved value basis. However, the concept of valuing land on the basis of its original state became increasingly unrealistic. Eventually the Valuation of Land Act 1951 was amended in 1970 to provide for the progressive elimination of 'unimproved value' as a basis for local taxation and for its replacement by 'land value'. Land value now includes the following 'invisible' improvements made to the land, drainage, excavation, filling or reclamation of land, grading or levelling, removal or destruction of vegetation, alteration of soil fertility and the elimination of flooding.

Land value

> ... in relation to any land, means the sum which the owner's estate or interest therein, if unencumbered by any mortgage or other charge thereon, might be expected to realise at the time of valuation if offered for sale on such reasonable terms and conditions as a bona fide seller might be expected to impose, and if no improvements (as defined) had been made. (Section 2, The Valuation of Land Act 1951).

Improvements

> ... in relation to any land, means all work done or material used at any time on or for the benefit of the land by the expenditure of capital or labour by any owner or occupier in so far as the effect of the work done or material used is to increase the value of the land and the benefit is unexhausted at the time of valuation.

> Provided that the work done or material used on or for the benefit of the land by the expenditure of capital or labour by any owner or occupier in the provision of roads or streets, or in the provision of water, drainage, or other amenities in connection with the sub-division of the land for

building purposes shall not be deemed to be improvements on that land or any other land.

Other improvements which are deemed to be indistinguishable from the land are deemed to be part of the land value include:

- the draining, excavation, filling or reclamation of land, or the making of retaining walls in pursuance to the forgoing;
- the grading or levelling of land or the removal of rocks, stone, sand or soil;
- the removal or destruction of vegetation;
- the alteration of soil fertility or the structure of the soil;
- the arresting or elimination of erosion or flooding.

Value of improvements

means the added value which at the date of valuation the improvements give to the land.

Advantages of land value

- it does not discourage the development of land as rates will be the same on a property whether or not it is developed;
- the system is more likely to produce the same rates on adjoining properties particularly in residential areas which tend to have standard section sizes;
- ratepayers have a good understanding of the land value given its history within local government finance in New Zealand;
- it is sometimes argued that it provides an incentive to develop property. It can result in relatively high holding costs for the owners of undeveloped land.

Disadvantages

- the level of land value in the market is determined by the fact that land is limited in quantity and varies with quality. The value is influenced by the characteristics of the land such as location, view, aspect and as such these characteristics may have more of an influence on the level of rates assessed than the level of services provided;

- there is a greater demand on services where there is a multi-unit development on the one rateable property in comparison to a single unit on similar land;
- high valued properties pay more for similar or identical services;
- the system favours residential property owners where the rateable land value is low;
- land values tend to fluctuate more than improved capital values;
- the system is not necessarily related to ability to pay;
- it is perceived by some to be unfair on the owners of undeveloped land. The owner of such land is likely to make less use of council services than the owner of a developed property;
- utilities are regarded as improvements and as such have no land value. Under a land value system no share of the general rate can be allocated to utility companies;
- rates are a tax on assets. From that perspective the land value system fails to take full measure of the ratepayer asset base as no account is taken of the improvements;
- as areas become urbanised it becomes increasingly difficult to separate off and value the land apart from its improvements.

Annual value

... in relation to any rateable property, means the rent at which the property would let from year to year, after deducting 20 per cent in the case of houses, buildings and other perishable property, and 10 per cent in the case of land and other hereditaments; but in no case shall it be less than 5 per cent of the capital value of the fee simple of the property.

Advantages of annual value

- recognises the use to which the property is put and the reduction in the need to apply differentials;
- a more transparent system where there is an abundant of open market rental transactions;
- closely aligned to capital value.

Disadvantages

- property being rented, relative to owner-occupied property, is low in New Zealand especially in the residential sector;

- the public are less familiar with rental values which would limit ratepayer's ability to understand rates assessments. This is contrary to mthe government's intention to create greater transparency in the application of funding mechanisms.

Capital value

... of land means the sum which the owner's estate or interest therein, if unencumbered by any mortgage or other charge, might be expected to realsie at the time of valuation if offered for sale on such reasonable terms and conditions as a bona fide seller might be expected to realise.

Advantages of capital value

- it is easier to establish capital values for properties as these can be based on recent sales at market values;
- ratepayers tend to understand this system better than any of the other options;
- it is more likely to better reflect the recovery through general rates of the cost of property based services;
- in a district experiencing rapid expansion and population growth, capital value will increase the rating base. This does not necessarily occur with land value based rating systems;
- capital value reflects the total value of a ratepayer's investment. Therefore, in newly developed areas, capital value is likely to reflect ability to pay as ratepayers will not generally purchase in areas they cannot afford;
- it allows utilities to be rated and for them to pay an appropriate amount towards the cost of services;
- it takes the fullest measure of a ratepayers asset base;
- gives a better indication of the demands that are likely to be placed on an authority's services such as water and sewerage systems;
- because capital values include land values it is always a larger tax base. On average the capital value base is 2 to 3 times the land value base. This means the rate in the dollar of value, will therefore be lower.

Disadvantages

- capital value systems require more frequent roll maintenance with respect to improvements;

- there will be more demands on the resources of the valuation service provider to value improvements;
- objections to the value of improvements can be time consuming and protracted;
- capital value rating can be a deterrent to improving properties. This could result in illegal buildings or improvements being made;
- adjoining properties using similar council services will have significantly different rate accounts if the capital values are significantly different, even though the land values may be the same;
- capital value enables a fairer and less complex system of rating to be established than does land value.

Funding mechanisms

The Local Government Act (2003) requires that each council formulate a funding policy which aims to map the cost of individual services to the most appropriate method of funding those services. The Act identifies three types of benefit/expenditure:

- that service which is independent of the number of persons who benefit from the expenditure, or generates benefits which do not accrue to identifiable persons or groups of persons, or which generates benefits to the community at large;
- that service which provides direct benefits to persons or categories of persons; and
- that service which is needed to control negative effects caused by the action or inaction of persons or groups of persons.

Following on from this the council must determine how the expenditure for each service is to be raised;

- expenditure which gives rise to general benefits may be funded from rates;
- expenditure which gives rise to direct benefits should be funded by means of user charges, uniform charges and/or targeted rates;
- expenditure necessary to control negative effects should be funded by those whose action or inaction caused the negative effects to occur or from general rates.

General rates

General rates can be arranged to price expenditure items efficiently or
otherwise recognise community values. Essentially, the general rate is the
preferred funding tool where benefits do not accrue to individuals. The
services provided are essentially 'property' related and hence one would
expect to add value to the property. The general rate has a certain degree of
flexibility in that local authorities have the power to vary the level of the
rate over different parts of the district. The ability to modify rates by
location is thought appropriate because councils are generally responsible
for a range of public good functions that are specific to different geographic
areas. In addition, there is the capability to vary the general rate according
to type or use of property.

The basis for the general rate is currently a matter for each local
authority to decide. Even if a uniform system were to be imposed upon
local authorities with regard to the general rate it would seem likely that all
the current valuation bases (land value, capital value, annual value), would
remain available for the use of targeted rates as a funding tool to target
more specific patterns of benefit for specific functions.

Differential rating

The ability to make rates differentially is a potentially valuable tool in
targeting the funding of particular functions. Differentials are traditionally
thought of as variations on value based rates. However they can also be
seen as a type of purpose designed proxy (albeit one which must be linked
to values). They are like proxies because they are levied/charged on
specific properties based on type, use or some other characteristic.

Differential rating enables a council to levy rates so that rates made
in respect of any one or more specified types or groups of property may
vary from those rates made and levied in respect of another specified type
or group of property. Essentially, differential rating allows a council to
develop a rating system which recognises the vagaries of valuation (in
relation to types or groups of properties as opposed to individual
properties). In addition, the council can reflect more fairly the rate burden
across groups of properties by such factors as type, location etc. The system
is seeking to ensure that different groups of property (residential,
commercial and rural) each contribute the same proportion of rates over
time. It is often argued that the commercial group should bear a
disproportionately greater share of the rates burden than other groups
because:

- rates are a tax deductible expense and businesses can claim back Goods and Services Tax (GST);
- businesses can affect the real incidence of rating by effectively passing on the cost to customers;
- businesses receive a higher level of service than other groups.

It can also be argued that differentials should be used to ensure that the rates levied on a particular group actually reflect the services received by properties in that group. This could be an argument for having a lower differential for the rural sector. It is important to recognise the fact that all groups of ratepayers or properties actually form part of the whole community. The degree to which it is sensible to dissect a community into differentially rated parts must be considered. A holistic view should be adopted.

Uniform annual general charges

Uniform annual general charges (UAGC) will generally be used as a mechanism for allocation of costs when the benefit is people related. The ability of having a flat per property tax, such as the uniform annual general charge allows councils to recover costs across whole communities. The flexibility of having both UAGCs and a general rate in the funding toolbox allows local authorities to much more closely design the impact of their funding systems to meet the perceived wishes of local communities. A UAGC per property tax also allows councils to set a de facto minimum rate so that even those with very low value properties make a minimum contribution to the funding of local public goods.

A flat per property tax also allows a number of equity objectives to be achieved. For instance it can ensure that ratepayers pay for public good functions more equally. However, there are a number of problems surrounding the application of UAGCs such as:

- the distortionary effects of such a tax, whereby land tenure can be arranged to avoid 'per property' taxes while value based taxes cannot be avoided in the same way;
- equity and fairness effects, especially as flat per property taxes may be regressive and impact more heavily on poorer households;
- flat taxes blunt accountability by limiting how much those with high value properties pay. The charge can be considered regressive in nature.

Currently there is a cap (expressed as 30 per cent of certain types of revenue) on the use of UAGCs and UACs, excluding those for water and sewerage. The current cap was inserted as a restraint on the use of a tax mechanism seen as regressive.

Targeted rates and charges

Targeted funding tools are funding instruments where payment is by a compulsory tax, but liability only arises from the use, consumption or availability of services. They represent a middle ground between:

•   taxes where payment is compulsory without relation to the consumption of services; and
•   prices which are voluntary upon consumption of the services.

The legislation contains a single, flexible generic targeted rate power, which replaces the range of separate rate and charge powers available under the current Local Government Act (LGA). Flexible, targeted charging mechanisms can be best used to target those who generate costs or benefit from functions. They in effect fall between the tax mechanisms for recovering costs across the whole community and prices charged to individuals. The key purpose of the provisions for targeted rates is to allow councils to align the nature of a service provided more closely with the manner of rating for that service. The provisions will allow more flexibility than the current system of separate rates. A local authority may set a single targeted rate for several functions, or several targeted rates for a single function.

Pricing and charging

A general pricing power provides for councils to:

•   recover appropriate economic costs;
•   apply efficient pricing principles; and
•   have regard to the purpose of the legislation governing the function being charged for.

The previous range of pricing and charging powers available to local authorities under the LGA, the Rating Powers Act (RPA) and other legislation was often unduly prescriptive and prevented local authorities from recovering full/appropriate costs from users. A general pricing power, supplemented by pricing and costing guidelines, provides local authorities with greater flexibility in setting prices while also ensuring that such prices are efficient and appropriate.

Tax base

As of 2003 there were approximately 1.5 million rateable properties in New Zealand. Figure 5.3 illustrates the distribution of properties between the categories rural, lifestyle, residential, commercial/industrial and other.

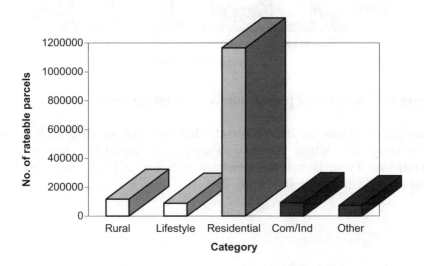

Figure 5.3   Distribution of rateable property by category

Of the total number of properties the largest category by far is residential representing some 76 per cent of the property tax base, next is rural property which accounts for 8 per cent.

The distribution of the property tax basis across those territorial authorities which have been given city status highlights the continued reliance on land value. Of the fifteen city territorial authorities nine utilise land value, five capital improved (Wellington) and one annual value (Auckland). Not with standing this distribution Figure 5.4 shows the number of properties assessed under each basis for the fifteen TAs. The number of parcels assessed under land value is only slightly greater than those assessed under a capital value approach.

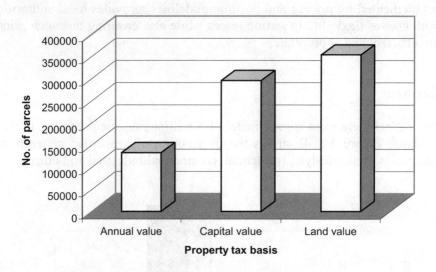

Figure 5.4   Number of parcels under each rating basis

However, in terms of the total split between the various basis when considering the whole country Figure 5.5 illustrates the relative proportions. There is still an important reliance on land value which is almost double that of capital value.

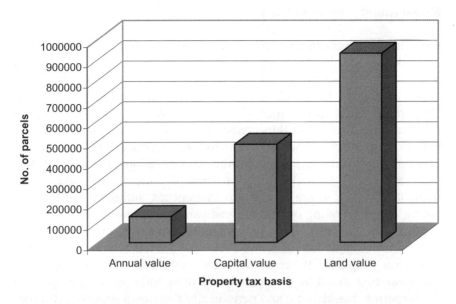

Figure 5.5 Parcel distribution by rating basis for entire country

In terms of the total value of all rateable property Figure 5.6 illustrates the capital value and the land value. The ratio of capital improved value to land value is in the region of 2.29:1 representing a fairly modest differential which could be interpreted as meaning the improvements generally do not add significantly to the total value of the property.

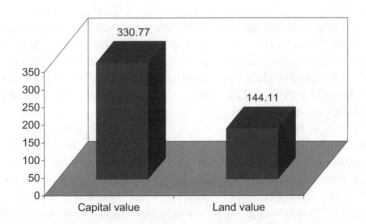

Figure 5.6 Capital improved value and land value of all rateable property: 2003

Responsibility for valuations

Early forms of government in New Zealand were funded from excise duty on traded goods, but the cost and practical difficulties of collecting such taxes prompted a search for a funding system which was easier to apply and more equitable. In 1844, the government introduced the Municipal Corporation Ordinance, which allowed local authorities to tax property to raise revenue. Parliament thus created the need for valuers, but failed, for a long time, to specify how valuations for tax purposes should be conducted, or who should carry then out. Further complications arose in 1893 when local authorities were permitted to compile their own valuation rolls without reference to the central government tax authority and three years later a system of rating on unimproved values was introduced involving yet another type of roll. The government responded in 1896 when the Government Valuation of Land Act was passed which established the Valuation Department as a separate department of the government administration to act as the central valuation authority with responsibility for preparing, maintaining and periodically revising a general valuation roll for the country. All local authorities who chose to rate on the basis of capital value or unimproved value were required to use the rolls prepared by the Valuation Department. Those electing to use annual rental values were required to employ there own valuers. In 1958 the Department was given the authority to undertake annual value assessments for local authorities. In 1987 the Department became Valuation New Zealand with sole responsibility for providing rating valuations for all territorial authorities (with the exception of Auckland).

In 1997 the government decided that effective from 1 July 1998 Valuation New Zealand should be replaced by two new organisations; an Office of the Valuer-General with responsibility for setting standards and auditing providers of valuations for rating purposes and by a crown owned company, Quotable Value New Zealand, which will provide contestable rating valuation services. The impetus for changes to the existing rating valuation provisions arose out of the following areas:

*   dissatisfaction from local government, the key user, about VNZ's monopoly pricing and service delivery arrangements. There was also a perception that the services being delivered by VNZ were above their requirements;
*   the emergence and growth of a non-core function within VNZ which conflicted with its non-commercial departmental environment.

The result of this split means that now the provision of land and capital rating valuations will no longer be the an exclusive central government function but will be devolved down to territorial authorities. Such authorities will in consequence have a greater choice over how and who is able to provide rating valuations on their behalf. Territorial authorities will therefore become responsible for ensuring that the rating valuations produced meet the rules set by the Valuer-General. The Office of the Valuer-General will have the following functions and responsibilities:

•   provide, technical advice to government on valuation issues and the regulation of the valuation services sector;
•   set minimum quality standards and specifications necessary to meet government outcomes;
•   monitor and audit the valuations provided by valuation providers against minimum standards;
•   certify to local authorities (and through them to ratepayers) that the resulting valuations meet the minimum standards for a fair and consistent property valuation system; and
•   set standards for, and act as custodian of, the National Property Database and valuers field notes previously held by VNZ.

In addition, authorities will be responsible for providing rating valuation services to Regional Councils as required on payment of a fee.

The Valuer-General regulates the rating valuation market through a series of rules (Rating Valuation Rules 1998 (as amended)). These effectively establish the minimum levels of performance that territorial authorities must achieve in the rating valuation environment. The overall objective is to provide a nationally consistent, impartial, independent and equitable valuation system at least cost which maintains the integrity of property valuation and underpins public confidence in the rating system. In addition, to provide an independent quality assurance of valuations for rating purposes.

Statistical rules

Table 5.4 details the statistical rules that are applied to all the properties on the district valuation roll (after a revaluation) including property groupings such as residential, lifestyle, and rural properties.

Table 5.4   VG statistical rules

Test	Tolerance	Capital value	Land value	Annual value
Coefficient of dispersion (COD)	Less than or equal to 12%	Yes	Yes	To be developed
Median ratio	0.90/1.10	Yes	Yes	
Price related differential (PRD)	0.98/1.03	Yes	Yes	
Comparison of average value changes	Less than 10%	Yes	Yes	

District valuation rolls

The Rating Valuations Act 1998 provides the amended legislation for the introduction of contestability into the provision of valuations for the purposes of rating. Territorial authorities will have responsibility to prepare and maintain a district valuation roll for its own district, with the roll containing prescribed information on each separate property. The required information includes:

- name of the owner(s);
- name of the occupier(s);
- address of the property;
- legal description;
- land area;
- nature and value of improvements;
- date of valuation;
- land value of the land;
- capital value of the property;
- where the annual rental value system is in force, the annual rental value;
- the special rateable value or rates postponement value of the land, where applicable.

It is incumbent upon the authority to revise the district valuation roll at intervals of not more than 3 years. After the new values have been established the authority must obtain the approval of the Valuer-General before the general revaluation may be implemented. The VG has the power to approve, or to decline to approve the revised valuation roll.

Appeal procedures

Upon the VG's certification of approval of the roll the authority must give the public notice of the new district roll detailing arrangements for its inspection. Objections to the roll can be made within the time limit specified and in the manner prescribed in the legislation.

An authority may at any time cause the roll to be altered, or on an application made by the owner or occupier of the land appearing in the roll make alterations to the current roll in order to readjust or correct valuations. Where an objection has been received the territorial authority must refer the objection to a registered valuer (this can be the same person who originally prepared the valuation). On conclusion of the review of the objection the authority has the following options:

• alter the valuation;
• decline to alter the valuation.

The result of the review process must be notified in writing to the objector and/or the owner or occupier. If any party is dissatisfied with the review an appeal can be made within 20 days to the Land Valuation Tribunal. The Valuer-General may at any time object to a valuation in the roll, object to the decision made on review and as of right join as a party in any proceedings in a Land Valuation Tribunal or any subsequent or related court proceedings.

Exemptions

The Local Government (Rating) Act (LGRA) 2002 currently provides for the exemption of a variety of types of land from rates. In general these exemptions relate to land used for public and community purposes. Some of the exemptions relate to land owned by the Crown or by Crown entities, and others relate to land in private or community ownership (see Tables 5.5 and 5.6). Exempt properties do not enjoy full exemption from local authority rates and charges. They are liable for any separate rates and charges that are made in respect of water supply, waste collection and sewerage disposal.

Some territorial authorities are characterised by the presence of very substantial areas of Crown land. For example, in the West Coast local authority area approximately 90 per cent of the land is classified as national parks and Department of Conservation land.

Table 5.5   Crown land exemption

Crown Land
Land for Vice Regal residences
Crown owned land used for state roads
National parks
Protected areas under legislation such as Reserves Act, Wildlife Act
Hospitals, schools and university hostels, child welfare homes
Land owned and occupied by the Crown used for certain operational elements of airports
Defence land
Land regarded as Crown land
Land used for the purposes of an education authority
Integrated schools
Universities
Hospital and health service land

Table 5.6   Non-Crown exemptions

Non-Crown exemptions	
Educational institutions	Kindergartens, playcentres, schools
Religious institutions	Churches, chapels, mosques, Sunday schools
Charitable	Properties used for the relief of the aged, infirm, mentally disabled
Health	Children's health camps
Others	Cemeteries, crematoria, land used for river control
Maori purposes	Marae (up to 2.03 ha), customary land, Maori burial ground
Heritage	NZ Historic Places
Community (50 per cent) LocalPublic authority land	gardens, sports grounds, public halls, libraries, swimming pools, cemeteries and crematoria.

Under the Second Schedule LGRA 2002 a local authority may remit or postpone rates. The following are some of the specified cases; land set aside for Maori reserve; land occupied by a trust used for the general public; land used for games and sport; charitable institutions and; places of public religious worship.

Rates postponement

Under the Rating Valuations Act 1998 the territorial authority has the power either under its own volition or on an application from the owner or occupier to determine the rates postponement value of any farmland whose value is in some way attributable to the potential use to which the land may be put for residential, commercial, industrial or other non-farming use. The rates postponement value of any land excludes any potential value at the date of valuation so as to preserve uniformity and equitable relativity with comparable parcels of farmland the valuations of which do not contain any potential value. Where farmland value has a value higher than existing use value then two valuations are required, one for the existing use and the other for the highest and best use. The difference between the rates assessed on the lower and higher values is postponed. The following conditions apply for rates postponement:

- the postponed rates become a charge on the property and become payable if the property is sold for non-farming uses;
- if the circumstances affecting the property remain unchanged for a period of five years the postponed rates over that period are written off;
- the postponement may be transferred to successive owners providing the farmland use does not change.

Postponement can also be applied to assist elderly ratepayers with a fixed level of income experiencing financial hardship. In this case only residential property is eligible and the owner must have owned the property for not less than five years. The postponed rates will be postponed until the death of the ratepayer, or until the ratepayer ceases to own the property, or until the ratepayer ceases to use the property as his/her residence, or until a date specified by the council.

Special rateable values

Under the Rating Powers Act (now repealed) and the Valuation of Land Act a regime was created that produced artificially low valuations for particular kinds of property (often called 'out of zone' properties). These are properties used for a range of purposes which are of lower value than the uses made of similar properties in the area. The kinds of properties involved are:

- farmland in urban areas;
- commercial or industrial properties in residential or rural areas;
- residential properties in commercial or industrial areas;
- single or double unit houses where values are influenced by the demand for multi unit housing;
- properties with existing use rights under the Resource Management Act; and
- properties subject to specific preservation conditions.

Such properties receive an artificially low valuation based on their actual rather than potential uses. This practice is inefficient since rates for public good functions should be levied on value and value will by definition be influenced by potential use. It also distorts against higher value uses of the land affected and increases the rates burden on the rest of the community. The practice blunts accountability. Local authorities should be accountable for the way the costs of their activities are allocated. Automatic discounting through the valuation system creates effects for which councils cannot be held responsible.

Remission of rates

A local authority may on application from an occupier may after investigation remit in full or in part the rates payable if financial hardship would result on payment. If part of the rates have been remitted the authority can postpone the remainder. Rates will automatically be remitted annually for those properties which had Special Rateable Values applied under section 24 of the Rating Valuations Act 1998 and where there is evidence that the land value has been affected by the zoning. The amount remitted is the difference in rates payable between the rates calculated on the special rateable value and the normal rateable value.

Critical review

Property taxes, in the form of rates and annual uniform charges, are the principal source of revenue for local government in New Zealand. Historically, as the primary focus of local government was for the provision of services to property (for example water supply, sewerage, stormwater drainage), rates were considered highly appropriate as a form of local tax, as property owners tend to be the direct beneficiaries of those services. However, the focus of service delivery is changing as councils are now providing a variety of 'people services', which include a range of cultural, social and economic development activities. This extension of focus does raise the question of whether property rates continue to be the most appropriate primary source of additional funding for local government going forward, or whether alternative options exist that would be preferable. This question is particularly relevant given that local government now have a power of general competence, which enables councils to further alter their focus if they so chose.

Rates have the important advantage of being locally derived, and as such are aligned, albeit imperfectly with the local community. Rates are also a highly transparent tax which is good for accountability, as rates and particularly rate increases are highly visible to ratepayers. At the same time this high level of visibility may contribute to the willingness to pay issues, particularly where the level of benefit received by ratepayers is often much less visible. A further contributor here may be a perception on the part of some ratepayers that rates are a charge for services rather than a tax.

The concept of contemporary equity embodies the principle that the level of tax levied should take into account the benefit received and the taxpayer's ability to pay. There tends to be a belief that some local government services (e.g. cultural and social services) benefit a wider group than just ratepayers, and should therefore be paid for over a wider tax base. This includes residents who are not property owners, as well as visitors to the district. This view implies non-property related services should be funded through a mechanism that draws on all potential users as the tax base. This view appears to be based on the legal incidence of rates, which falls solely on property owners. In practice, the economic incidence of rates is likely to be wider. Rates will be passed on in property rentals and in prices for goods and services to some extent, depending on the particular conditions of the market.

Property values are not always a good proxy for ability to pay. Property values in general do not increase in direct proportion to increases in income. In some cases an individual may own a high value property, but may have a low cash income (pensioners and occasionally farmers may fall in this category). Rates therefore tend to have a regressive impact overall. This issue however, can be addressed if sufficiently flexible powers for waiver and postponement are available.

Uniform rating basis

Early attempts to establish a uniform basis of rating in New Zealand were negated as early as 1896 when the freedom to choose between annual value, capital value and unimproved value was clearly established. The Officials Co-ordinating Committee Report (1988) drew attention to the various ways that the property valuation focus had been shifted, by bringing in differentials and uniform annual charges. The report suggested the introduction of capital value rating would reduce some of the pressures giving rise to the use of differential rating. Mainly for reasons of local autonomy there has been a perception that a choice of systems was needed. It is claimed either capital value rating or land value rating may be more appropriate for an individual authority because of the character of the district. It could be argue that land value rating is better for rural areas and capital value rating is more appropriate for cities. The report concluded that there were good reasons for having one form of rating system nation-wide, but if government had no clear preference, then there should be access to both land and capital value rating systems. The 1988 Committee indicated the following:

- capital values are readily established by reference to direct market data whilst land values are more difficult to demonstrate and are consequently less readily understood;
- capital values will continue to be required for other purposes;
- there is more correlation between ability to pay and capital values than is the case with land values;
- many local authorities ostensibly rating on land value nevertheless derive a significant proportion of their rating income from capital value levies.

Would the move to a uniform system be less expensive? There would be a saving in costs if the land value system as discontinued (VNZ, 1992). Although not exactly quantified it could be in the order of 5 per cent of expenditure related directly to the provision of valuation roll services. This represents the marginal cost of maintaining detailed assessments of land values for improved properties.

As the capital value system is better understood it is likely that there would be less time spent in advising ratepayers about the system than is the case with those districts where land value rating is used. Land value as a system is not well understood by ratepayers particularly with respect to the development improvements and structural improvements.

It was one of the conclusions of the 1988 report that generally speaking sharp changes in value arise in respect to land values, rather than to buildings and other improvements. Valuations based on land alone are therefore more likely to increase more than capital improved values.

While the land value rating system has been a valued system in the past, its benefits are increasingly being questioned. Even if one accepts that its strength is the encouragement that it brings to develop property it is questionable whether New Zealand is in a developing mode. In addition, land use planning through the rating system is not the most efficient mechanism to attain proper land use controls.

Differential rating

Differential rating was initially used to reduce the rating burden on farm land where pressures for urban expansion was pushing values, and therefore rates, upwards. Their use was later extended to recognise differences in the cost of servicing differing parts of a district. Valuations fix property prices at a point in time and release them suddenly into rating systems. Local authorities can react to these shocks by altering their rating systems to avoid sudden changes to the bills faced by individual ratepayers.

They do this by adjusting the relationship between property value and rates, usually by altering differentials. This practice is inefficient since rates for public good functions should be proportional to value. Frequent adjustments set up expectations of further adjustments in the future making it politically difficult to maintain a clear proportional relationship between property values and rates for public good functions. More frequent variations could reduce this behaviour. It is significant that annual valuations are now undertaken for Wellington City. Wellington is a local authority whose rating policy has been strongly influenced by the valuation driven cycle described.

Differential rating severely compromises the role which valuations play in determining rating liability. Local authorities have the ultimate sanction subject to ratepayer rights to determine what is, in their opinion, the most equitable way of distributing the local tax burden among ratepayers. Most authorities which have implemented a differential rating system have done so in the belief that they have introduced greater equity into the rating system. Studies have shown that certain systems have altered the burden of rates so that a larger contribution is obtained from low-valued properties and multi-unit residential property which has had the result of increasing the regressive nature of rates (Scott, 1979). A further trend which is noticeable is the shift in the burden of rates from residential to the commercial and industrial sectors. Such shifts are of two types; those which are trying to counteract the effects of revaluations and; those concerned with an attempt to extract a greater contribution from the business sector.

The first type of shift is important because due to inflation different property sector values have changed by differing amounts. In general residential property values have increased at higher rates than commercial and industrial and therefore differential rates are used to restore the relative contribution of the different sectors which existed prior to the revaluation. In terms of the second shift, it is argued that as commercial and industrial rates are tax deductible they should contribute a heavier rate than for example owner occupied residential property.

In addition, Dowse and Hargreaves (1999) suggest that the differential rates have been manipulated so far away from land value to make the result approximating to capital value rating. Although they are commonly introduced to redress perceived inequities, differentials can have the effect of moving away from equity and fairness issues and the 'each according to his ability to pay' aspect. Put simply, differentials operate to ake the rating system more regressive rather than less. It places a heavier burden on those with limited resources whose property assets may be of lesser value.

Maori land rating

The rating and valuation of Maori land raises significant legal and constitutional issues. Maori freehold land is rateable and is valued and rated in accordance with the relevant legislation. Special rules however, often apply such as the exemption of particular types of Maori land (e.g. Marae, reserves set aside under the Maori Affairs Act). The normal enforcement mechanisms are modified so that Maori land cannot be sold for unpaid rates. This results in situations where the owners of multiply-owned Maori land do not pay their fair share of rates. It is often argued that the following factors need to be considered when Maori land is being valued and taxed:

The valuation system does not sufficiently recognise the restrictions on the sale inherent in the tenure of multiply-owned Maori land;

- the cultural values which attach to land which is not considered as a tradable commodity;
- rates on Maori land can be seen as a disincentive to its development.

References

Audit Commission (1993), '*A Study of New Zealand Local Government Following Reorganisation*', Occasional Paper, no 19, pp.1-22.

Brown, B.J. (1971), 'A Review of the Valuation of Land and Rating Acts Amendments 1970', *New Zealand Valuer*, vol 21, no 8, pp. 304-311.

Bush, G. (1995), '*Local Government and Politics in New Zealand*', Auckland University Press, New Zealand.

Dowse, G. and Hargreaves, B. (1999), 'Rating Systems in New Zealand', in W.J. McCluskey (ed.), *Property Tax: An International Comparative Review*, Ashgate Publishing Limited, UK, pp. 283-312.

Groves, H.M. (1949), 'Impressions of Property Taxation in Australia and New Zealand', *Land Economics*, Feb., pp. 22-28.

Keall, R.D. (2000), 'New Zealand: Land and Property Taxation', *American Journal of Economics and Sociology*, December.

Kerr, S., Aitkin, A. and Grimes, A. (2003), '*Land Taxes and Revenue Needs as Communities Grow and Decline*', Lincoln Institute of Land Policy Working Paper, Cambridge, MA, United States, pp. 1-36.

McCluskey, W.J., Grimes, A. and Timmins, J. (2002), '*Property Taxation in New Zealand*', Lincoln Institute of Land Policy, Working Paper WP02WM1, Cambridge, MA, United States, pp. 1-21.

McCluskey, W.J. and Franzsen, R.C.D. (2001), '*Land Value Taxation: A Case Study Approach*', Lincoln Institute of Land Policy Working Paper

WP01WM1, Lincoln Institute of Land Policy, Cambridge, MA, United States, pp. 1-109. (see http://www.lincolninst.edu/publications).

McCluskey, W.J. and Franzsen, R.C.D. (2004), '*The Basis of the Property Tax: A Case Study Analysis of New Zealand and South Africa*', Lincoln Institute of Land Policy Working Paper WP04WM1, Lincoln Institute of Land Policy, Cambridge, MA, United States, pp. 1-48 (see http://www.lincolninst.edu/publications).

New Zealand Local Government Association (1992), '*Principles and Guidelines for Local Government Revenue Systems*', Discussion paper, Wellington.

O'Regan, R. (1973), '*Rating in New Zealand*', Baranduin Publishers Limited, New Zealand.

Robertson, J.S.H. (1966), '*Local Rating in New Zealand: A Study of its Development*', Valuation Department, Research Paper 663, Wellington.

Scott, C. (1979), '*Local and Regional Government in New Zealand: Function and Finance*', George Allen and Unwin, Sydney.

Valuation New Zealand (1988), '*A Proposal for a Uniform System of Rating Based on Capital Value: A Discussion Paper*', Wellington.

Legislation referred to:

Rating Powers Act, 1988 (and amendments).
Rating Valuations Act, 1998.
The Valuation of Land Act, 1951.
The Land Valuation Proceedings Act 1948.
The Local Government (Rating) Act 2002.

Chapter 6

Property Taxation in South Africa

Riël C.D. Franzsen

Introduction

South Africa covers an area of 1,123 million square kilometers and has a population of approximately 45 million (est. 2004). The new constitutional dispensation that became effective on 27 April 1994 saw the disappearance of the former four provinces and the ten self-governing black homelands, and the creation of nine new provinces under a supreme Constitution.

Brief history of local government in South Africa

Comprehensive reforms of the local government sphere in South Africa has had a significant impact on local government funding, and necessitated the reform of the property tax regime. Before the property tax is discussed, however, it is necessary to provide a brief overview of local government structures – and their reform in recent years.

Local government reforms

Since the first democratic elections were held at national level in April 1994, South Africa has experienced dramatic local government reforms. Actually reforms started even before April 1994 with the enactment of the Local Government Transition Act 209 of 1993 (the 'LGTA'). The politically negotiated LGTA set the ball rolling for the transition to a new, non-racial and democratic system of local government.

Firstly, there was the amalgamation of racially segregated urban municipalities. This happened in the wake and context of the LGTA. Secondly, so-called transitional representative councils or transitional rural councils were established after the first non-racial local government elections held country-wide in 1995 in an attempt to provide some semblance of local governance to rural areas where primary local government has been absent. Thirdly, national government published its vision for future local government, originally in the Green Paper on Local Government (October 1997), and thereafter in a comprehensive White Paper on Local Government (March 1998). Almost seven years of transition culminated in a new local government dispensation that became effective after the second democratic local government elections were held on 5 December 2000. Since 1998 five key statutes have been enacted to give effect to the broad principles envisioned in the White Paper, namely the:

*   Local Government: Municipal Demarcation Act 27 of 1998;
*   Local Government: Municipal Structures Act 117 of 1998;
*   Local Government: Municipal Systems Act 32 of 2000;
*   Local Government: Municipal Finance Management Act 56 of 2003; and
*   Local Government: Municipal Property Rates Act 6 of 2004.

In terms of the Local Government: Demarcation Act of 1998 the Municipal Demarcation Board (MDB) was established at the end of 1998. In February 2000 the MDB completed the task of demarcating the boundaries of the three categories of municipalities provided for in the Local Government: Municipal Structures Act of 1998 (read with section 155 of the Constitution of the Republic of South Africa of 1996). A primary objective of the initial demarcation process was to substantially reduce the number of municipalities. As a result, in December 2000, the former 843 transitional municipalities were abolished and replaced by 284 new-look municipalities. This rationalization had a significant impact in both metropolitan and non-metropolitan areas. These 284 municipalities furthermore ensure that local government now extends to every square metre of South Africa.

Under the new local government dispensation a distinction must be drawn between metropolitan and non-metropolitan areas. Six single-tier metropolitan municipalities were established in the areas demarcated as metropolitan (so-called Category A municipalities). In non-metropolitan areas a two-tier structure was retained. Across the nine provinces there are 47 district municipalities (so-called Category C municipalities) and within each district municipality there is one or more of the 231 local municipalities (so-called Category B municipalities). The significant rationalization was primarily achieved by amalgamating the primary-tier local councils (traditional urban municipalities) with transitional rural municipalities into the new-look local municipalities. In other words, local municipalities now consist of urban as well as rural properties.

Tables 6.1 and 6.2 present an overview of the changes regarding municipal structures.

Table 6.1   The 'Old', 'Transitional' and 'New' Municipalities

Apartheid Municipalities (Pre-1994)	Transitional Municipalities (1994-December 2000)	'New-look' Municipalities (Post-December 2000)
White local authorities (urban)	Metropolitan (two-tier): Transitional metropolitan councils (5)	Metropolitan (single-tier):
Black local authorities (urban)	Metropolitan local councils (24)	Metropolitan municipalities (6)
Regional services councils or joint services boards (urban and rural)	Non-metropolitan (two-tier): District councils (42) Transitional local councils (for urban areas) and transitional representative or rural councils (for rural areas) (771)	Non-metropolitan (two-tier): District municipalities (47) Local municipalities (231)

Table 6.2 presents a summary of the 'new' municipalities that now provide wall-to-wall local government countrywide on a province-by-province basis.

Table 6.2　　Post-December 2000 South African municipalities

Province	Metro (Category A)	Local (Category B)	District (Category C)	Total Number of Municipalities per Province
Eastern Cape	1	38	6	45
Free State	-	20	5	25
Gauteng	3	9	3	15
KwaZulu-Natal	1	50	10	61
Limpopo	-	26	6	32
Mpumalanga	-	17	3	20
Northern Cape	-	27	5	32
North West	-	20	4	24
Western Cape	1	24	5	30
Total	6	231	47	284

Source: Intergovernmental Fiscal Review 2003

Despite the fact that the amalgamation became effective on 5 December 2000, most if not all of these newly established municipalities are still facing considerable challenges such as financial stress, inadequate management practices, dysfunctional institutional systems, inefficient service delivery and disproportionately high operating costs. To all of this must be added the difficulties presented by integrating budgets, staff, IT systems and the alignment of assets and liabilities (*Budget Review*, 2001).

Local government finances

Although there has been a substantial increase in grant support from the national sphere in recent years (as evidenced by Table 6.3), South African municipalities collectively provide a significant percentage (on aggregate about 90 per cent) of total operating income from own sources of revenue. In metropolitan areas the average is closer to 95 per cent. As indicated in Table 3, the primary sources of revenue for funding municipal operating expenditure are, in order of importance, the following:

- user charges (especially for four main services, namely electricity, water, sanitation and refuse removal);
- rates on property (i.e. property tax);

- regional services council (RSC) levies (i.e. levies on payroll and turnover); and
- Intergovernmental grants

Table 6.3   Budgeted municipal operating income: 2001-2002 to 2003-2004

Revenue Sources	2001-2002		2002-2003		2003-2004	
	R Bn	%	R Bn	%	R Bn	%
User charges	25.0	46	28.0	46	31.0	42
Rates on property	11.5	21	12.5	20	14.3	20
RSC levies	3.9	7	4.4	7	5.2	7
Intergovernmental grants	3.6	7	6.7	11	8.1	11
Other sources (e.g. fines)	10.3	19	10.0	16	14.3	20
Total	54.3	100	61.6	100	72.9	100

Source: Trends in Intergovernmental Finances: 2000/01-2006/07

'Other sources' of funding, which collectively also constitute a significant percentage on aggregate, include traffic fines, interest on investments, recovery of outstanding debt, rental income (e.g. on municipal housing stock) and the use of previous years' surplus funds.

Importance of property tax

Rates on property have remained relatively constant at approximately 20 per cent of total operating income for the local government sphere. Rates on property are only levied by metropolitan and local municipalities and not by district municipalities.

Table 6.4   Rates on property by category of municipality: 2001-2002 to 2003-2004

Municipalities	2001-2002		2002-2003		2003-2004	
	R Bn	%	R Bn	%	R Bn	%
Metropolitan Municipalities	6.3	67	8.9	71	10.1	70
Local Municipalities	3.1	33	3.7	29	4.3	30
Total	9.4	100	12.6	100	14.4	100

Source: Trends in Intergovernmental Finances: 2000/01-2006/07

It is noteworthy that the six metropolitan municipalities are responsible for approximately 70 per cent of the total revenue from rates on property, with the 231 local municipalities on aggregate responsible for only 30 per cent.

Presently rates on property are still levied, assessed and collected in terms of pre-1994 provincial legislation in all nine provinces. Table 6.5 provides a breakdown of rates on property per province for the 2003-2004 financial year.

Table 6.5   Rates on property by province: 2003-2004

Province	Rates on Property ('000)	Operating Income: Total ('000)	Rates as a percentage
Eastern Cape	889,489	6,520,034	13.64
Free State	583,919	4,150,868	14.07
Gauteng	5,674,598	26,911,288	21.09
KwaZulu-Natal	3,228,463	12,985,185	24.86
Limpopo	264,291	2,718,022	9.72
Mpumalanga	503,490	3,135,529	16.06
Northern Cape	179,015	1,460,982	12.25
North West	350,037	3,034,165	11.54
Western Cape	2,670,095	12,070,117	22.12
Total	14,343,399	72,986,189	19.65

Source: Trends in Intergovernmental Finances: 2000/01-2006/07

Although property rates have remained relatively constant as a percentage of operating income, there has been marked growth in the total nominal amount raised through the property tax in recent years. Table 6.6 illustrates the levels of municipal operating income for the provinces.

Table 6.6   Municipal operating income: 2002-2003

Municipalities	Rand millions					
Metropolitan Municipalities	RSC Levies	Property Tax	Electric	Water	Other	Total
Johannesburg	1,050	2,196	2,569	2,163	1,751	9,730
Cape Town	654	1,897	2,370	689	2,249	7,861
Ethekwini (Durban)	322	2,072	2,526	1,040	1,581	7,543
Ekurhuleni (East Rand)	418	1,148	2,241	1,200	2,351	7,360
Tshwane (Pretoria)	407	1,207	1,930	649	987	5,182
Nelson Mandela (PE)	148	372,	826	206	500	2,054
Total	3,001	8,894	12,464	5,950	9,421	39,732
Local Municipalities	-	3,644	6,669	3,034	10,178	23,526
Total	3,001	12,538	19,133	8,984	19,600	63,259

Source: 2003 Intergovernmental Fiscal Review

For local municipalities collectively property tax represented 15.5 per cent of total operating income, whereas for the six metropolitan municipalities it represented 22.4 per cent.

Property-related taxes: brief overview

Historically land-related taxation in South Africa can be traced as far back as 1677, when the Dutch East India Company introduced an agricultural tithe on small-scale farmers who had been settling down in the fledging colony located at the Cape of Good Hope. Various land-related charges were introduced with regard to agricultural land. The Dutch introduced recognition fees on farms in 1714 and the British (after annexing the colony in 1806) introduced quitrent, hut taxes, various forms of land taxes and eventually property rates in the Cape colony (and their various other colonies in southern Africa). Introduced in the Cape Colony in terms of the Municipal Ordinance in 1836, rates on property have been a source of revenue for primarily urban municipalities in South Africa ever since.

Property tax was an important local tax during the (pre-1994) apartheid era. It was levied by all former white urban local authorities and only in some instances in Coloured and Indian townships. It was not levied by former black local authorities, despite the fact that the necessary enabling legislation was, in principle, in place. In the case of the white local authorities generous rebates were generally granted to residential ratepayers, shifting much of the tax burden to commercial and industrial properties. In many instances especially larger local authorities could also afford to set low property tax rates because they were realising substantial profits on the provision of certain trading services (such as the provision of electricity and water). These profits on trading services allowed many urban councils to 'cross-subsidise' the general rates account. Property tax rates were set annually, after the revenue from all other sources were considered – in essence making up the shortfall.

Transfer duty, a tax on the acquisition of immovable property, was introduced to the Cape Colony in 1686, making it the oldest land-related tax still levied in South Africa at present. Presently the following land-related taxes are levied:

National sphere

The most important property-related tax levied by the national sphere of government is transfer duty. Transfer duty, levied in terms of the Transfer Duty Act 40 of 1949, is payable on the acquisition of 'property' as defined (in essence it means immovable property, i.e. land and improvements, as well as limited real rights pertaining to land and improvements). Tax rates are high. From 1 March 2004 natural persons pay transfer duty as follows: 0 per cent on the first R150,000; 5 per cent on the value from R150,001 to R320,000 (i.e. the next R170,000); 8 per cent on the rest (i.e. above R320,000). Persons other than natural persons (e.g. companies, close corporations and trusts) pay transfer duty at a uniform tax rate of 10 per cent. Where value-added tax (VAT) is payable on the acquisition of 'property' (typically where property is acquired from a property developer), no transfer duty is payable.

Provincial sphere

At the provincial sphere of government no property-related taxes are levied. Section 228 of the 1996 Constitution furthermore explicitly prohibits provinces from levying 'rates on property' (i.e. a tax on the ownership of immovable property).

Local sphere

In South Africa 'property tax' – in a narrow sense – refers to a tax called 'rates on property' which is an annual tax on the owners of immovable property (i.e. land and, where applicable, improvements).

Property tax systems in present-day South Africa

Rates on property, as an annual tax payable by the owner on the market value of property situated within municipal boundaries, is levied in terms of one of the following three systems:

- a site rating system (i.e. taxing only the land, excluding improvements);
- a flat rating system (i.e. taxing the improved value of the land); or
- a composite rating system (i.e. taxing both the land and the improvements, but at separate tax rates)[1]

The White Paper, published in March 1998, also proposed material changes to the manner in which local government is to be financed, citing certain features of the property rates dispensation that required reform. And indeed the White Paper (i.e. government policy advisors) suggested a simpler and uniform valuation system with regards to tax base is one of the key policy objectives of a future rating dispensation. It is, however, also stated that a 'key decision that needs to be taken is whether there should be uniform national system, or whether there should continue to be local choice in this matter'. In essence the White Paper suggested uniformity, but leaves the question which of the three systems in operation in South Africa is to be preferred, unanswered.

At the time when the reform of the local government sphere commenced in al earnest in 1994, the use of the three rating system was

---

[1] In the United States such a tax is referred to as a 'split-rate property tax'.

rather evenly spread amongst municipalities throughout the country, i.e. a third each. The distribution within former provinces however indicate a general preference for one or at most two out of the three systems, as indicated in Table 6.7.

Table 6.7   Rating systems used by pre-1994 municipalities in 1993-1994

Province	Site Rating		Flat Rating		Composite Rating		Total
	No.	%	No.	%	No.	%	
Cape	4	2.4	89	54.0	72	43.6	165
Natal	34	50.7	1	1.5	32	47.8	67
Orange Free State	10	19.6	8	15.7	33	64.7	51
Transvaal	78	88.6	2	2.3	8	9.1	88
Total/ Percentage	126	34.0	100	27.0	145	39.1	371

Source: Bell and Bowman, 2002

The amalgamation of municipalities in December 2000 has reduced the number and nature of municipalities significantly. Although the exact numbers for each of the three systems at present are not known (as some of the new municipalities are still in the process of harmonising their systems), suffice it to say that all three systems are still used in meaningful numbers. The mere existence and perseverance of the three systems in South Africa for almost 100 years, each with a significant following, suggest that there must be some merit in all three systems. This is enforced by the significant number of municipalities throughout the country where the current tax bases have been operational for longer than 25 years.

Traditionally, legislation prescribed that the municipal valuer has to value land, improvements and the total value of each rateable property. Thereafter the municipal council must choose a tax base – in other words the choice of tax base was primarily a political decision.

Property tax reform: need and process

As a constitutionally-guaranteed source of local government revenue, the importance of property tax is entrenched and is bound to increase over time. However, the significant constitutional, institutional and socio-economic changes that have occurred inevitably result in a need for reforms of the current property tax system(s) in South Africa. The following reasons should suffice:

- the four provincial ordinances regulating rates on property which date from the (pre-1994) apartheid era, are out-dated in the context of the new constitutional dispensation and lack uniformity;
- municipalities have been saddled with an important developmental role in terms of sections 152(1) and 153 of the 1996 Constitution;
- municipalities now cover South Africa's surface area wall-to-wall, in other words all formerly untaxed rural land is in principle included within the jurisdiction of a taxing authority);
- although 'surcharges on fees for services' (i.e. what used to be referred to as profits on trading services – see above) are also mentioned as own sources of revenue for municipalities in the Constitution (section 229(1)), the general trend is to become less reliant on surcharges for a variety of reasons (e.g. material changes to the manner in which electricity will be distributed in future).

The Department of Provincial and Local Government (DPLG) held a first exploratory workshop on property tax reform in November 1997. Various draft bills followed which were discussed within DPLG and other government departments (e.g. National Treasury, Department of Public Works, Department of Land Affairs) and at workshops and meetings held with various other stakeholder groups (e.g. organised local government, civics groups, traditional leaders, the valuers' profession, agricultural unions, the tourist and mining industries). Eventually the 11th draft of the Local Government: Property Rates Bill was published in the Government Gazette in August 2000, inviting public comment. Some aspects were left unresolved in the Bill (e.g. how land under the control of traditional authorities was to be treated). Numerous submissions were received and together with the unresolved policy issues forced DPLG back to the drawing board.

A further draft of the Bill (the 18th), as approved by Cabinet, was published once more in the Government Gazette in March 2003. In April 2003 Parliament's Portfolio Committee for Local Government held a 'closed' workshop with invited stakeholders to thrash out policy issues and practical problems relating to the Bill. As a next important step, public hearings were held in Parliament at the instance of the Portfolio Committee for Local Government in May 2003.

After further technical work the Bill was at last tabled in Parliament in February 2004. It was passed by Parliament and the Local Government: Municipal Property Rates Act 6 of 2004 was published in the *Government Gazette* in May 2004. It is envisioned that the Act will become operational on 1 July 2005, to coincide with the local government sphere's 2005-2006 financial year. Therefore, the first valuation rolls to be prepared in terms of this legislation will most likely only be implemented on 1 July 2006.

It is noteworthy that early drafts of the Property Rates Bill (the last being the 10th) retained the present three options of tax base and the freedom of local choice in this regard. The 11th draft (published in August 2000) provided that a rate levied on property must be an amount in the Rand determined by the municipality on the improved value of the property. Although it insisted on the inclusion of improvements in the tax base, it however still provided for the possibility of split rating and therefore still required three values per property.

The major policy shift to tax only the improved value of land, in later drafts providing for only one value (i.e. the 'market value' of the property) has been maintained in all the drafts since, and was finally confirmed with the promulgation of the Local Government: Municipal Property Rates Act 6 of 2004 (MPRA). This will bring to an end a century of 'value separation' as the new rating base will require one value only (i.e. the capital improved value of the rateable property). The primary reason given for adopting a single system on a national basis is the need for uniformity across the country (White Paper, 1998; Bell and Bowman, 2002; Manche, 2003).

Although in line with international trends (McCluskey and Franzsen, 2001), the commencement of the MPRA will obviously result in major shifts in tax incidence in those municipalities (especially in Gauteng, Limpopo and Mpumalanga provinces, see Table 6.7) where site rating is used and, to a lesser extent, in those municipalities (especially evident in the Free State, KwaZulu-Natal and Western Cape provinces, see Table 6.7) where composite rating is used and improvements taxed at a significantly lower rate than the land. Municipalities have generally not been pro-active in undertaking studies on the shifts in incidence that will result from migrating to capital improved values, and how to counter the impact of this change through phasing-in provisions and/or the use of differential rates for different property categories.

Review of land value taxation ('site rating') and its demise

The statutory imperative to have at least two or three separate values reflected on the valuation roll for each rateable property, a prerequisite for local choice as regards a rating system, dates back to 1903. Table 8 presents a summary of the legislation that mandated separate values and sanctioned the use of different tax bases as a result of these separate values with regards to the former four (i.e. pre-1994) provinces of South Africa. In each case the sanctioning of separate values pre-dates the allowance for different rating system by a number of years.

Table 6.8 **Legislative origins of differential values and different tax bases**

Province	Year	Enabling Legislation for Allowing Site Valuation	Year	Enabling Legislation for Allowing a Choice of Rating System
Transvaal	1903	Local Authorities Rating Ordinance	1916	Local Authorities Rating (Amendment) Ordinance
Orange Free State	1903 1904	Bloemfontein Municipal Ordinance (1903) and the Municipal Corporations Ordinance (1904)	1920	Local Government Further Amendment Ordinance
Natal	1911	Municipal Corporations Law Amendment Ordinance	1924	Boroughs Ordinance
Cape	1912	Cape Municipal Ordinance	1917	Cape Municipal (Amendment) Ordinance

Source: McCluskey and Franzsen, 2004

For valuation purposes, legislation in all four the former provinces of the pre-1994 South Africa (namely the Cape of Good Hope, Natal, Orange Free

State and Transvaal), has dictated a 'separation' of values (i.e. the need for land values and the value of improvements to be reflected separately in a valuation roll) as far back as 1903 as indicated by Table 6.8. Under the present provincial ordinances still regulating rating throughout South Africa, municipalities still have a choice between at least two of the above-mentioned three tax bases. Local choice as regards these three possible tax bases dates back to as early as 1916 (Table 6.8).

Tax base

The introduction of a land value tax was introduced as far back as 1916 in the old Transvaal province, with other provinces following suit (see Table 6.8). Although the split was surprisingly even before amalgamation started in 1993 (as reflected in Table 6.7), 'site rating' was the predominant system in at least the former Transvaal where some municipalities have been using this base for more than 80 years.

Basis for valuation

Irrespective whether a municipality utilizes flat rating, composite rating or site rating, the basis for valuation for rating purposes in South Africa has always been market value. This was confirmed by various decisions of the provincial courts. For example, in *SA Breweries Ltd v Kroonstad Municipality* 1913 OPD 34, Maasdorp C.J. in the Orange Free State stated (p 35):

> But it was left to the court to decide what was meant by the word 'value' and the court decided last year [1912] that 'value' meant, in the ordinary signification of the word, 'market value'.

It was also emphatically confirmed by the Appellate Division of the Supreme Court (as it was known then) in *Durban Corporation and Another v Lincoln* 1940 AD 36. Watermeyer J.A. (delivering the majority judgement) states the following in this regard (p 41):

> It is important to notice that rates may be levied on the whole property, or the land alone, or diversely on the land and the buildings but not on the buildings alone… To arrive at the *fair market value* of the property as a whole does not present any insuperable difficulties… (my emphasis)

This is a confirmation of the *locus classicus* in South Africa as regards 'market value' as basis of the valuation of immovable property, *Pietermaritzburg Corporation v SA Breweries Ltd* 1911 AD 501 (at 516).

Site (i.e. land) value

The earliest legislative provision for so-called 'site value of land' dates back to 1903 (see Table 8). The Transvaal's Local Authorities Rating Amendment Ordinance, 1 of 1916 defined 'site value of land' (in section 4) as follows:

> 'Site value of land' shall mean the capital sum which the land or interest in land might be expected to realise if offered for sale on such reasonable terms and conditions as a bona fide seller would require assuming that the improvements, if any, thereon or appertaining thereto… had not been made. The site value of land shall include any value due to any licence privilege or concession attached to the site for the time being.

In the same ordinance the 'value of improvements' in relation to land 'shall mean the added value which the improvements give to the land at the date of valuation irrespective of the cost of improvements'.

The relevant part of section 104 of Ordinance 4 of 1913 in the former Orange Free State read as follows:

- the value of the ground [i.e. land], by which shall be understood the estimated value which such ground would realise if placed in the open market for voluntary public sale.
- The value of the buildings by which shall be understood the making of a valuation based on the estimated cost of replacement, at the time of such valuation, due allowance being made for any depreciation existing at the time of such valuation, either in the buildings themselves or in the marketable or rental value thereof.

In *Durban Corporation and Another v Lincoln* Watermeyer J.A. states the following in regarding valuing land on which improvements have been effected (p 43):

> The market value of land, separated from the building that stands upon it, is not an incomprehensible idea… The market value, therefore, of land separated from the building which stands upon it, when determined in the only way it is possible to determine it, is seen to be the equivalent to the market value of the land regarded as a vacant site. [The valuation board]

determined the market value of the land, and in the course of doing so, in order to arrive at an attainable result, they regarded the land as a vacant site. And (p 45):

> In my opinion the only practical and logical view to take is that land regarded as a vacant site has a determinable market value, that the building placed upon it is a physical addition to the land and that thereafter the market value of the property (land and building) may be greater or theoretically it may even be less than the market value of the land alone. The difference – the increase or the decrease – is due to the building, and can be regarded as the value of the benefit or of the burden of the building. It is, of course, not the market value of the building: there is no such thing.

In *Kleinfontein Estate and Township Co v Benoni Municipality* 1918 TPD 193 Gregorowski J., referring with approval to the Australian case of *Nathan v The Commissioner of Land Tax* (reported in the Second Annual Report of the Commissioner of Land 1911-1912, p 48), states the principle clearly (at p 202):

> The definition of 'site value' indeed says that the assessment is to be made 'assuming that the improvements if any thereon or appertaining thereto had not been made,' but this cannot be construed to require the assessment to be made quite irrespective of the profitable use to which experience or history has proved that the property can be put, by certain improvements.

Value of improvements

In the case of *SA Breweries Ltd v Kroonstad Municipality* 1913 OPD 34, Maasdorp C.J. in the Orange Free State stated the following (p 36-37):

> The Council have gone back upon the procedure they adopted last year, that is to say they again made a valuation of the building according to a very abnormal way of making valuations, namely, by calculating how much brick, mortar and timber there is in the building, and by finding out how much it would cost to put the same bricks and mortar and timber there to-day. Well that is not value; that is the cost – the cost of construction...

Regarding the manner in which the value of improvements should be established, Watermeyer J.A. decided the following in the *Lincoln* case (p 42):

> But when the next step has to be taken and the total market value of the whole property has to be divided into two and allocated in part to the land and in part to the buildings upon the land, a very much more difficult

problem arises... A building standing upon a piece of land is like a picture painted upon a piece of canvas; and just as it is impossible to sell the picture apart from the canvas on which it is painted, so it is equally impossible to sell a building apart from the land. It is possible to scrape the paint from the canvas, and it is possible to pull the building down and sell the material, but then the work has been destroyed and what is sold is not the building but building material... It is, therefore, idle to attempt to find the market value of the building separated from the land on which it stands, and any valuator who is attempting to do so is pursuing a will of the wisp. The value, therefore, which has to be assigned to buildings... is not market value but value determined in some other way.

If the position of the other component part, the land, be examined, it will be seen that, though there are difficulties with regard to its valuation, they are nothing like so formidable as those connected with the building, and it is not necessary to abandon entirely the idea of market value...

In summary: In terms of the current provincial legislation in all the new provinces, except KwaZulu-Natal, the value of improvements is arrived at by deducting the site value from the total value, in other words the value of the improvements for rating purposes is indeed a residual value.

However, legislation in the former Cape Ordinance (which applied until the enactment of the 1993 Valuation Ordinance in 1994) also allowed for the value of improvements to be arrived at on the basis of replacement cost minus depreciation. This methodology is indeed still used in certain jurisdictions (e.g. Buffalo City (formerly known as East London) in the Eastern Cape). The 1974 Natal Ordinance (still applicable throughout the province of KwaZulu-Natal) only provides for improvements to be valued on the basis of replacement cost at the date of valuation less depreciation. It also provides that this value must then be added to the value of the land (as if unimproved) to get to a total rateable value. This aggregated value (land value plus the value of improvements) does not necessarily equate to market value (see *Durban Corporation and Another v Lincoln* 1940 AD 36 on 45; Ethekwini Metropolitan Council, 2003).

Definitions from provincial legislation

Cape Province

Section 14(1) of the Property Valuation Ordinance of 1993 states that:

a valuer shall, for the purposes of this Ordinance, determine:

- the improved value of land, which shall be the amount which such land would have realised if sold on the date of valuation in the open market by a willing seller to a willing buyer;
- the site value of land which shall be the amount arrived at in the same manner as that referred to in paragraph (a) but on the assumption that the improvements, if any, had not been made; and
- the value of improvements, which shall be arrived at by subtracting the site value of the land from the improved value thereof;

provided that where the land or improvements, if any, is or are of such a nature that there is no open market value therefor, the improved value or site value, as the case may be, may be determined therefore:

- on the basis of the amount it would cost to replace the improvements in, on or under the land, having regard to the depreciation thereof for any reason, as determined on the date of valuation; or
- in any other suitable manner.

Section 44 of the Cape Valuation Ordinance 26 of 1944, which was only repealed by the 1993 Ordinance with effect from January 1994, only provided for depreciated replacement cost as method of valuing improvements.

Therefore there are some municipalities in the Eastern Cape, Northern Cape and Western Cape still utilising depreciated replacement costs for buildings, whereas others – under the 1993 Ordinance, arrive at the 'value' of improvements by deducting the land value from the improved value. Since 1912 the value of land has always been the market value as if unimproved.

Natal

Section 155(5) of the Local Authorities Ordinance 25 of 1974 states:

The value of land shall be the ordinary price which a buyer would have been willing to give and a seller would have been willing to accept if the land to be valued had been brought to a voluntary sale on the fixed date.

Section 155(6)(a) states:

The value of building shall be the estimated cost of erection at the fixed date, and in determining that value the valuator shall take the estimated cost of erection at the fixed date and from it shall deduct the amount determined by him in respect of depreciation.

Section 155(7) provides that:

> Where, owing to the infrequency of sales or other reasons, the purchase price obtained or obtainable in any locality, or in the case of buildings, the cost of erection, will not, in the opinion of the valuator, serve as a sufficient guide to enable him to arrive at a fair and equitable valuation of any property (whether land or buildings), then the rental and productivity and the possibilities of any such property as an investment shall be considered in establishing the basis of and finally determining the valuation of the property.'

In present day KwaZulu-Natal, the position has remained the same since 1911. Land is valued at market value, whereas buildings and other improvements are valued with reference to the depreciated cost of construction as a general rule.

Ethekwini Metropolitan Council (formerly known as the Durban City Council) makes it clear to ratepayers that adding the (market) value of the land to the depreciated replacement cost of the building(s) on a rateable property does not equate to the market value of the improved property (Ethekwini Metropolitan Council, 2003).

Orange Free State

In section 106(1) of the Local Government Ordinance 8 of 1962, the following definitions are given:

> For the purposes of section 105 (i.e. preparing a valuation roll):
>
> •   'value of the rateable property' means the amount which such property without any improvements, would have realised if sold on the date of valuation in the open market by a willing seller to a willing buyer;
> •   'value of improvements' means the amount obtained by subtracting the amount referred to in paragraph (a) from the amount which the rateable property, including any improvements, would have realised if sold on the date of valuation in the open market by a willing seller to a willing buyer.

In brief, in the Free State land was always valued (as if unimproved) at market value. For a number of years (since 1913 until the 1962 Ordinance was enacted) buildings were valued at replacement cost minus depreciation, whereas since the enactment of the 1962 Ordinance the value of improvements would again constitute the residual value, arrived at by deducting the value of the land from the improved value of the rateable property.

Transvaal

Section 9(1) of the Local Authorities Rating Ordinance 11 of 1977 states that:
> a valuer shall, for the purposes of this ordinance, determine:

- • the improved value of land or the improved value of a right in land which shall be the amount which such land or right in land would have realized if sold on the date of the valuation in the open market by a willing seller to a willing buyer;
- • the site value of land or the site value of a right in land which shall be the amount arrived at in the like manner to that referred to in paragraph (a), but on the assumption that the improvements, if any, had not been made; and
- • the value of improvements which shall be arrived at by subtracting the site value of the land or the site value of the right in land from the improved value thereof.

In the provinces of Gauteng, Limpopo, Mpumalanga and that part of the Northwest that formerly constituted part of the Transvaal, land has been valued at market value for the past century, and the value of buildings has always been arrived at by subtracting the 'site value' (i.e. the value of land as if unimproved) from the improved value i.e. it constitutes the residual value.

The beginning of the end for site rating: Local Government: Property Rates Bill, 2000 (11th Draft)

Since the inception of the drafting process of the Local Government: Property Rates Bill in 1998, echoing a principle stated in the White Paper (1998), Government was adamant about the need to create a simplified, and preferably a uniform rating dispensation for the whole of South Africa.

Despite the policy to establish a uniform system, earlier drafts of the Bill all maintained the various options (i.e. site rating, flat rating and composite rating). For example, the following relevant definitions for rating were contained in the 11th draft of the Bill, published in the Government Gazette in August 2000 as the Local Government: Property Rates Bill, 2000. The 'General basis of valuation' is stated as follows in clause 33:

(1)   Subject to section 51(3) of the Sectional Titles Act, 1986, and other provisions of this Act:

- the improved value of property must be determined as an amount equal to what the property would have realised if sold on the date of valuation in the open market by a willing seller to a willing buyer;
- the site value of land must be determined as an amount equal to what the property would have realised if sold on the date of valuation in the open market by a willing seller to a willing buyer but *on the assumption* that:
    (i)   there are no improvements to the property; and
    (ii)   *only the existing improvements may be erected* on the property
- the value of improvements must be determined by subtracting the site value of the property from its improved value.' (my emphasis)

The definition of 'site value' (clause 33(1)(b)) made little sense and would have resulted in the demise of site rating as a matter of course as it, in essence, limited the valuer to 'current use' instead of 'highest and best use' in determining the value of land. Clause 33(1)(c) maintained the principle applied throughout most of the country (except in KwaZulu-Natal and some jurisdictions in the former Cape of Good Hope) that the value of improvements will be a residual value.

Local Government: Municipal Property Rates Act 6 of 2004

With the enactment of the MPRA the principle of uniformity has now been extended to the basis of valuation for rating purposes. Site values (and therefore site rating) as well as separate values for building (and therefore the possibility of composite rating) will belong to a century-long past as soon as the transition period lapses four years after the commencement of the MPRA.

In section 1 'market value' is defined as:

in relation to a property, means the value of property determined in accordance with section 46.

Under the heading 'General basis of valuation' section 46 provides as follows:

(1)   Subject to any other applicable provisions of this Act, the market value of a property is the amount the property would have realised if sold on the date of valuation in the open market by a willing seller to a willing buyer.

In determining the market value of a property, the following must be considered for purposes of valuing the property:

- the value of any license, permission or other privilege granted in terms of legislation in relation to the property; and
- the value of any immovable improvement on the property that was erected or is being used for a purposes which is inconsistent with or in contravention of the permitted use of the property, as if the improvement was erected or is being used for a lawful purpose; and
- the value of the use of the property for a purpose which is inconsistent with or in contravention of the permitted use of the property, as if the property is being used for a lawful purpose.

The MPRA thus brought clarity after initial ambivalence about the possible retention of multiple tax bases and local choice in this regard.

Valuation methodology

There are several accepted valuation methodologies that can be used to determine the land value component of a particular property. The choice of a particular method is largely dependent upon the quality and quantity of transaction evidence available at the time of the valuation as well as what may be dictated by law.

Feetham J.A. states the following in *Durban Corporation v Lincoln* 1940 AD 36 at 54:

> It seems to me clear that neither in the Natal legislation, nor in the legislation of any of the other provinces in the Union, did the mere requirement that the values of land and building should be shown separately introduce any new principle of valuation, or make any difference whatsoever in the principles of valuation to be applied: in all cases property had to be valued either under the express terms of the governing statute, or in accordance with its necessary implications, at its fair market value, taking the condition of the property as it actually existed at the time of the valuation.

In establishing market value generally, various methods may be used of which the following have been accepted by the South African courts, namely:

*   comparable sales method, also referred to as 'direct sales comparison';[2]
*   income capitalisation method;
*   rentals; and
*   land residual approach.[3]

For rating purposes the preferred method used in practice is that of direct comparable sales. However, where comparable sales are not in evidence, alternative methods, such as the income capitalisation method, are also used to determine the value of land.

Valuation data

For the largest part of the country, the Deeds Office keeps accurate and up to date records of any transfers of ownership or limited real rights in land. Where a property is sold, the sales price will also be reflected. Sales data is not confidential under South African law. The details of any property parcel registered as such in the Deeds Office can be accessed electronically

---

[2] This particular approach involves the assessment of land value based on the direct comparison of the subject land with other comparable land sales. It does not utilise a unit of comparison but rather takes the land as a block or parcel with individual adjustments for size, location, road frontage, topography etc being made holistically by the valuer. This method is often used when there is a lack of market transactions or where a particular parcel is unique in size, shape or location. The determined value is largely subjective being based upon the experience and knowledge of the valuer. The application of this approach is well suited to valuing rural/residential property on the periphery of urban areas and low cost housing areas within large towns and cities (McCluskey and Franzsen, 2004).

[3] In the absence of open market transactions it is possible to estimate the land value of a property by analysing improved value sales. These techniques are generally subjective and rely heavily on the skill and experience of the valuer. But in the absence of other evidence they do provide a reasonable approach to determining the land value of a particular property. In South Africa the land residual approach has been criticised by Ogilvie-Thompson J.A. in *Estate Marks v Pretoria City Council* 1969 (3) SA 227 (A) at p 248 as 'a complicated exercise involving specialised skills in several spheres', and as a result are not often applied in practice (Gildenhuys, 2002).

as can a list of recent property transactions. This generally provides municipal valuers with sufficient sales data and market evidence for rating valuations.

Within the areas which formerly constituted 'white South Africa' there are well functioning capital and rental markets. This applies to urban and rural land. However, in the black townships property markets only started to develop when it became possible (in the mid-1980s) for black South Africans to acquire ownership. A brief study by Franzsen and McCluskey in 1999 of valuation rolls for two rural towns (Leandra and Wakkerstroom) in the province of Mpumalanga indicated that the first attempts to include township properties in municipal valuation rolls resulted in inconsistencies and different approaches (McCluskey and Franzsen, 1999).

The fact that all rural land is now within municipal boundaries also provides valuers with new challenges. The methodologies now being used for the valuation of communal land tenure have not yet been tested in the courts.

Whether site rating provides the best option for rating purposes, especially where there is at least some doubt about the capacity within the valuers profession, is not clear. The problem, as is the case in New Zealand (see McCluskey and Franzsen, 2004), is not the extension of valuation rolls to the relatively few rural properties, but how to deal with the substantial numbers of built-up urban properties. Generally speaking the assessment of site value is usually straightforward where evidence of demand is present and good sales data are available. However, in the highly developed inner cities of South Africa, vacant land sales are indeed posing a problem for municipal valuers. A paucity of undeveloped sites may also have the result that those remaining sites command very high, somewhat unrealistic comparable values. Valuers will sometimes have to rely on sales from adjacent neighbourhoods to provide an indication of land values. Figure 6.1 illustrates the sales of vacant and improved residential properties over the period 1999-2002 for the Tshwane Metropolitan Council. Whilst there are no fundamental conceptual problems in valuing land for taxation, there can be difficulties in practice particularly for commercial areas (McCluskey and Franzsen, 2001; Bell, 2002; McCluskey and Franzsen, 2004).

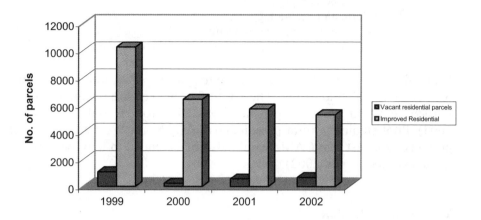

**Figure 6.1   Sales of vacant and improved residential parcels:
Tshwane Metropolitan Area**

Computer generated valuations have not been used in South Africa until recently, although some automation has been in place in the case of the larger metropolitan municipalities. Outdated provincial laws stipulated that each rateable property had to be physically inspected by the municipal valuer, severely hampering the use of computer assisted mass appraisal techniques. This however, did not prevent the extensive use of computers in data collection and maintenance and in the preparation and manipulation of valuation rolls – especially in the case of some of the larger municipalities (e.g. the City of Tshwane).

In 2000 section 10G of the Local Government Transition Act 209 of 1993 – which applies country-wide – was amended by the insertion of subsection (6A). Section 10G(6A)[4] states:

> Despite anything to the contrary in any other law, a municipality must value property for purposes of imposing rates on property in accordance with generally recognised valuation practices, methods and standards. For purposes of paragraph (a):
>
> •   physical inspection of the property to be valued, is optional; and
> •   in lieu of valuation by a valuer, or in addition thereto, comparative, analytical and other systems and techniques may be used, including:

---

[4] Section 45 of the new MPRA replicates section 10G(6A) of the Local Government Transition Act.

- aerial photography;
- information technology;
- computer applications and software; and
- computer assisted mass appraisal systems or techniques.

Under this legislation it is now possible to utilise CAMA in the preparation of municipal valuation rolls. The City of Cape Town has completed and introduced its first CAMA-generated valuation roll in 2002 (Weichardt, 2003). Pilot studies in rural jurisdictions in the North West and Free State provinces suggest that CAMA could also be extended to non-metropolitan municipalities (Ward, 2002).

Valuation profession

Maintaining the status quo, the MPRA (section 39(1)(a)) stipulates that only valuers registered with the South African Council for the Property Valuers Profession may be appointed as municipal valuers. The question therefore arises whether there are enough qualified valuers to undertake the task of preparing and maintaining valuation rolls that – in principle – need to cover almost the total surface area of the country and will they be able to adhere to the maximum four-year valuation cycle? Of the approximately 2,000 registered valuers, associated valuers and valuers in training, at most 20 per cent are presently involved in municipal valuations (Zybrands, 2003b).

Some commentators argue that the number of rural properties (e.g. commercial farms) is not too large to present insurmountable problems. Furthermore, a number of local municipalities have been pro-active and have already started preparing new valuation rolls that extend to rural properties albeit under present provincial laws (Zybrands, 2003b).

In terms of section 27(4) of the recently enacted Property Valuers Profession Act 47 of 2000 it will be possible for valuers, who are not registered in South Africa, to work 'in the service of or by the order of and under the direction, control, supervision of or in association with a registered person entitled to perform the work identified and who must assume responsibility for any work so performed'. The City of Cape Town, using international consultants and local private valuers to assist its in-house valuation department, completed a computer-assisted mass appraisal (CAMA) general revaluation of more than 500,000 residential properties in June 2002 (Weichardt, 2003).

Both the South African Council for the Valuers Profession (the statutory regulatory entity) as well as the South African Institute of Valuers (a voluntary professional association for the valuers profession) seem confident that although the new property tax dispensation provides the profession with a huge challenge, there is sufficient capacity to take on the task at hand. Much depends, however, on the attitudes and vision of municipal councils and municipal valuers.

The metropolitan municipalities and some of the other larger primarily 'urban' municipalities (mostly secondary cities under the previous local government dispensation) have in-house valuation departments. These departments have developed their own unique in-house methodologies – which could suggest a reluctance to change. However, Tshwane Metropolitan Municipality (formerly Pretoria City Council) did, for a two-year period also rate improvements. Because the valuation roll contains at least two values for all rateable in any event, migrating to another system does not depend too heavily on the valuation profession's preference generally, or that of the municipal valuer more specifically, but rather on how to spread the burden more effectively (not necessarily more fairly) amongst the ratepayers. In the case of smaller municipalities, valuation service providers are selected through a process of private tendering.

Individual owners can object and appeal individual values. However, until the MPRA becomes operational, external, independent quality control of valuation rolls as such do not exist.

Critical overview

In South Africa, property taxation – including the choice of tax base – has become highly politicised in recent years. Although all three traditional tax bases are presently still being used extensively, the commencement of the MPRA (probably by July 2005) will result in a single, uniform rating system. Site rating and composite rating will then belong to the past.

In a recent review of property tax trends in New Zealand and South Africa, McCluskey and Franzsen (2004) obtained feedback from a number of municipal valuers in South Africa who responded to a questionnaire that dealt with valuation and rating issues in respect of each of the three rating systems currently still in place. Although the sample is too small to be of any statistical relevance or to draw any meaningful conclusions, it does provide an interesting perspective on the debate on property tax reform in South Africa. It does show that there are differences of opinion, even within the valuers' profession. The fact that the Institute of Valuers officially support flat rating as opposed to site rating, and that individual valuers responsible for site value valuation rolls also support the valuation of improvements did not seem to have influenced those municipal councils still using site rating. Table 6.9 provides an overview of the six municipalities for which the municipal valuer responded to the questionnaire.

Table 6.9   Municipalities that responded to the questionnaire

Municipality	Province	Rating system	How long?	Review in last 10 years?
Dihlabeng LM	Free State	Composite	25 years +	No
George LM	Western Cape	Composite	25 years +	No
Greater Tubatse LM	Limpopo Mpumalanga	Site	80 years +	No
Polokwane LM	Limpopo	Site	50 years +	No
Potchefstroom LM	Northwest	Site	25 years +	No
Tshwane MM	Gauteng	Site	50 years +	Yes[5]

Source: McCluskey and Franzsen, 2004

The first striking feature is that all six councils have been using their current system for a considerable time (more than 25 years) and without contemplating any self-imposed changes – except for the Tshwane Metropolitan Municipality (Pretoria City Council as it then was) where a tax on the value of improvements was levied as a temporary measure for a two-year period only.

The fact that no reviews as regards an appropriate base have been undertaken in the last five years seems to confirm the statement that councils were generally adopting a 'wait-and-see' approach – awaiting the outcome of the property tax reforms as these would play out in the MPRA. However, it must be remembered that – from a valuation point of view – valuation rolls generally already contain at least two values (i.e. land value and value of improvements) or three values (i.e. land value, value of improvements, and the improved value). Therefore, changing to a new basis will not be too difficult. From a taxation point of view, however, changing the tax base may have a significant impact on tax incidence.

---

[5] Tshwane introduced composite rating as a temporary measure for a two-year period only (1997/1998 and 1998/1999).

Of the three systems in South Africa, responses were significantly in favour of flat rating, or, as a second alternative, composite rating. In other words, a system that also taxes the value of improvements was preferred by a majority of the respondents. Only one respondent favoured site rating on the grounds of its administrative simplicity in comparison to a system that includes improvements.

It is often claimed that taxpayers will have less trouble to understand capital values as tax base than site value. However, in a South African context where the vast majority of ratepayers are not familiar with even the concept of 'market value' (as markets in former townships are only now emerging and in tribal areas the concept of private ownership is foreign and sale of property not possible) or with the concept of any form of rating, this argument may be less convincing. Some respondents to the questionnaire suggested that site rating could actually be the easier in a rural setting.

The majority of respondents were of the view that land value tended to encourage development or rather strongly felt that site value does not penalise the development of land and that a system that taxes improvements, especially at the same rate as the land, may indeed be a disincentive to develop land. However, one respondent pointed out that rating is usually a relatively minor consideration when a decision is made to develop or not develop land. Other factors drive these decisions.

A number of large urban municipalities in South Africa (e.g. Johannesburg and Pretoria) have been using site rating for many years. In the late 1990s Cape Town contemplated a change from capital improved rating to site rating. The Western Cape legislator actually amended the Valuation Ordinance of 1993 to provide that should site rating be selected as the tax base, it was no longer required to also value the improvements (Van Ryneveld and Parker, 2002). Site rating was however not implemented, as it became clear that a change in the base would have resulted in tremendous shifts in incidence – which would have been economically and politically unacceptable. Other reasons for retaining the flat rating system in Cape Town included (Van Ryneveld and Parker, 2002):

- delays with the national framework legislation on local government generally;
- the creation of single-tier metropolitan municipalities which necessitated a single, uniform rating system throughout the metropolitan area; and
- national government indicated its preference for a rating system based solely on the improved value of property.

In South Africa the view is held in some circles that property tax is a wealth tax and that improvements should therefore be included in the base as these usually represent a considerable portion of the total value of a developed property (Manche, 2003). However, Bahl (2002) points out that there:

> is another perceived advantage of a capital value tax (probably wrongly held) that a tax on land and structures will fall more heavily on businesses, landlords, and wealthy residential homeowners, than will a land value tax, i.e., it will be more progressive. This perception could resonate well with the large population of South African poor. However, contrary to intuition, taxing land and improvements may be less progressive than a land-only tax. For one thing, landowners are heavily concentrated in the upper income brackets. Another issue is that a tax on improvements could drive investment away from real estate, reducing the supply of structures and forcing up rents. Vertical equity may be an argument in [favour] of the land value base.

It must also be kept in mind that a tax on business properties can more readily be shifted onto consumers (Bahl, 2002) – including the poor who supposedly benefit from taxing these properties more heavily.

An advantage that a capital value tax base has, in comparison to a land-only base, is that it allows for lower nominal tax rates (Bahl, 1998; Bahl, 2002). This makes it politically more acceptable.

However, certain interest groups argue against the taxation of improvements, claiming that it would stifle development or even result in the demolition of existing improvements (e.g. farm labourer dwellings). Various international studies indicate that there are inconclusive results about whether a land-value only tax base leads to the more efficient use of urban land (Bahl, 2002).

Probably the most-often cited argument in favour of a site-value tax is its assessment advantage (McCluskey and Franzsen, 2001; Bahl, 2002; Bell, 2002; Van Ryneveld and Parker, 2002). In the context of the new local municipalities that consists of urban and rural properties, it could possibly be argued that a land value system could indeed be less cumbersome. Clearly the valuation roll can be prepared and maintained more cheaply and uniformly if improvements are not included in the tax base. However, this very real advantage is not presently available in the context of South Africa. The current provincial laws require that irrespective of the tax base utilised in practice, the valuation roll must reflect two (i.e. land and improvements) or three values (i.e. land, improvements and capital value). Only in the Western Cape did the legislator amend the Cape Valuation Ordinance, 1993 to make it possible to value only land should a municipal council opt for site rating.

As valuation rolls must of necessity include two or three values, irrespective of the actual tax base utilised by a municipality, valuers in some of the councils using site rating admit that they place less emphasis on the accuracy of the values of improvements and rather ensure that the value of the land is at least an accurate approximation of market value.

A system requiring the valuation of improvements has a more significant resource cost as it requires a more significant initial input, regular supplementary valuations (i.e. more extensive maintenance) and regular revaluations. However, many municipal valuers in South Africa (admittedly mostly those operating in metropolitan areas) have been arguing for uniformity and also for the migration to capital values. Not surprisingly, the principle argument used is the paucity of reliable data within built-up areas (especially CBD areas) in especially the larger urban jurisdictions. Policy makers within the relevant government department, the Department of Provincial and Local Government, also canvassed strongly for uniformity. Furthermore it was argued that capital improved values provide a more equitable, more buoyant and broader tax base that also reflects a taxpayer's ability to pay rates more appropriately. So the tide was turning against site rating.

Despite the dramatic political and constitutional changes, South African municipalities seem to have retained the pre-1994 systems that were in place before the transformation process commenced and with which they were familiar.

As mentioned above, it is generally argued that as areas are developed there is a dearth of sales evidence of undeveloped land. The lack of evidence of sales in inner city suburbs may not be as convincing with regard to less developed urban and especially rural areas. However, the suitability of a LVT in rural areas was not endorsed by respondents in a recent survey in South Africa (McCluskey and Franzsen, 2004). It was found that as there are generally few improvements in rural areas, the inclusion of improvements in these areas do not pose a major problem to valuers.

It is suggested that South Africa's property tax reforms are not primarily driven by valuation considerations, but rather by constitutional, institutional and socio-political considerations. In reality, historic patterns as well as social and political realities are the more important factors that a specific municipality or a government will consider in deciding on the most appropriate system. Familiarity with an existing system should not be discarded as an important factor.

The Local Government: Municipal Property Rates Act 6 of 2004 (MPRA) was passed in Parliament and signed into law by the President on 11 May 2004 and published in the Government Gazette (No. 26357) on 17 May 2004. The Preamble of the MPRA confirms the Constitutional imperative regarding the developmental nature of local government and municipalities' right to impose rates on property, and confirms that property tax is a critical source of own revenue municipalities. The Preamble also states the following overall principles:

- certainty;
- uniformity;
- simplicity;
- addressing historical imbalances; and
- addressing the impact of rates on the poor.

Tax base

The MPRA clearly states that rates are determined with reference to the 'market value' of the property. It furthermore allows for the categorization and differential rating of different categories of property on the basis of use or ownership.

As a result of the wall-to-wall coverage of the total surface area of the country by one or more municipalities, comprehensive property tax coverage is attainable under the MPRA. The nature of local municipalities implies that rates on property can now be extended to formerly untaxed rural properties. While this did occur historically in some parts of the country until the late 1980s,[6] in many areas rates on property will constitute a new tax, with the associated challenges this entails.

Extension of the tax base

State-owned property: State-owned land is presently taxed, although a 20 per cent rebate applies. State-owned properties will remain taxable. Whether an individual municipality will grant an exemption, rebate or reduction under section 15 of the MPRA will be a local decision. The

---

[6] A form of property tax was levied by so-called divisional councils in the former Cape Province, but was abolished together with divisional councils between 1987 and 1989 (see Katz, 1998; Franzsen, 2002).

national government may however issue guidelines to municipalities in this regard (see section 3(5)).

Public service infrastructure: In terms of the MPRA (see section 1 definitions of 'property' and 'public service infrastructure' read with section 17) public service infrastructure (PSI) will, in principle, have to be valued and become rateable.

In section 1 'public service infrastructure' is defined to refer to:

> publicly controlled infrastructure of the following kinds:
>
> * national, provincial or other public roads on which goods, services or labour move across a municipal boundary;
> * water or sewer pipes, ducts or other conduits, dams, water supply reservoirs, water treatment plants or water pumps forming part of a water or sewer scheme serving the public;
> * power stations, power substations or power lines forming part of an electricity scheme serving the public;
> * gas or liquid fuel plants or refineries or pipelines for gas or liquid fuels, forming part of a scheme for transporting such fuels;
> * railway lines forming part of a national railway system;
> * communication towers, masts, exchanges or lines forming part of a communications system serving the public;
> * runways or aprons at national or provincial airports;
> * breakwaters, sea walls, channels, basins, quay walls, jetties, roads, railway or infrastructure used for the provision of water, lights, power, sewerage or similar services of ports, or navigational aids comprising lighthouses, radio navigational aids, buoys, beacons or any other device or system used to assist the safe and efficient navigation of vessels;
> * any other publicly controlled infrastructure as may be prescribed; or
> * rights of way, easements or servitudes in connection with infrastructure mentioned in paragraphs *(a)* to *(i)*…

Section 17(1)(a) provides that the first 30 per cent of the market value of PSI is to be excluded for rating purposes, although section 18 provides for a possible ministerial override of this exclusion. As PSI will in most instances constitute 'newly-rateable property' (as defined in section 1), it implies that the rating of PSI will have to phased in over three years (in terms of section 21).

The impact of the extension of the tax base to PSI has not been measured and the methodologies to be utilised to value PSI still have to be negotiated with the valuers profession. It is likely that ministerial regulations will provide for statutory values for certain types of PSI (e.g. the national railway network).

Communal land: Communal land is an area of major concern, fraught with problems. The rating of 'land tenure rights' under the Communal Land Rights Act 16 of 2004 is not yet clear. The problems regarding communal land are not only rural issues. For example, there are pockets of communal land within Pretoria (i.e. Tshwane Metropolitan Council) and Durban (the Ethekwini Metropolitan Council). Municipalities with communal land located within its municipal area will have to confront one or more of the following issues (Franzsen, 2002):

•   ownership of communal land is not uniform and the market value of
        land tenure rights need to be established;
•   co-operation of traditional authorities is imperative;
•   identifying the taxpayer within the context of a complex system of
        tenure rights of those individuals entitled to the use of that land;
•   the abject poverty in many tribal areas will require extensive poor
        relief programmes;
•   extensive taxpayer education will be required regarding concepts
        such as valuation, market value and taxation;
•   billing and collection will present formidable logistical challenges.

Few traditional authority areas presently receive municipal services that could justify the introduction of a property tax. In many instances residential properties on communal land will fall below the statutory value threshold (currently set at R15,000) and will thus be excluded. Furthermore, those above the threshold will generally qualify as 'newly-rateable properties' implying a compulsory phase-in period of at least three years.

Agricultural properties: Empirical research undertaken on the behalf of the subcommittee on land tax of the *Commission of Inquiry into certain aspects of the Tax Structure* (Katz Commission) indicated that a land tax on the market value of commercial farms may have a significant impact on land values and a distortionary effect on the agricultural sector. Equity concerns suggest that the value of agricultural land is best reflected in applying current use values.[7] In many cases the market value of land would equal its current use value and therefore few problems should arise as regards tax base. However, it is where agricultural land is located on the urban fringe and the market value is affected by non-farm factors, such as development pressures, that a marked divergence between use value and market value is encountered The subcommittee therefore suggested a unique tax that assesses the *use value* rather than the *market value* of land (Katz, 1998 at pp. 51-52).[8]

In its report to government the Katz Commission recommended that use value should be accepted, but for municipalities that can justify its use, market value should remain an option (Katz, 1998 at p. 5). It has been suggested that both values can be shown in the valuation roll, but only the current use should be used to determine the actual tax payable. However, with the extension of municipal boundaries in 2000 to included all rural properties, and with the promulgation of the MPRA, this recommendation was nullified.

The MPRA does not provide for use values. It only provides for 'market value'. The negative impact of using market values in certain areas (e.g. agricultural land on the urban fringe) rather than use values, could however to some extent be countered by carefully selected property categories and differential tax rates. These will have to be justifiable in terms of the municipality's rates policy (as required by section 3).

Valuation

Market value

Market value has been retained as the basis for establishing rateable values. In the case of PSI it may be necessary for national government to provide guidelines and/or publish regulations that could assist municipal valuers in

---

[7] Nketoana Municipality in the Free State province has recently introduced a 2 per cent property tax (on market value) on all rateable properties, including farmland, within its jurisdiction. Not surprisingly, the farmers successfully contested the validity of this tax. If it is accepted that the average annual yield on agricultural land in this area of the country is between 4 per cent and 5 per cent of capital value (and land typically accounts for 70 to 80 per cent of the value of a farming enterprise), a 2 per cent property tax equates to a 40-50 per cent income tax.

[8] This recommendation was made before the enactment of the Local Government: Municipal Structures Act of 1998 and the publication of the 11th draft of the Property Rates Bill in August 2000.

determining the 'market value' of PSI in a uniform manner. Probably the best way of achieving this goal will be to ascribe statutory values to certain types of PSI. The valuation of PSI could be done in various ways. Section 46(5) states the following:

> Where the available market related data is not sufficient to determine the market value of public service infrastructure, such public service infrastructure must be valued in accordance with any other method of valuation as may be prescribed.

Where another method or methods are prescribed, this may indeed impact on the assessed values of PSI and therefore the rates payable by the owners thereof. Typically, network-type utilities (such as those providing electricity, water and gas, or a rail network) prove difficult to value using conventional methodology.

Valuation cycles

The MPRA prescribes a valuation cycle of one, or more, but up to a maximum of four years (section 32(1)). However, under exceptional circumstances and only with the permission of provincial government, it could be extended for a further financial year. In other words, a general revaluation needs to be undertaken at least every four years, or in exceptional cases, five years.

Mass valuation including property banding

A novel development that will be introduced in South Africa when the MPRA commences, is a provision for the use of a 'mass valuation system or technique' where 'the available market related data of any category of rateable property is not sufficient' for the use of techniques to determine discrete values. Section 45 of the MPRA makes specific mention of a banding system as one such option.[9]

The use of mass valuation should be strictly regulated. Ideally government should provide guidelines or a framework when a municipality can use such a system and how it should be applied, so as to avoid a proliferation of a variety of systems from developing over time.

---

[9] Property banding may indeed be an option deserving further study in a South African context. (See McCluskey, Plimmer and Connellan, 2002.)

Objection and appeal

The MPRA extensively regulates the right to object and appeal values reflected on the valuation roll. However, in terms of section 82 monitoring the integrity and quality of valuation rolls will be introduced when the MPRA commences. This form of control has to date not existed in South Africa.

Tax rates

The MPRA retains the right of municipalities to strike their own rates as specified amounts in the Rand. Rates are determined annually. The MPRA allows for differential rating, i.e. different rates could apply to different categories of property. Section 19(1)(b) provides that a municipality may not levy a rate on non-residential properties that exceeds a prescribed ratio to the rate levied on residential properties.[10] The Minister for Local Government must prescribe a ratio, but may only do so with the concurrence of the Minister of Finance (s 19(2)).

Property tax administration

Most aspects of property tax administration (i.e. billing, collection and enforcement) are not dealt with in the MPRA, but rather in the Local Government: Municipal Systems Act 32 of 2000.

Only a few provisions in the MPRA deal with rates administration, such as those dealing with aspects of payment, issuing of accounts and the recovery of rates from third parties.

Municipal Rates Policy: transparency and accountability

A welcome novelty in a South African context that can do a lot to educate ratepayers and to ensure responsible municipal governance, is the so-called 'rates policy'. The MPRA compels a municipality to adopt a rates policy and levy its rates accordingly. The rates policy must be reviewed annually. The first rates policy to be adopted under the MPRA must take effect on the same date the first valuation roll created in terms of this Act becomes

---

[10] This ratio still has to be determined.

effective. The adoption of a rates policy must be preceded by compliance with the principles in Chapter 4 of the Local Government: Municipal Systems Act 32 of 2000 – i.e. a municipality must follow a process of community participation.

A rates policy must:

- be adopted as prescribed;
- accompany the annual budget for the financial year concerned;
- treat ratepayers equitably;
- determine criteria for:
  - differential rates;
  - exemptions, rebates and reductions;
  - increases in rates;
- determine criteria for:
  - property categorisation – for purposes of differential rating;
  - owner categorisation – for purposes of exemptions, rebates or reductions;
- determine the rating of properties used for multiple purposes;
- identify and quantify the cost to the municipality and benefit to the community of exemptions, rebates and/or reductions, as well as exclusions under section 17(1), as well as the impact of the phasing in of rates in terms of section 21;
  - take into account the effect of rates on:
  - the poor (s 3(3)(f));
  - public benefit organizations;
  - public service infrastructure;
- allow the municipality to promote local, social and economic development;
- identify all rateable property not rated;
- take into account the impact of rating on agricultural properties

By-laws must be adopted to give effect to the rates policy. The Minister for Local Government may make regulations regarding the preparation, contents, adoption and enforcement of a rates policy.

Rates policies should significantly enhance the transparency and accountability of municipal councils. It could and should be used to explain the rationality of a municipality's property categorisation and its use of differential rates (e.g. by pointing out differences in service levels).

The rates policy (especially if read with the credit control and debt collection policy provided for in the Local Government: Municipal Systems Act) goes some way to address the too often neglected issue of taxpayer education. If the rating system is better understood and perceived to be equitable, compliance should be enhanced. Section 4 of the MPRA also mandates community participation before a rates policy is adopted. If this is done properly, it should further enhance compliance.

Various 'checks and balances'

Apart from the rates policy, the MPRA also provides other safeguards against over-zealous municipal councils, for example by capping annual increases in rates (section 20), compulsory phasing-in provisions (section 21) and through external valuation quality controls which could provide protection against manipulation of the valuation roll(section 82).

Additional relief mechanisms that could be utilised to ensure that property tax is levied equitably include:

- 'exclusions' (as defined in section 1) of a municipality's rating power as regards certain types of 'property', i.e. a restriction on the power of a municipality to tax property (currently provided for in section 17);
- 'reductions' (as defined in section 1) of the 'amount' (i.e. the rateable value) for which a property is valued in accordance with the provisions of the MPRA in terms of section 15 – thereby applying the rate struck by a municipality to the lower amount;
- 'rebates' (as defined in section 1), i.e. a discount granted in terms of section 15 on the amount of the rate payable;
- 'exemptions' (as defined in section 1), fully or partially, being granted by municipalities in terms of section 15;
- 'rate-capping', i.e. stipulating a maximum allowable tax rate or tax rates; the MPRA provides for this option in section 16(2) or section 16(3) if the criteria set out in section 16(1) are met.

The appropriateness and availability of these options may vary depending on circumstances and the mischief or need to be addressed. However, utilisation of any one or more of these mechanisms are bound to complicate the administration of the tax and therefore comes with a cost. Apart from the MPRA and ultimately the Constitution (e.g. section 229(2)(a)), political parties, the press, ratepayers associations and community forums can also function as watchdogs to ensure that property taxes are properly levied, collected and enforced.

Assistance to municipalities during the transitional phase

Municipalities will probably require assistance to enable them to implement the MPRA in an orderly and timely manner. It must be appreciated that the commencement of this Act (if it is to be 1 July 2005) will follow shortly after the commencement of the Local Government: Municipal Finance Management Act and the Local Government: Municipal systems Act. Whereas the policies contained in these Acts may generally be sound, some municipalities are finding it difficult to implement the wide-ranging provisions of these Acts due to capacity constraints.

In the context of the complexity of the migration to a new system of property taxation within the larger framework of municipal financial management, it would be appropriate for the Department of Provincial and Local Government (DPLG) and, where relevant, National Treasury to provide training and assist with capacity building so as to enable municipalities to comply with the new legislation. Especially important would be to map out clear time lines with respect to the key steps required to implement the MPRA (especially when read with the other two Acts referred to in the previous paragraph).

The successful implementation of the MPRA will require wide political support and proper 'marketing. This presupposes that national, provincial and local politicians are well informed about its aims and goals. They need to understand what a property tax is, and probably equally as important, what it is not.

It is the politicians who will be primarily responsible for educating taxpayers specifically and local communities generally on property taxation. In all of this the municipal rates policy will play a pivotal role. As indicated above, section 4 mandates that the community must participate in the process of adoption of a municipal rates policy. This, however, presupposes a properly informed community that can indeed participate in a meaningful manner. A well-informed community presupposes proper taxpayer and community education – which is the responsibility of the council, led by the local councillors and a well-informed municipal manager.

Conclusions

The enactment of the MPRA brought about substantial reforms of the property tax dispensation in South Africa. Earlier calls for a uniform tax base have indeed triumphed. The South African Institute of Valuers, representing the valuers' profession, officially also support capital improved values as the preferred tax base, citing lack of public understanding of a land value system, as well as the lack of vacant sales within CBD areas as primary reasons. Further reasons cited include that with capital improved values the valuation roll automatically provides data on all improvements and other new developments, capital values provide a more buoyant revenue base than land only and can achieve a better distribution of the tax burden.

Despite the fact that South Africa is about to do away with land value taxation, its long and unique history of site, flat and composite rating may indeed provide valuable lessons for jurisdictions contemplating a change of their system(s), be it to a land, a split-rate or capital improved value system.

References

Bahl, R.W. (1998), 'Land vs Property Taxes in Developing and Transition Countries', in D. Netzer (ed.), *Land Value Taxation: Can it and Will it Work Today?*, Lincoln Institute of Land Policy, Cambridge, MA, United States, pp. 141-171.

Bahl, R.W. (2002), 'Fiscal Decentralization, Revenue Assignment, and the Case for the Property Tax in South Africa', in M.E. Bell and J.H. Bowman (eds), *Property Taxes in South Africa: Challenges in the Post-Apartheid Era*, Lincoln Institute of Land Policy, Cambridge, MA, United States, pp. 21-44.

Bell, M.E. (2002), 'Property Tax Structure and Practice', in M.E. Bell and J.H. Bowman (eds), *Property Taxes in South Africa: Challenges in the Post-Apartheid Era*, Lincoln Institute of Land Policy, Cambridge, MA, United States, pp. 59-75.

Bell, M.E. and Bowman, J.H. (2002a), *'Property Taxes in South Africa: Challenges in the Post-Apartheid Era'*, Lincoln Institute of Land Policy, Cambridge, MA, United States.

Bell, M.E. and Bowman, J.H. (2002b), *'Extending the Property Tax into Previously Untaxed Areas in South Africa'*, paper presented at the 95th Annual Conference of the National Tax Association, Orlando Florida, United States.

Bowman, J.H. (2002), 'Current Property Tax Laws', in M.E. Bell and J.H. Bowman (eds), *Property Taxes in South Africa: Challenges in the Post-*

Apartheid Era, Lincoln Institute of Land Policy, Cambridge, MA, United States, pp. 45-56.

Budget Review (2001), National Treasury, South Africa.

Budget Review (2003), National Treasury, South Africa.

Craythorne, D. (1997), '*Municipal Administration: A Handbook*' (4th ed.), Juta: Kenwyn, Cape Town, South Africa.

Ethekwini Metropolitan Council (2003), 'Real Estate: Valuation Roll – Frequently Asked Questions' (http://www.durban.gov.za/treasury/valroll/faq.htm).

Franzsen, R.C.D. (1998), 'Commentary', in D. Netzer (ed.) *Land Value Taxation: Can it and Will it Work Today?*, Lincoln Institute of Land Policy, Cambridge, MA, United States, pp. 172-182.

Franzsen, R.C.D. (1999), 'Property Taxation in South Africa', in W.J. McCluskey (ed.), *Property Tax: An International Comparative Review*, Ashgate Publishing Limited, Aldershot, pp. 337-357.

Franzsen, R.C.D. (2001), '*Property Tax Reforms in South Africa*', Lincoln Institute of Land Policy and City of Porto Alegre Conference on Property Taxation, Porto Alegre, Brazil.

Franzsen, R.C.D. (2002), 'The Taxation of Rural Land', in M.E. Bell and J.H. Bowman (eds), *Property Taxes in South Africa: Challenges in the Post-Apartheid Era*, Lincoln Institute of Land Policy, Cambridge, MA, United States, pp. 215-231.

Franzsen, R.C.D. and McCluskey, W.J. (2000), 'Some Policy Issues Regarding the Local Government: Property Rates Bill' *South African Mercantile Law Journal, v*ol. 12 no. 1, pp. 209-223.

Gildenhuys, A. (2002), 'Valuations, Valuers and Appraisers', in *The Law of South Africa*, vol. 30 (First Reissue), Butterworths, Durban, pp. 156-205.

*Intergovernmental Fiscal Review (*2003), National Treasury, South Africa.

Jonker, A.J. (1984), '*Property Valuation in South Africa*', Juta and Co, Kenwyn.

Kapp, C.J. (1998), 'Property Rates Survey undertaken in South Africa', in M.E. Bell and J.H. Bowman (eds), *A Framework for Strengthening Local Property Tax Administration in South Africa: Final Report*, Department of Constitutional Development, South Africa.

Manche, J. (2003), '*Towards understanding Key Aspects of the Property Rates Bill*', paper presented at the Property Rates Bill Workshop, Benoni.

McCluskey, W.J. and Franzsen, R.C.D. (1999), '*Local Government: Property Rates Bill*', Unpublished report for the Department of Finance, South Africa.

McCluskey, W.J. and Franzsen, R.C.D. (2001), '*Land Value Taxation: A Case Study Approach*', Lincoln Institute of Land Policy Working Paper WP01WM1, Lincoln Institute of Land Policy, Cambridge, MA, United States, pp. 1-109. (see http://www.lincolninst.edu/publications).

McCluskey, W.J. and Franzsen, R.C.D. (2004), '*The Basis of the Property Tax: A Case Study Analysis of New Zealand and South Africa*', Lincoln Institute of Land Policy Working Paper WP04WM1, Lincoln Institute of Land Policy, Cambridge, MA, United States, pp. 1-48 (see http://www.lincolninst.edu/publications).

McCluskey, W.J. and Williams, B. (1999), 'Introduction: a Comparative Evaluation', in W.J. McCluskey (ed.), *Property Tax: An International Comparative Review*, Ashgate Publishing Limited, Aldershot, pp. 1-31.

Slack, E. (2004), 'Property Taxation in South Africa', in R.M. Bird and E. Slack (eds), *International Handbook of Land and Property Taxation*, Edward Elgar Publishing Limited, UK, pp. 199-204.

Trends in Intergovernmental Finances, 2000/01-2006/07, National Treasury, South Africa.

Van Ryneveld, P. and Parker, M. (2002), 'Property Tax Reform in Cape Town', in M.E. Bell and J.H. Bowman (eds), *Property Taxes in South Africa: Challenges in the Post-Apartheid Era*, Lincoln Institute of Land Policy, Cambridge, MA, United States, pp. 157-173.

Ward, R. (2002), 'Demonstration of Computer-assisted Mass Appraisal', in M.E. Bell and J.H. Bowman (eds), *Property Taxes in South Africa: Challenges in the Post-Apartheid Era*, Lincoln Institute of Land Policy, Cambridge, MA, United States, pp. 113-137.

Weichardt, E. (2003), '*Innovation from the City of Cape Town – Western Cape*' (http://www.sacities.net/left/studies.stm).

White Paper on Local Government (1998), Government Printers, Pretoria.

Zybrands, A. (2003a), '*Comments by the Property Valuers*' Profession on the Property Rates Bill', paper presented at the Property Rates Bill Workshop, Benoni.

Zybrands, A. (2003b), Personal communication on 10 July 2003.

Legislation and proposed legislation referred to:

Local Government Ordinance 8 of 1962 (Orange Free State).

Municipal Ordinance 20 of 1974 (Cape).

Local Authorities Ordinance 25 of 1974 (Natal).

Local Authorities Rating Ordinance 11 of 1977 (Transvaal).

Property Valuation Ordinance, 1993 (Cape).

Local Government Transition Act 209 of 1993.

Local Government: Municipal Demarcation Act 27 of 1998.

Local Government: Municipal Structures Act 117 of 1998.

Local Government: Municipal Systems Act 32 of 2000.

Local Government: Municipal Finance Management Act 56 of 2003.

Local Government: Municipal Property Rates Act 6 of 2004 (see www.gov.za/gazette/acts/2004/a6-04.pdf).

Local Government: Property Rates Bill, 2000 (11th draft: 4 August 2000).

Local Government: Property Rates Bill, 2003 (18th draft: 18 March 2003) (see www.gov.za/gazette/bills/2003/b19-03.pdf).

Chapter 7

Land Value Taxation in Western Australia

Riël C.D. Franzsen

Introduction

Although first discovered by Dutch seafarers, Western Australia was established as a British colony in the 1820s. It became part of the Commonwealth of Australia with its establishment on 1 January 1901. Western Australia has a surface area of approximately 2.5 million square kilometres, but a population of less than 1.9 million of which approximately 1.3 million live in the Perth Metropolitan Region. Perth is the capital of Western Australia.

Overview of local government

In 1838 the Town Improvement Act was passed. Through the authorisation of so-called town trusts and country trusts, a first tentative step towards local government was given. The Perth Town Trust was established in 1838 with the first property tax (in the British tradition called 'rates') levied in 1839. Perth became a city in 1856. By 1871 there were seven town trusts (namely Perth, Fremantle, Albany, Bunbury, Busselton, Geraldton and Guilford). In that year the Municipalities Act was passed, giving increased functions and powers to the 'municipalities'. The 1871 Act was repealed by the Municipal Corporations Act and the latter by the Local Government Act of 1960 (WALGA, 2004). The Local Government Act, 1995 which presently regulates local government in Western Australia replaced the 1960 Act.

The Road District Act, also passed in 1871, provided that locally-elected road boards would replace the Crown as the primary authority responsible for communications in the colony. Their primary powers revolved around the construction of roads, bridges and related drainage works. Road boards had rating powers too. Road boards were given the power to use a site value or an annual value system to raise revenue, with the majority of boards opting for a site rating system (Hornby, 1999). A new, consolidated Road Districts Act was passed in 1905 and again in 1911 and 1919.

The most important functions provided by local government in Australia are road maintenance; refuse collection and disposal, street lighting, primary health care, libraries and recreational facilities (Forster, 2000). Public security and education are not regarded as local functions.

In 1902 municipalities collected £94,894 through rates. A hundred years later (2001/2002) rates revenue in Western Australia amounted to $722 million. Local governments are presently represented collectively through the Western Australia Local Government Association (WALGA).

Local government structures

In terms of the Local Government Act, 1995 (LGA) the Governor, acting upon the recommendation of the Minister responsible for local government in the State, makes an order declaring areas to be districts. Such an order of the Governor also designates the district to be a city, a town or a shire. Together cities, towns and shires cover the total surface area of the State.

Section 2.4 of the LGA states that a district can only be designated a city if the district is in the metropolitan area and has more than 30,000 inhabitants more than half of whom live in an urban area. If it is not in the metropolitan area, a district can only be designated a city if it has more than 20,000 inhabitants more than half of whom live in an urban area. A district can only be designated a town if more than half of its inhabitants live in an urban area. A district that is not designated a city or a town is designated as a shire. Shires will typically consist of one or more small towns and their surrounding rural areas.

Section 3.1 of the LGA stipulates that the general function of a local government is to provide for the good government of persons in its district. The scope of the general function of a local government is to be construed in the context of its other functions under the LGA (or any other written law and any constraints imposed by the LGA or any other written law) on the performance of its functions. However, a liberal approach is to be taken to the construction of the scope of the general function of a local government.

Section 3.5 of the LGA sets out the legislative powers of local governments in Western Australia, stating that a local government may make local laws under this Act prescribing all matters that are required or permitted to be prescribed by a local law, or are necessary or convenient to be so prescribed, for it to perform any of its functions under this Act.

According to section 3.61 of the LGA two or more local governments may, with the Minister's approval, establish a regional local government to do certain things for the participating local governments, in other words for any regional purpose. The LGA apply to a regional local government as if it were made up of a single district. Section 3.66 precludes the application of certain provisions of the LGA to a regional government, amongst these the power to levy and collect rates.

There are 144 local governments of which 30 are urban local governments located in the Perth Metropolitan Region. Local governments range in size from the minute Shire of Peppermint Grove (a mere 1.5 square kilometres) within the Perth Metropolitan Area, to possibly the largest municipality in the world today, namely the Shire of East Pilbara (378,553 square kilometres).

The City of Perth itself is a small council, consisting primarily of the central business district. Its surface area is 8.8 square kilometres and its population approximately 6,000. Although local governments cover the total surface area of Western Australia, where applicable, local governments do not exercise any control over aboriginal land. Generally aboriginal land is not presently rated.

Local government finances

By 31 August in each financial year, or such extended time as the Minister may allow, a local government must prepare and adopt (by an absolute majority), in the form and manner prescribed, a budget for its municipal fund for the financial year ending on the next following 30 June. As part of the annual budget a local government must prepare a detailed estimate for the current year of:

- expenditures;
- revenue and income, independent of general rates; and
- the amount required to make up the deficiency, if any, shown by comparing the estimated expenditure with the estimated revenue and income.

Furthermore, the annual budget is to incorporate particulars of the estimated expenditure proposed to be incurred by the local government, the fees and charges proposed to be imposed by the local government, detailed information relating to the rates and service charges which will apply to land within the district including:

*   the amount it is estimated will be yielded by the general rate; and
*   the rate of interest (if any) to be charged by the local government on unpaid rates and service charges.

In terms of section 6.15(1) of the LGA a local government is entitled to the receive revenue and income as follows:

*   rates;
*   service charges;
*   fees and charges;
*   borrowings;
*   investments; or
*   any other source.

Authorised by or under this Act or another written law.

*   dealings in property; or
*   grants or gifts.

Section 6.32(1) of the LGA states:

When adopting the annual budget, a local government:

*   in order to make up the budget deficiency, is to impose a general rate on rateable land within its district, which rate may be imposed either:
    (i)   uniformly; or
    (ii)   differentially;
*   may impose on rateable land within its district:
    (i)   a specified area rate; or
    (ii)   a minimum payment;
*   may impose a service charge on land within its district.

An absolute majority (that is 50 per cent of the votes) is required before a council can levy any one or more of the above rates. Section 6.38(1) of the LGA states:

A local government may impose on:

- owners; or
- occupiers,

of land within the district or a defined part of the district a service charge for a financial year to meet the cost of providing a prescribed service in relation to the land.

Any service charge must either be used in the financial year in which the charge is imposed; or placed in a reserve account established and to be used exclusively for the purpose of that service. In some instances service charges are also determined with reference to the property tax base, for example sewerage rates.

Importance of rates

All local governments in Western Australia charge and collect rates. Traditionally revenue from rates makes up the shortfall between revenue from all other sources and the expected expenditures in the operating budget. For those local governments with limited access to other revenue sources, rates is an important source of revenue. This is generally the case throughout Western Australia.

Section 6.34 of the LGA states that unless the Minister otherwise approves, the amount shown in the annual budget as being the amount it is estimated will be yielded by the general rate is not to be:

- more than 110 per cent of the amount of the budget deficiency; or
- less than 90 per cent of the amount of the budget deficiency.

In 1998/1999 rates revenue as a percentage of total local government revenue averages 42 per cent for Western Australia (the median, however, was 34 per cent). In the case of Stirling council (within the Perth Metropolitan Region), 75 per cent of its revenue is derived from rates, whereas in the case of the Shire of Upper Gascone, only 4.5 per cent of its total revenue is from rates (the rest primarily comes from Commonwealth grants).

Table 7.1 provides an overview of the importance of rates as a source of revenue for four Western Australian local governments. The City of Perth and Shire of Peppermint Grove are both small, densely urbanised local governments located within the Perth Metropolitan Region, whereas the Shire of Augusta-Margaret River is a relatively well-developed, albeit primarily rural, rating authority consisting of two rural towns (the coastal town of Augusta and Margaret River which is a service town for the Western Australian wine industry) and a diverse tourism and agricultural sector in the south-western corner of the State. The Shire of East Pilbara is the largest local government in Western Australia. Covering a vast and mostly pristine area of 378,553 square kilometres, but sparsely populated (with fewer than 10,000 inhabitants), it has a limited property tax base.

Table 7.1   Importance of rates: 2003-2005

	2003/2004 (actual, 000)			2004/2005 (budgeted, 000)		
Local Government	Total revenue	Rates	Rates as %	Total revenue	Rates	Rates as %
City of Perth	88.320	40.980		95.418	44.334	
Shire of Peppermint Grove	2.079	1.158	55.7	2.072	1.199	57.9
Shire of Augusta-Margaret River	14.134	6.569	46.5	16.311	8.314	51.0
Shire of East Pilbara	12.387	2.935	23.7	13.771	3.033	22.0

Source: Western Australian Local Government Association, 2004

As is to be expected the more rural local governments have to rely more heavily on grants and subsidies from the State and Commonwealth as the traditional services (e.g. fire prevention, town planning, recreation centres, libraries, building services, etc.) funded by rates are less readily available and property values tend to be considerable lower than in urban or metropolitan areas.

Tax base for rates

All land parcels in Western Australia has been surveyed and assessed. There are approximately 740,000 property parcels in total. All relevant and applicable information pertaining to land is transferred by computer linkages among the offices of the Department of Land Information, the State Revenue Office and Valuer General's Office. Records are frequently updated by computer. In Western Australia the separation between the provider (Valuer General's Office) and the user (taxing and rating authorities) of valuations is important. This ensures the independence of valuations, the basis for a sound and legitimate valuation roll.

The Valuation of Land Act, 1978 provides the following relevant definitions:

> 'land' means lands, tenements and hereditaments, and any improvements to land, and includes any interest in land;

> 'rateable land' means land in respect of which any rate or tax is assessed under any of the rating and taxing Acts or is, in the opinion of the Valuer-General, reasonably likely to be assessed under any of those Acts prior to such land being valued in a general valuation;

Presently the tax base for all land situated within a 'townsite' (i.e. all land within the 30 councils in the Perth Metropolitan Region, all land within towns, as well as urban properties within the jurisdiction of shire councils) is gross rental values, whereas, unimproved values are used by shire councils for rural properties. In other words, two tax bases are utilised simultaneously by shire councils. Section 6.32(2) of the LGA provides as follows:

Where a local government resolves to impose a rate it is required to:

- set a rate which is expressed as a rate in the dollar of the gross rental value of rateable land within its district to be rated on gross rental value; and
- set a rate which is expressed as a rate in the dollar of the unimproved value of rateable land within its district to be rated on unimproved value.

Furthermore a local government:

- may, at any time after the imposition of rates in a financial year, in an emergency, impose a supplementary general rate or specified area rate for the unexpired portion of the current financial year; and
- is to, after a court or a Land Valuation Tribunal has quashed a general valuation, rate or service charge, impose a new general rate, specified area rate or service charge.

An absolute majority is required before a council can levy any of the above rates. Where a court or a Land Valuation Tribunal has quashed a general valuation, the quashing does not render invalid a rate imposed on the basis of the quashed valuation in respect of any financial year prior to the financial year in which the legal proceedings which resulted in that quashing were commenced.

As mentioned before, in some instances service charges (e.g. sewerage rates) are also based on the same tax base (i.e. gross rental value or unimproved value – as the case may be) as rates. A new State tax, the emergency services levy, introduced on 1 July 2003 is also assessed on a local government's rates base. Although a State tax levied by the Fire & Emergency Services Authority (FESA), it is charged and collected through the rating system by all local governments throughout the State.

Valuation

The Valuation of Land Act, 1978 regulates the valuation of land in Western Australia for all public purposes including rating. However, this Act must be read with the Local Government Act, 1995. Section 6.28 of the LGA states:

> The Minister is to:
>
> • determine the method of valuation of land to be used by a local government as the basis for a rate; and
> • publish a notice of the determination in the *Government Gazette*.
>
> In determining the method of valuation of land to be used by a local government the Minister is to have regard to the general principle that the basis for a rate on any land is to be:
>
> • where the land is used predominantly for rural purposes, the unimproved value of the land; and
> • where the land is used predominantly for non-rural purposes, the gross rental value of the land.
>
> The unimproved value or gross rental value, as the case requires, of rateable land in the district of a local government is to be recorded in the rate record of that local government.
>
> Subject to subsection (5), for the purposes of this section the valuation to be used by a local government is to be the valuation in force under the *Valuation of Land Act 1978* as at 1 July in each financial year.

Where during a financial year:

- an interim valuation is made under the *Valuation of Land Act 1978*;
- a valuation comes into force under the *Valuation of Land Act 1978* as a result of the amendment of a valuation under that Act; or
- a new valuation is made under the *Valuation of Land Act 1978* in the course of completing a general valuation that has previously come into force, the interim valuation, amended valuation or new valuation, as the case requires, is to be used by a local government for the purposes of this section.

The legislated tax bases for rating purposes are gross rental value (for predominantly urban land) and unimproved value (for predominantly rural land). How these are to be determined is regulated by the Valuation of Land Act, 1978 and will now be discussed in more detail.

The Valuation of Land Act, 1978 states that for the purposes of a general valuation, the Valuer-General shall determine, or cause to be determined, with respect to rateable land, the gross rental value or the unimproved value, as the case requires, so far as that value is required by a rating or taxing authority for the purpose of assessing any rate or tax or is, in the opinion of the Valuer-General, reasonably likely to be so required before the next general valuation of the land is made.

Gross rental value

'gross rental value' of land means:

… the gross annual rental that the land might reasonably be expected to realize if let on a tenancy from year to year upon condition that the landlord were liable for all rates, taxes and other charges thereon and the insurance and other outgoings necessary to maintain the value of the land, provided that:

- where the gross rental value of land cannot reasonably be determined on such basis, the gross rental value shall be the assessed value;
- the gross rental value of any land not used for residential purposes only shall, where the value of the improvements on the land is less than one-third of what would have been the value of the land if it were vacant land, in any event, be not less than what would be the assessed value of the land if it were vacant land;
- the gross rental value of any land separately valued shall, in any event, be not less than $20; and

•   calculation of the gross rental value of any land shall include any
       payment normally or usually made for or in relation to a tenancy of
       the kind in question but shall not include any allowance, by
       discounting or otherwise, for advance payment or late payment of
       rent that may apply...

In terms of section 24(2) of the Valuation of Land Act, 1978 any
improvements on any land that are, in the opinion of the Valuer-General,
not capable of occupation shall not be included for the purposes of
determining the gross rental value of the land. However, the gross rental
value of any land shall include the value of such of the items set out below
as are fixed to the land, namely:

•   lifts, escalators or hoists of any description;
•   air conditioning, cooling, heating or circulating equipment;
•   water heating, cooling or pumping equipment;
•   sewerage or drainage pumps;
•   vehicle turntables; and
•   door control and surveillance equipment of any nature, including the
       control equipment used therewith and whether provided by the
       landlord or not.

In terms of section 17 of the Valuation of Land Act, 1978 the Valuer-
General may from time to time reconstitute valuation districts for the
purpose of determining gross rental values. In doing so, the Valuer-General
shall have regard to the boundaries of areas defined under the rating and
taxing Acts for rating or taxing purposes.

Unimproved value

In terms of section 17 of the Valuation of Land Act, 1978 the whole of the
State is constituted into a valuation district for the purpose of determining
unimproved values.

       'unimproved value' means:

•   in relation to any land situate within a townsite, except land referred
       to in paragraph (b)(ii), the site value;

The value of the site is then:

•   the capital amount that an estate in fee simple in the land not
       including improvements might reasonably be expected to realize
       upon sale; or

- where the unimproved value cannot reasonably be determined on the basis of the above — the percentage of the capital amount that an estate in fee simple in the land might reasonably be expected to realize upon sale assuming that the land has been developed, without buildings, to the standard generally prevailing in the part of the State in which the land is situated and taking into account any restriction on the land imposed under any written law, such percentage being that prescribed for land in that part of the State.

In short, unimproved value is the market value of a land (a lot) assuming that no physical improvements have ever been made to it, but assuming that the surrounding land is indeed developed as it stands at the date of valuation. What is being valued, is a 'vacant lot'. However, through the passage of time, pure unimproved value has become unworkable for 'townsite' land, in other words, in an urban environment. Therefore, improvements which were made when the land was being developed for sale (i.e. defined as 'merged improvements'), are deemed to have effectively merged with the land to such an extent that they cannot be separately identified.

The following definitions in section 4 of the Valuation of Land Act, 1978 are relevant in the context of determining either gross rental value or unimproved value for rating purposes:

'improvements' in relation to land means the value of all works actually effected to land, whether above or below the surface, and includes fixtures, but does not include:

- machinery, whether fixed to the land or not; or
- any below ground works used in the extraction of minerals or petroleum...

'merged improvements' means any works in the nature of draining, filling, excavation, grading or levelling of the land, retaining walls or other structures or works for that purpose, the removal of rocks, stone or soil, and the clearing of timber, scrub or other vegetation...

'site value' of land means the capital amount that an estate of fee simple in the land might reasonably be expected to realize upon sale assuming that any improvements to the land, other than merged improvements, had not been made and, in the case of land that is reserved for a public purpose, assuming that the land may continue to be used for any purpose for which it is being used or could be used at the date of valuation...

'townsite' means:

- all land within the metropolitan region;
- all land within a district that is a city or town outside the metropolitan region;
- any land that is currently a townsite within the meaning of the *Land Administration Act 1997* or any Act repealed thereby; and
- any land, including privately owned subdivided land, in an area that has been, or is to be regarded as having been, constituted a townsite, and given a name, under section 10 of the *Land Act 1933*.

'vacant land' means land on which there are no improvements other than merged improvements.

'value' in relation to land means the assessed value, the capital value, the gross rental value, the site value, the unimproved value and a value determined or assessed under section 39(1) of the land or any one or more of those values; "to value" means to determine or assess those values or any one or more of them; and "determination of value" or "valuation" means a determination or assessment of those values or any one or more of them.

Valuation methodology

In the case of gross rental values the Valuer General's Office assembles a database of rental evidence. This database is based on information on actual market rentals provided by property owners, property managers and from other sources. A schedule of all rented properties at the date of valuation is then prepared for the relevant valuation district (DLI, 2004). Rented properties are then inspected and the data obtained regarding rents analysed. Unsuitable rental evidence (e.g. rental agreements between related parties) is discarded. A final list of acceptable rentals are then used as a basis for determining fair gross rental values, defendable with sufficient actual market evidence, for all properties in the valuation district, after making allowances for special property-specific features. Where an annual rental cannot reasonably be determined, the Valuation of Land Act, 1978 stipulates that the gross rental value will then be the 'assessed value' (as defined). Assessed value is a set percentage of the capital value of the specific property (DLI, 2004). Gross rental value in essence represents the annual equivalent of a fair weekly rental.

In the case of unimproved values, property values are determined with reference to the capital market at the date of valuation. All actual sales, excluding unsuitable ones (e.g. between connected parties), relevant to the predetermined date of valuation are investigated and the sales evidence analysed (DLI, 2004).

Vacant land sales are not a problem in most of the jurisdictions in Western Australia.

Frequency of general valuations

In terms of section 22(1a) of the Valuation of Land Act 1978 the Valuation-General shall make or cause to be made a general valuation for the whole State for the purposes of determining unimproved values, so far as is practicable, every financial year. A general valuation within the valuation district constituted for the purpose of determining unimproved values, so far as practicable, every financial year. As the whole State is constituted as a valuation district, this implies that unimproved values are determined annually for all approximately 740,000 rateable properties.

A general valuation shall be made within each valuation district constituted or reconstituted for the purpose of determining gross rental values at such times as the Valuer-General shall determine. The Valuer-General shall ensure that, so far as practicable, the valuations comprising a general valuation shall at all times be accurate and up-to-date. In the Perth Metropolitan Area gross rental values are determined every three years. In the rest of Western Australia (i.e. for towns in rural areas) gross rental values are determined every four to five years (DLI, 2004). Despite the regularity of general revaluations, the Valuer-General also undertake interim valuations (e.g. where land has been subdivided) as and when required.

Responsibility for valuations

No person shall be engaged as a valuer for a rating or taxing authority unless he or she is licensed under the Land Valuers Licensing Act 1978, or qualified for membership of the Australian Institute of Valuers (incorporated) as a Fellow or Associate of that Institute (section 25(2) of the Valuation of Lands Act, 1978).

Under the Valuation of Land Act, 1978 the Valuer-General is responsible for the completion and maintenance of valuation rolls of rateable land. The Valuer-General's Office is a division of the Department of Land Information. It is the task of this State government agency to undertake independent and impartial valuations.

Furthermore, section 16 of the Valuation of Lands Act, 1978 states that the Valuer-General may contract for services of private valuers as well as professional, technical or other assistance as may be necessary to enable him to perform his duties and functions effectively. The Valuer-General may not engage the services of a valuer if he or she is employed by, or a member of, a rating or taxing authority. Such a valuer shall be deemed to be an officer assisting the Valuer-General in the administration of this Act.

Section 25 of the Valuation of Land Act, 1978 states that a rating (i.e. local government) or taxing authority (i.e. the State Revenue Department) may engage valuers to make general or interim valuations. They may furthermore, subject to the approval of and conditions set by the Valuer-General, engage a private valuer to make a general valuation of rateable land within a valuation district or to value specified land within a valuation district in respect of which the relevant authority considers that an interim valuation is necessary or expedient. Any valuer engaged in this manner is deemed to be an officer assisting the Valuer-General in the administration of the Valuation of Land Act.

Where a private valuer is contracted to prepare a valuation roll, the Valuer-General has to specify, in respect of each valuation district in which the valuer shall make valuations, the date of valuation. Once the valuation roll has been prepared or the specified interim valuation has been made, the relevant authority must submit it to the Valuer-General for approval. If the Valuer-General approves the valuation roll or specified interim valuation, the Valuation of Land Act shall apply to the valuation as if it were a general valuation or an interim valuation made by the Valuer-General. Although the Valuation of Land Act, 1978 allows local governments to use their own valuers to prepare a valuation roll, in practice, however, all local governments use the values of the Valuer-General. Should a local government choose to use the services of a private valuer, the office of the Valuer-General will be responsible for extensive quality control and setting conditions regarding the work to be done.

Valuation rolls

The valuations comprising a general valuation relating to land shall come into force on such day as is determined by the Valuer-General and supersede any previous valuations of gross rental value or unimproved value, as the case may be, in force under this Act relating to that land.

Valuation rolls are, in essence, formal records of all rateable land throughout the State, shall be in such form as the Valuer-General may determine and shall contain the following particulars in respect of rateable land:

- a description of every portion of land separately valued sufficient to identify it;
- the gross rental value or the unimproved value of the land that has been determined by the Valuer-General;
- the date on which the valuation or valuations shall, or shall have, come into force; and
- such additional particulars as the Valuer-General may determine.

There must, so far as practicable, be a separate valuation roll for each valuation district. Every valuation roll shall for all purposes and in all proceedings be evidence of every valuation recorded in that roll and of the particulars in respect of rateable land set out in the roll as required and until the contrary is proved every valuation recorded in a valuation roll shall be presumed to have been duly made under the Valuation of Land Act, 1978 and to have force according to the particulars so set out. Copies of the relevant valuation rolls are supplied (by the Valuer-General's Office) to local governments and are available for public inspection.

Mass appraisal and a geographic information system (GIS)

The introduction of annual revaluation of land in 1993 to provide unimproved values, necessitated the use of modern mass appraisal techniques. However, these techniques are used for all of the different valuations for which the office of the Valuer-General is responsible. Values are provided by using a fully computerised valuation system. (The alternative was a substantial increase in manpower to complete the task manually – which was not cost efficient.) All the analytical tools necessary for setting value levels, using property attributes which are linked with value charts and reference files are provided.

When land is first subdivided, this fact is added to the database and a manually-assessed unimproved value (following an inspection of the land) is entered to maintain the computer database for future use. All the attributes/detriments (being the positive or negative factors that influence the value of the land, e.g. view, soil types, size, frontage, etc.) of the individual plots are stored in the database for the future, automatic calculation of values.

The assumptions for the mass appraisal of values, is that established values in a homogeneous area will increase or decrease in value from year to year in a relatively uniform and coordinated manner. These homogeneous areas are referred to as 'sub market areas' (SMAs). Valuers have to interpret the applicable sales evidence within each SMA to determine the change in value level. Valuation charts are then constructed from these sales and entered into the computer. The 'old values' are compared with the sales from which the charts are constructed, and replaced with 'new values'. This method has been proven to be the most reliable and appropriate (VGO, 1998). Unique property types are assessed manually, in order to maintain a high degree of accuracy.

Since 1993 a geographic information system (GIS) has been developed to assist valuers with the mass appraisal exercise. Cadastral plans of areas to be valued are produced from the GIS, displaying land details, zoning, sales information, unimproved values, etc. The displayed information all assist valuers to ensure that coordination is correct. Coordination is of vital importance in the Western Australia context. Section 32(3) of the Valuation of Land Act, 1978 requires values to be correct '...by [themselves] or in comparison with other values in force...'. Incorrect coordination with adjacent properties may result in taxpayers objecting against their property values (VGO, 1998).

The Valuer General's Office tests the outcomes of values assessed by mass appraisal, by comparing their accuracy and coordination levels within the framework of internationally accepted standards (as set and accepted by – amongst other countries – the United States, Canada and New Zealand). As stated above, the Valuation of Land Act, 1978 also requires a high level of accuracy and currency as regards values.

Mean ratio and coefficient of dispersion tests are applied to the values produced. The Means Ratio measures the overall levels of values adopted, by comparing the assessed values against the sales evidence. The office of the Valuer-General aims to be within the band of 85-100 per cent of fair market evidence. (In the three years preceding 1997/98, the percentages achieved were 90 per cent, 91 per cent and 92 per cent respectively – VGO, 1998.) The Coefficient of Dispersion measures the uniformity of the valuations across all local governments, and should be less than 15 per cent. In 1996/97 VGO achieved 6.64 per cent, in 1995/96 it was 6.63 per cent and in the first year of measurement, 1994/95, it was 15 per cent (VGO, 1998).

Queries, objections and appeals

As is customary in respect of any *ad valorem* property tax, formal objections and appeals may be lodged against general and interim valuations for both gross rental values and unimproved values. However, in Western Australia an informal system is in place in terms of which a disgruntled person my query a valuation on the valuation roll. This system of informal queries is working well. The outcome costs of this less time consuming option is almost half that of formal objections. The response times of 86 per cent for gross rental values and 69 per cent for unimproved values in 90 days reflects the benefits of this system (VGO *Annual Report*, 1997).

The number of objections, appeals and queries obviously depends on the number of valuations that become effective and the impact of charges raised by the taxing and rating authorities utilising the Valuer-General's office's values. The regularity of general revaluations ensure that relatively few queries, objections and appeals are lodged in Western Australia.

Section 32 of the Valuation of Land Act, 1978 states that any person liable to pay any rate or tax assessed in respect of land (or his or her authorised representative) who is dissatisfied with a valuation of such land made under Part III of the Valuation of Land Act, 1978, may serve upon the Valuer-General or any rating or taxing authority a written objection to the valuation:

- in the case of land the subject of a general valuation, within 60 days after the date on which the making of the valuation was published in the *Government Gazette* as prescribed; and
- in any case where the valuation is the basis of the assessment by a rating or taxing authority of any rate or tax, within 60 days after the issue of such an assessment.

An objection to a valuation of land must properly identify the relevant land, identify the valuation objected to and comprehensively state the grounds of objection. Grounds for objection include that the valuation is not fair or is unjust, inequitable or incorrect, whether by itself or in comparison with other valuations made under the Act. A person may not make more than one objection to a specific valuation during any period of twelve months.

Where an objection to a valuation is served on the local government, it must, as soon as practicable, refer the objection to the Valuer-General and advise him of the date on which the objection was served. The Valuer-General must, with all reasonable despatch, consider any objection and may either disallow or allow it, wholly or in part. The Valuer-General must provide written reasons for his decision.

Should the Valuer-General allow an objection, wholly or in part, he must advise the person who objected of any consequent amendment of the valuation. Where the Valuer-General disallows an objection, wholly or in part, he must also advise the person who objected of the time and manner in which an appeal against the decision may be lodged.

In terms of section 34 of the Valuation of Land Act the Valuer-General must promptly advise a local government (or other rating or taxing authority) obliged to adopt or use, or which has adopted, any valuation of:

- receipt by him of an objection to the valuation;
- any allowance by him of an extension of time for service of an objection to the valuation;
- his decision on an objection to the valuation and the reasons therefor;
- any amendment of the valuation consequent upon his allowance, wholly or in part, of an objection to the valuation; and
- receipt by him of a notice requiring him to treat an objection to the valuation as an appeal.

Any person who is dissatisfied with the decision of the Valuer-General on an objection by that person may, within 60 days (or such further period as the Valuer-General may allow for reasonable cause shown) after service of notice of the decision of the Valuer-General, serve on the Valuer-General a notice requiring that the Valuer-General treat the objection as an appeal against the valuation. The Valuer-General must promptly refer the objection to a Land Valuation Tribunal, as established in terms of the Land Valuation Tribunals Act, 1978, as an appeal.

Any amendment of a valuation following the allowance (wholly or in part) of an objection to or an appeal against a valuation shall not apply for the purposes of any rating or taxing year prior to the year in respect of which the objection was served.

General appeal against valuation roll

Section 36 of the Valuation of Land Act, 1978 determine that 'where there is a question of general interest as to whether proper principles have or have not been applied in the valuation under this Act of the whole or a definable part of the land in a valuation district, a rating or taxing authority having an interest in the valuation or any person liable to pay any rate or tax on the basis of the valuation of any part of the land may appeal to a Land Valuation Tribunal to have the question resolved'.

An appeal cannot be brought under this section where a ratepayer wants to have a question relating to his or her own individual case resolved. The Land Valuation Tribunal may give such directions in relation to a valuation, or a part thereof, as it considers fit, including making an order quashing, wholly or in part, any valuation which, in the opinion of the Tribunal, has not been properly made.

Other valuations for public purposes

Apart from the valuations made for rating and land taxation purposes, the Valuer-General may make valuations of land for:

- any department, agency or instrumentality of the Crown in right of the Commonwealth, the State, or any other State; and
- any person, body or authority performing any public function which, under any written law:
  - has among his, her or its functions the power to acquire or dispose of land; or
  - has the power to impose a rate or tax on land.

The Valuer-General may also raise appropriate charges for any such valuations.

In most instances the value required for these other valuations is market value (i.e. 'capital values') which is defined in the Valuation of Land Act, 1978 as follows:

> 'capital value' of land means the capital amount which an estate of fee simple in the land might reasonably be expected to realize upon sale — provided that where the capital value of land cannot reasonably be determined on such basis, the capital value of such land shall be the sum of, first, the unimproved value of the land, and, secondly, the estimated replacement cost of improvements to the land after making such allowance for obsolescence, physical depreciation, and such other factors as are appropriate in the circumstances...

Administration of rates

Exemptions

Other than the exemptions provided for in section 6.26 of the LGA, all land within a district (i.e. city, town or shire) is rateable. Section 6.26(2) states that the following land is not rateable land:

- land which is the property of the Crown and:
  - is being used or held for a public purpose; or
  - is unoccupied (except for certain specified types of land).

- land within the district and owned by the local government or a regional local government which is used for the purposes of that local government or regional local government (other than for purposes of a trading undertaking of that local or regional local government);
- land used or held exclusively by a religious body as a place of public worship or in relation to that worship, a place of residence of a minister of religion, a convent, nunnery or monastery, or occupied exclusively by a religious brotherhood or sisterhood;
- land used exclusively by a religious body as a school for the religious instruction of children;
- land used exclusively as a non-government school within the meaning of the *School Education Act 1999*;
- land used exclusively for charitable purposes;
- land vested in trustees for agricultural or horticultural show purposes;
- land owned by Co-operative Bulk Handling Limited or leased from the Crown or a statutory authority (within the meaning of that term in the *Financial Administration and Audit Act 1985*) by that company and used solely for the storage of grain where that company has agreed in writing to make a contribution to the local government;
- land which is exempt from rates under any other written law; and
- land which is declared by the Minister to be exempt from rates.

The Minister may from time to time, declare that any land or part of any land is exempt from rates and by subsequent declaration cancel or vary the declaration. A notice of any such declaration is to be published in the *Gazette*.

Furthermore, land does not cease to be used exclusively for a purpose mentioned in section 6.26 (2) merely because it is used occasionally for another purpose which is of a charitable, benevolent, religious or public nature (e.g. a church hall being used for a concert to raise funds for the homeless).

Tax rates

Local governments determine their own tax rates, either as a uniform rate for all land categories, or as differential rates for different categories. There is a clear trend to move towards the utilisation of differential rates. To comply with the notion that all property owners should be expected to make at least some contribution to the cost of local public services, local governments are also entitled to implement a minimum rate. In practice local governments avail them of this right.

Differential and minimum rates

Before a differential rate is imposed, the local government is required to give public notice of its intention to do so. It must invite submissions from ratepayers and the electorate in general within 21 days from the date of the notice. A document explaining the objects and reasons for each proposed rate (or minimum payment) must also be made available for inspection by the electorate and ratepayers.

In terms of section 6.33 of the LGA a local government may impose differential general rates according to any, or a combination, of the following characteristics:

- the purpose for which the land is zoned under a town planning scheme in force under the *Town Planning and Development Act 1928*;
- the predominant purpose for which the land is held or used as determined by the local government;
- whether or not the land is vacant land; or
- any other characteristic or combination of characteristics prescribed.

In imposing a differential general rate a local government is not to, without the approval of the Minister, impose a differential general rate which is more than twice the lowest differential general rate imposed by it.

A local government may impose on any rateable land in its district a minimum payment which is greater than the general rate which would otherwise be payable on that land. A lower minimum payment may be imposed in certain areas. However the local government is to ensure the general minimum is imposed on not less than 50 per cent of the number of separately rated properties in the district on which a minimum payment is imposed. Minimum payments may be applied separately, in accordance with the principles set forth in section 6.35 (2), (3) and (4) of the LGA, to:

- land rated on gross rental value;
- land rated on unimproved value; and
- each differential rating category where a differential general rate is imposed.

Before imposing any differential general rates or a minimum payment applying to a differential rate category, a local government must properly (i.e. as prescribed in the LGA) give public notice locally of its intention to do so. The local government is required to consider any submissions received before imposing the proposed rate or minimum payment with or without modification.

Differential rates were introduced for the first time by the Perth City Council in 1996/1997. Table 2 indicates the differential rates for the 2004/2005 financial year.

Table 7.2   City of Perth rates for 2004-2005

Land use category	Rate (cents per $ of gross rental value)	% increase from 2003/2004
Residential	5.313	3.2
Hotel	7.277	0.0
Commercial	7.156	2.7
Retail	7.232	0.7
Office	4.816	3.2
Industrial	8.031	1.2
Vacant land	9.632	3.2

Source: www.perth.wa.gov.wa (2004)

In all categories the minimum rate is $380. The overall increase in rates income budgeted is 2.4 per cent. The low rate on residential properties is aimed at attracting persons to inner city living. (The relatively small Perth City Council is within the heart of the Perth Metropolitan Area – consisting of 30 different local governments.) A larger residential population is perceived to be beneficial to all other sectors in the city.

The high rate on the rather small industrial sector is defended by the 'greater demand on the City's special services such as health, building and compliance…'. The highest rate on vacant land is explained by the council as follows: 'Vacant land is of little benefit to the community and is not encouraged by the Council. Accordingly, those few properties in this category attract the highest rate.'

The Shire of Augusta-Margaret River also makes extensive use of differential and minimum rates. The rates for the 2004/2005 financial year are set out in Table 7.3.

Table 7.3   Shire of Augusta-Margaret River for 2004-2005

Land use category	Tax base	Rate (cent per $)	Minimum rate
General – Zone 1	Gross rental value	9.6569	$700
Vacant land – Zone 1	Gross rental value	9.6569	$1,200
Industrial – Zone 1	Gross rental value	10.4768	$700
Commercial – Zone 1	Gross rental value	13.6660	$850
Special rural – Zone 2	Gross rental value	11.1113	$850
Special rural vacant land – Zone 2	Gross rental value	11.1113	$1,200
Rural farming – Zone 3	Unimproved value	0.3596	$850
Rural cellar door – Zone 4	Unimproved value	0.7178	$1,622

Source: www.amrsc.wa.gov.au (2004)

Indicative of the dual nature of the Western Australian property tax system, gross rental values are used for townsite properties (i.e. properties mostly located in towns) and unimproved values are used for properties used predominantly for rural purposes. However, some rural properties (those in zone 2) have been rated on gross rental values because their predominant use was not deemed to be rural. (Typically these are small rural plots under 4 hectares in size and used for residential purposes or vacant small rural lots held for speculative purposes).

The Shire is in the process of developing a comprehensive rating policy for rural properties with the aim of creating greater equity between urban and rural ratepayers.

In the Shire of Wyndham-East Kimberley the two towns of Kununurra and Wyndham are rated on gross rental values whereas the rural properties (i.e. land outside the towns) are rated on unimproved values.

Differential rates are not applied to town sites, but have been introduced in the 1999/2000 financial year to rural property categories. A distinction is drawn – and different rates in the $ charged for three categories of rural land:

- pastoral land;
- agricultural land; and
- mining tenements.

Minimum rates apply to all categories of property in the two towns and in rural areas.

The Shire of Peppermint Grove (within the Perth Metropolitan Area) applies a uniform rate (of 6.8040 per cent of gross rental value for 2004/2005) for the six property use categories within the shire. The minimum rate applied in this Shire is a high $618.

Specified area rates

Section 6.37(1) of the LGA states that a local government may impose a specified area rate on rateable land within a portion of its district for the purpose of meeting the cost of the provision by it of a specific work, service or facility if the local government considers that the ratepayers or residents within that area have:

- benefited or will benefit from;
- access to or will have access to; or
- contributed or will contribute to the need for, that work, service or facility.

A specified area rate may only be used for the purpose for which the rate is imposed in the financial year in which the rate is imposed, or must be placed it in a reserve account established for that purpose. If a local government receives more money than it requires from a specified area rate on any land or if the money received from the rate is no longer required for the work, service or facility, it:

- may, and if so requested by the owner of the land is required to, make a refund to that owner which is proportionate to the contributions received by the local government; or
- is required to allow a credit of an amount proportionate to the contribution received by the local government in relation to the land

on which the rate was imposed against future liabilities for rates or service charges in respect of that land.

Rate record

In terms of section 6.39 of the LGA a local government must, as soon as practicable after a it has resolved to impose rates in a financial year, ensure that a record is compiled, at the time and in the form and manner prescribed, for that financial year of all the rateable land in its district; and all land in its district on which a service charge is imposed.

Liability and payment of rates

The owner for the time being of land on which a rate has been imposed is liable to pay the rate or service charge to the local government. If there are two or more owners of the land they are jointly and severally liable to pay the rate.

A rate is ordinarily payable to a local government by a single payment but the person liable for the payment of the rate may elect to make payment thereof to the local government by four equal or nearly equal instalments, or such other method of payment by instalments as is set forth in the local government's annual budget.

Local governments generally provide for a variety of payment options to ease compliance by ratepayers. For example, in the Shire of Wyndham-East Kimberley ratepayers can pay their rates in any of the following ways:

- in cash or by credit card in person at shire offices;
- by mail by credit card (maximum $4,000), cheque or money order direct bank deposit into the Shire's account (details on rate notice);
- instalments (implying that the early-payment discount will not be available).

The City of Perth provides even more options, such as payment at any Australia Post Office, any branch of the Commonwealth Bank, online or telephonically by credit card or by EFTPOS at council offices.

Discounts and penalties

Section 6.46 of the LGA stipulates that, subject to the *Rates and Charges (Rebates and Deferments) Act 1992*, a local government may, when imposing a rate or a service charge, resolve to grant a discount or other incentive for early payment. However, an absolute majority (i.e. 50 per cent) is required before a council can grant a discount. For example, the City of Perth provides an incentive to ratepayers paying the full amount owing within 35 days of issuance of the rate notice by automatically entering the names of these ratepayers into an early payment prize draw. The Shire of East Pilbara offers as early-payment incentive a maximum $800 refund on rates as a first prize and five-night, two-night and one-night holiday packages as second, third and fourth prizes respectively.

Local governments charge penalty interest on late payment. For example, the City of Perth, Shire of Augusta-Margaret River and the Shire of Wyndham-East Kimberley charge interest at a rate of 11 per cent.

Tax relief

Local governments can provide limited hardship relief measures on application. For example, the City of Perth will consider the provision of a rebate or concession to qualifying pensioners or senior citizens. To encourage people to relocate to the inner city, purchasers of new residential property within a specified area of the City of Perth will also qualify for a rebate for three consecutive financial years.

The Shire of Augusta-Margaret River provides for the option of tax deferral for pensioners meeting the eligibility criteria.

Recovery of rates

Rates are generally recoverable by a local government from:

* the owner at the time of the compilation of the rate record; or
* a person who subsequently, whilst the rates are unpaid, becomes the owner of the land.

If a rate remains unpaid after it becomes due and payable, a local government may recover it, as well as the associated legal costs of any proceedings, if any, for that recovery, in a court of competent jurisdiction. Rates or service charges due by the same person to the local government may be included in one writ, summons, complaint, or other process.

Where the payment of a rate imposed in respect of any land is due and payable, notice may be given to the lessee of the land requiring the lessee to pay to the local government any rent as it falls due in satisfaction of the rate. Where an amount pertaining to a rate is paid by the lessee, that payment discharges the lessee from any liability to the lessor in the same amount. Where the amount paid by the lessee exceeds the rent due, or if there is no rent due, the amount may be set off by the lessee against accruing rent, or the balance recovered from the lessor in a court of competent jurisdiction.

If any rates which are due to a local government in respect of any rateable land have been unpaid for at least three years, the local government may, in accordance with the appropriate provisions of the LGA take possession of the land and hold the land as against a person having an estate or interest in the land and:

- from time to time lease the land;
- sell the land;
- cause the land to be transferred to the Crown; or
- cause the land to be transferred to itself.

When land is possessed by the local government, it must give to the owner of the land such notification as is prescribed and then to affix on a conspicuous part of the land a notice, in the form or substantially in the form prescribed.

Where payment of any rates imposed in respect of any land is in arrears, the local government has an interest in the land and may therefore lodge a caveat to preclude dealings in respect of the land. It also has the power to withdraw any caveats lodged by it.

Where, within twelve years of the taking of possession of any land by a local government an entitled person (i.e. the person who would be entitled to possession but for the fact that the local government took possession) pays to the local government all rates and service charges due and payable in respect of the land, the local government is required to give up possession of that land to the person where the local government has leased the land. However, if the land has been sold, or transferred to the Crown or to the local government itself, the twelve-year rule cannot apply.

A local government is entitled to exercise its power to sell the land, unless, within the three-year period prior to the exercise of the power of sale, the local government has at least once attempted under section 6.56 of the LGA (i.e. court proceedings) to recover money due to it. However, if the local government has a reasonable belief that the cost of the proceedings under that section will equal or exceed the value of the land, it is not required to proceed with recovery via the court, but can sell the land forthwith.

Prior to the time of the actual sale of any land by local government it may, upon such terms and conditions as are agreed between the parties, accept payment of the outstanding rates or service charges. If payment is made, the proceedings relating to the proposed sale are stayed and the local government is required to make such notifications and take such measures as are prescribed in relation to the payment and the cancellation of the proposed sale. A sale or transfer of the land discharges the outstanding liability for rates. If land is:

- rateable land;
- vacant land; and
- land in respect of which any rates or service charges have been unpaid for a period of at least three years

The local government in whose district the land is situated may apply in the form and manner prescribed to the Minister to have the land revested in the Crown in right of the State. The Minister is to consider the application and the surrounding circumstances and may grant or refuse the application. In terms of section 6.76 of the LGA the person named in the rate record as the owner of land may, within 42 days of the service of a rate notice, object to the rate record of a local government on the ground:

that there is an error in the rate record:

- with respect to the identity of the owner or occupier of any land; or
- on the basis that the land or part of the land is not rateable land;
- if the local government imposes a differential general rate, that the characteristics of the land recorded in the rate record as the basis for imposing that rate should be deleted and other characteristics substituted.

The local government is to promptly consider any objection and may either disallow it or allow it, wholly or in part – giving reasons in writing for its decision. An appeal to a Land Valuation Tribunal may be lodged within 42 days after service of notice of the decision.

The LGA reconfirms that there is not to be an objection or appeal in respect of a valuation of rateable land appearing in a rate record except in accordance with the *Valuation of Land Act 1978*.

The making of an objection or an appeal against the data contained in the rate record does not affect the liability to pay any rate imposed under the LGA pending determination of the objection or appeal.

General appeal on a rate

Should a question of general interest as to whether a rate was imposed in accordance with the LGA arise, the local government or any person may appeal to a Land Valuation Tribunal to have the question resolved. This avenue of appeal is however not available to any person to have a question relating to that person's own individual case resolved. The Land Valuation Tribunal hearing a general appeal on a rate may make an order quashing a rate which in the opinion of the Tribunal has been improperly made or imposed.

Overall performance of the present rating system

The Western Australian property information system is excellent. Generally all land in Western Australia is assessed for purposes of rates, although not all land is rateable. This ensure that the coverage ratio (i.e. the percentage of properties captured in the tax base as a percentage of total properties) is very high.

Unimproved values are assessed annually throughout the State and gross rental values are determined every three years in the Perth Metropolitan Area and on a four- to six-yearly cycle in respect of towns in rural areas. Mass appraisal techniques are used for both all valuations for rating purposes. Regular revaluations imply fewer significant shifts in tax incidence. The few queries, objections and appeals received by the Valuer General's Office suggest that the quality of assessment is generally very high.

Councils are increasingly opting for differential rating. Perth City Council utilises seven land use categories and introduced differential rating as far back in 1997/98. The majority of local governments now utilise differential rating to spread the rates burden more equally amongst different property use categories. Differentiation is accompanied by vigorous public awareness campaigns.

The collection ratio (i.e. rates collected as a percentage of collectable rates) is on average very high, with no serious problems being reported by any of the local governments.

It is a somewhat unique feature to have two different systems (one based on gross rental values and the other on unimproved values) operate within a single rating authority as is indeed the case in most of the shires in Western Australia.

Land value taxation at state level

Land taxes were introduced throughout Australia at state level in all six states between 1877 (Victoria) and 1915 (in Queensland). A land tax was first introduced in Western Australia by the Land Tax Act of 1907. A federal land tax was introduced in 1911 (Herps, 1988). The combined effect of federal and state land taxes was rather severe, even at its highest it was still below 100 per cent of the economic rental value (Smith, 2004). The federal land tax was abolished in 1952 (Herps, 1988; Forster, 2000). In 1996/1997 the revenue from land tax in Western Australia amounted to $165,340 million. Currently land tax is assessed in terms of the Land Tax Assessment Act, 2002, Land Tax Act, 2002 and Taxation Administration Act, 2003.

Tax base

Land tax is payable, in accordance with the land tax Acts, for each financial year for all land in the State except land that is exempt under section 17 on the unimproved value of the land.

Valuation

The Valuer General determines the unimproved value of all taxable land throughout the State on an annual basis.

Assessment

Except where this Act specifically provides for a concession or rebate of land tax, the amount of land tax payable for taxable land for an assessment year is the amount calculated by applying the rate fixed in relation to the land under the *Land Tax Act 2002* to the amount equal to the unimproved value of the land according to the valuation in force under the *Valuation of Land Act 1978* at midnight on 30 June in the previous financial year.

Section 11 states that if a person owns 2 or more lots or parcels of taxable land, land tax is payable on the aggregated unimproved value of all the taxable land owned by the person in the State.

Where land is owned jointly by two or more persons, the land tax payable is assessed as if the land were owned by one person. When determining the extent (if any) to which the land is exempt or subject to a concession, the following matters are to be taken into account:

- each joint owner's use of the land by virtue of which the land is exempt or subject to a concession (whether or not the use is common to any of the other joint owners);
- each joint owner's interest in the land by virtue of which the land is exempt or subject to a concession (whether or not the interest is common to any of the other joint owners).

Where a person is taken to be the owner of a portion of a lot owned by the Crown, a Crown agency or a local government, then a reference in a land tax Act to the unimproved value of the land is a reference to the amount, as determined by the Valuer-General, that bears the same proportion to the unimproved value of the lot as the portion of the lot bears to the total potential lettable area. The total potential lettable area of a lot is the total area of the lot that is capable of being let, as determined by the Valuer-General on the assumption that none of the land is used for an exempt purpose and having regard to the lease conditions of the portion of the lot for which a value is required.

Specific assessment rules apply to newly-subdivided private residential property and to newly-subdivided rural business land.

In terms of section 16 the Commissioner may assess the amount of land tax payable on land on which a building containing non-strata home units is situated in accordance with this section if, apart from the building, no other improvements have been effected on the land except:

- improvements in the nature of draining, filling, excavation, grading or levelling of the land, retaining walls or other structures or works for that purpose, the removal of rocks, stone or soil, and the clearing of timber, scrub or other vegetation; or
- outbuildings, fences, garages or other improvements that are, in each case, designed for the use or enjoyment of the home unit owners.

A home unit owner who is a registered proprietor of an undivided share in the land is liable to pay land tax on the proportion of the unimproved value of the land that bears to the unimproved value of the land the same proportion as the owner's share in the land bears to the land.

If the owner of a home unit is liable to pay land tax assessed on a proportion of the unimproved value of the land under subsection (6) or (7), and is also the owner of any other land, then the part of the value of the land on which the home unit is erected is taken to be land for the purposes of a land tax Act and is taken to have the value assessed under the respective subsection.

Tax liability

Land tax payable on land for an assessment year is payable by the person who is or was the owner (or in some instances the deemed owner) of the land at midnight on 30 June in the previous financial year. In terms of section 8 a person is taken to be the owner of land for the purposes of tax liability if that person is entitled to:

• the land under any lease or licence from the Crown with or without the right of acquiring the fee simple; or
• use the land for business, commercial, professional or trade purposes under an agreement or arrangement with the Crown, with an agency or instrumentality of the Crown, or with a local government or public statutory authority.

Joint owners of land are jointly and severally liable for land tax payable on the land regardless of each of the joint owner's respective interests in, or use of, the land. A person who is liable to pay land tax is also liable to pay any additional taxes, interest, penalties or charges payable under a land tax Act in relation to the land tax.

If an agreement has been made for the sale of land, whether or not the agreement is completed by transfer or conveyance, and whether or not it was made before or after this Act commenced, then for the purpose of ascertaining who is liable to pay land tax on the land the seller is taken to be the owner of the land until the purchaser obtains possession of the land. From the date of possession the purchaser is taken to become the owner of the land.

Exemptions from land tax

Land is exempt from land tax for an assessment year if the Commissioner grants an exemption or partial exemption. The Commissioner has wide-ranging powers to grant exemptions. The Commissioner requires an owner of land to lodge an application in the approved form for an exemption or concession under Part 3 of the Act and to give any information within the owner's knowledge or control that is relevant to deciding whether or not the land is eligible for an exemption or concession. The Commissioner may grant the exemption, concession or further concession for the whole or part of the land if satisfied that there are reasonable grounds for doing so.

If the Commissioner refuses to grant the exemption or concession, the applicant may appeal to the Minister against the Commissioner's decision. An appeal may be made within 60 days after the date on which notice of the Commissioner's decision was issued, or within any further time allowed by the Minister for reasonable cause shown by the applicant. The obligation to pay, or the right to receive and recover land tax, is not affected by any appeal to the Minister.

Tax rates

For the 2004/2005 financial year the Land Tax Act, 2002 provides for the rates set out in Table 7.4.

Table 7.4   Land tax rates for 2004-2005

Unimproved value of land		Rate of land tax
Exceeding ($)	Not exceeding ($)	
0	100,000	Nil
100,000	220,000	$150 + 0.15 cent for each $1 in excess of $100,000
220,000	570,000	$330 + 0.45 cent for each $1 in excess of $220,000
570,000	2,000,000	$1,905 + 1.76 cent for each $1 in excess of $570,000
2,000,000	5,000,000	$27,073 + 2.30 cent for each $1 in excess of $2,000,000
5,000,000		$96,073 + 2.50 cent for each $1 in excess of $5,000,000

Date of payment

Land tax payable on an original assessment is due for payment on the 49th day after the date of the assessment notice. On a reassessment land tax is due for payment on the date specified in the assessment notice in accordance with the *Taxation Administration Act 2003*.

Present status of land value taxation

In 1980 the McCusker Committee of Inquiry was established to examine problems related to rating and taxation. Amongst other things, this committee recommended that only one valuation base should be used for rating purposes. The base should be capital value for improved properties and site value for unimproved properties. Prior to the McCusker Committee the Keall Report recommended that assessed value should be a certain percentage of capital value. These recommendations have not been implemented (Hornby, 1999).

Gross rental values are done on a triennial cycle in the metropolitan region and a four- to five-yearly cycle in country towns. These values are supplied to the metropolitan councils and the Water Corporation. For rating purposes, the gross rental value is multiplied by a factor determined by the Water Corporation (to calculate the sewerage rates) and by a factor determined by individual local governments to calculate their council rates. These factors are a ratio in the form of cents in the Dollar of the total budget required by the rating authorities and the total gross rental value of the rated district. Gross rental values are also used to determine the new Emergency Services Levy introduced on 1 July 2003. This State levy is forwarded to the Fire and Emergency Services Authority (FESA) to fund its services throughout Western Australia.

Unimproved value is a vacant land value which is applied to every property (lot) in Western Australia. Unimproved values are used by the State Revenue Department as a basis for the land tax and by some local governments, namely the shires for rural properties.

As pure unimproved value became unworkable for town site land, due to the nature of certain improvements (defined as 'merged improvements'), the tax base as regards taxes on unimproved value is actually 'site value'. The site value of land is defined (in the Valuation of Land Act 1978) as 'the capital amount that an estate of fee simple in the land might reasonable be expected to realize upon sale assuming that any improvements to the land, other than merged improvements, had not been made...'.

Land tax is currently levied in terms of the Land Tax Act, 2002. It is levied at progressive rates (ranging between 0.15 per cent – 2.5 per cent). The 30 local governments within the Perth Metropolitan Region and the vast majority of town councils elsewhere in the State, presently utilise gross rental values as tax base for rating. Some urban local governments and all the rural shires still use unimproved values for rating purposes.

A metropolitan region improvement tax (at a tax rate of 0.15 cents in the A$) is collected by the State Revenue Department on all land within the Perth Metropolitan Region which is also liable for the State's land tax and on the same tax base – i.e. unimproved value.

The future of land value taxation

In recent years there has been a noticeable move away from unimproved values as a tax base for local government rating in respect of land situated within a 'townsite' (i.e. land in an urban area). However, unimproved values are still utilised for all properties throughout the State for purposes of Western Australia's land tax and for the rating of rural land within the jurisdiction of the shire councils.

References

DLI (2004), '*Valuer General's Rating and Taxing Values (updated in June 2004)*', Department of Land Information.

Forster, G.A. (2000), 'Australia – Land and Property Tax System', *American Journal of Economics and Sociology*, December.

Herps, D. (1988), '*Land Value Taxation in Australia and its Potential for Reforming our Chaotic Tax System*', Walsh Memorial Bequest Address, Macquarie University School of Economics, reprinted by Earthsharing in 2001. (see www.earthsharing.org.au/herps.html).

Hornby, D. (1999), 'Property taxes in Australia' in W.J. McCluskey (ed.), *Property Tax: An International Comparative Review*, Ashgate Publishing Limited, Aldershot, pp 313-336.

Local Governments (2004), City of Perth (www.perth.wa.gov.au), Shire of Augusta-Margaret River (www.amrsc.wa.gov.au), Shire of East Pilbara (www.eastpilbara.wa.gov.au), Shire of Peppermint Grove (www.peppermintgrove.wa.gov.au).

McCluskey, W.J. and Franzsen, R.C.D. (2001), '*Land Value Taxation: A Case Study Approach*', research paper for the Lincoln Institute of Land Policy, Cambridge, Massachusetts, United States.

Slack, E. (2004), 'Property Taxation in Australia' in R.M. Bird and E. Slack (eds), *International Handbook of Land and Property Taxation*, Edward Elgar Publishing Limited, UK, pp. 91-97.

Smith, J. (2004), '*Land Value Taxation*' (www.earthsharing.org.au).

Valuer General Office (1997), *Annual Report, 1997*.

Valuer General Office (1998), Perth, WA.

Worrall, A. (1981), 'Land-locked! Why Australia turned to Land Value Taxation', *Land & Liberty* (July-August).

Legislation referred to:

Land Valuation Tribunals Act, 1978.
Valuation of Land Act, 1978.
Local Government Act, 1995.
Land Tax Act, 2002.
Land Tax Assessment Act, 2002.

Chapter 8

Site Value Taxation in Queensland

William J. McCluskey

Introduction

Queensland is the third largest state in Australia and has approximately 19 per cent of the population. The current state population stands at around 3.84 million, with Brisbane, the capital city having just less than one million (DLGPSR, 2004).

Queensland is now the only state in Australia which uses the original concept of 'unimproved' value for the rating of all property including urban and rural land (Trickett, 1982). The system is of some antiquity in the history of local government finance. After an initial attempt to use annual values local authorities have been leving rates on unimproved values since 1887. Initially, unimproved value was used only by the shires, but, the success of this change of rating base led to the adoption in 1890 of the unimproved value system for cities and towns as well. The Queensland Valuation of Land Act 1944 was modelled on the earlier New South Wales and New Zealand valuation legislation and also drew heavily on the Federal Land Tax Act. It is quite easy to understand why unimproved value was adopted by most states in the early stages of their development as it has a particular philosophical attraction to those responsible for the development of a largely undeveloped state.

Legislation

The Queensland Valuation of Land Act 1944, as amended, defines unimproved value in relation to both unimproved and improved lands.

Unimproved value means (Section 12(1)):

- In relation to unimproved land, the capital sum which the fee simple of the land might be expected to realise if offered for sale on such reasonable terms and conditions as a bona fide seller would require; and

• In relation to improved land, the capital sum which the fee simple of the land might be expected to realise if offered for sale on such reasonable terms and conditions as a bona fide seller would require, assuming that, at the time as at which the value is required to be ascertained for the purposes of this Act, the improvements did not exist. Provided that the unimproved value shall in no case be less than the sum that would be obtained by deducting the value of the improvements from the improved value at the time as at which the value is required to be ascertained for the purposes of this Act.

Section 12(1A):

Notwithstanding anything contained in this section, in determining the unimproved value of any land it shall be assumed that:

• the land may be used, or may continue to be used, for any purpose for which it was being used, or for which it could be used, at the date to which the valuation relates;
• such improvements may be continued or made on the land as may be required in order to enable the land to be continued to be so used.

But nothing in this subsection prevents regard from being had, in determining that value, to any other purpose for which the land may be used on the assumption that any improvements referred to in subsection (1) of this section had not been made.

Section 12(2):

For the purposes of this Act:

• improved value means, in relation to land, the capital sum the capital sum which the fee simple of the land might be expected to realise if offered for sale on such reasonable terms and conditions as a bona fide seller would require;
• the value of improvements means, in relation to land, the added value which the improvements give to the land at the time as at which the value is required to be ascertained for the purposes of this Act, irrespective of the cost of the improvements, including in such added value the value of any hotel licence the value of which has been included in the improved value.

- provided that the added value shall in no case exceed the amount that should reasonably be involved in effecting, at the time as at which the value is required to be ascertained for the purposes of this Act, improvements of a nature and efficiency equivalent to the existing improvements; and

- improvements means, in relation to land, improvements thereon or appertaining thereto, whether visible or invisible, and are made or acquired by the owner or his predecessor in title, and includes all such destruction of suckers and seedlings as is incidental to the destruction of timber and also includes the destruction of other vegetable growths and of animal pests on the land to the extent to which such destruction retains its utility, but does not include the destruction by any person of such growths or pests which are allowed to establish themselves on the land during his ownership, except to the extent (if at all) to which it restores wholly or partly so much of the utility of a previous improvement in the nature of the destruction of such growths or pests as is, by the subsequent provisions of this definition, deemed to have been lost, and any improvement consisting of the destruction of such growth or pests, by whomsoever the same may be effected, shall be deemed to have lost its utility to the extent to which, after it has been made, other growths or pests (as the case may be) are allowed to establish themselves on the land.

- provided that in the determination of the unimproved value of the land the term does not include invisible improvements other than timber treatment, where such invisible improvements have been made by the Crown (including a statutory body representing the Crown), a local authority or a Harbour Board.

A number of significant amendments have been made to the Act in recent years. Some of these in summarised form are listed below:

- a valuation of the unimproved value of land shall take into account the existence and effect of any easement, registered under any Act, in respect of which such land is the dominant or the servient tenement;

- a valuation of the unimproved value of any land shall not include the value of any timber on or any metals, minerals or coal in the land;

- in determining the unimproved value of land used exclusively for purposes of a single dwelling house or for the business of primary production, any enhancement in that value because the land has a potential use for industrial, sub-division or any other purposes shall be disregarded irrespective of whether or not that potential use is lawful when the valuation is made.

In the case of an improved property it must be assumed that all improvements on the land do not exist at the given date. However, any improvements to the land i.e. roads, power, telephone, sewerage etc. are taken into account. In other words surrounding infrastructure is reflected in the unimproved value.

Valuation issues

The Queensland Valuer-General's Department was established in 1946 as a result of the Valuation of Land Act 1944. Previously, valuations for rating were made by valuers appointed by the individual local authorities. By establishing the Valuer-General Department the government acknowledged the need for a central valuation authority with a co-ordinating function to remove disparities and inconsistencies which then existed and to establish an equitable basis for rating in accordance with sound principles of valuation. Currently, valuations are undertaken by the Department of Natural Resources and Mines (DNRM). Under the 1944 Act valuations were conducted every five to eight years. However, changes to the valuation system were introduced in 1985 (amendment passed to the VLA 1944) which provided for annual valuations. The change was as a result of trying to reduce the impact of very large increases in unimproved values which was a characteristic of the previous system. This should eliminate the excessive fluctuations which at times accompanied valuations which were reviewed at periods of up to eight years. All local governments in Queensland were valued annually by 1989 as opposed to the prior general revaluations which were carried out in each local government every 5 to 8 years.

Annual valuations avoid the huge variations that occurred under the previous system, however, it is questionable whether such a system is needed for the entire state. Clearly, it is of more practical relevance in urban areas which are experiencing rapid development and urban growth (such as Brisbane, Gold Coast and Cairns). On the other hand remote rural regions may not need such a frequent system of revaluation.

It has been found that annual valuations for the whole state is not appropriate as there is often insufficient sales evidence in some areas to allow an accurate reflection of he market. On the other hand three to five year valuation cycles particularly in rural areas would permit a more accurate and valid assessment of sales.

Valuation provision

The Department of Natural Resources and Mines currently provides all valuations for rating and other statutory purposes for the entire state including local governments. The valuation provision prior to a departmental reorganisation was conducted by the Valuer-General. Indeed one of the recommendations arrived at from the valuation review was the need to reintroduce the position of Valuer-General. As of June 2004 Queensland had 1.35 million parcels with an aggregate unimproved value of $105 billion. The centralised system at present provides for a system which enhances consistency, credibility and impartiality. In addition, given the tradition of the Department in providing valuations a unique knowledge and understanding of the valuation process has developed.

The question of out-sourcing the rating valuations has been considered in a Review of the States Valuation System (1996). It was one of the conclusions that if the valuation delivery was to be commercialised or out-sourced the regulatory function should remain within government.

Valuation process

It is considered impractical to carry out individual inspections of every property each year. Instead, market trends in unimproved values are calculated from property transactions for each land category. These land use categories would normally include residential, multi-unit residential, commercial, industrial, rural residential and various classes of agricultural land. There are essentially three stages in the valuation process:

- the basis;
- processing the valuation; and
- notification of the new valuations.

Basis

Sales information is analysed for each land category in each local government area. By comparing the analysed unimproved values with the existing unimproved values, the market movement in overall land values can be determined.

Processing the valuation

A sophisticated computer system, the Integrated Valuation and Sales System (IVAS) was developed in the early 1990s and came into full operation in 1994 (Kirby, 1997). The system provides support in the processes of valuation administration and valuation and contains a number of sub-systems including property update, objections, appeals, issues and information provision.

Based on comparative sales information the IVAS provides predicted values based on a pre-specified percentage factor applied to the current value on the properties. The factor can result in either an increase or decrease in the value. The predicted values are then subject to manual and statistical review prior to the issue of the valuation. For uniformity, these valuations are required to reflect the market as at 1 October of the year prior to a valuation becoming effective on the 30 June.

Notification

The IVAS generates an updated list of unimproved values for each local government area. This list is known as the valuation roll and includes such factors as:

- property address;
- ownership;
- property description;
- area;
- unimproved value.

Owners are notified of the valuation by mail and the new valuation rolls are placed on public display for six weeks from the date of issue at the relevant Department of Natural Resources and Mines offices. On the 30 June following the date of valuation, the new valuations come into effect for local government rating purposes, and for the assessment of Land Tax by the Office of State Revenue.

Objection and appeal procedures

Land owners have 42 days from the date of receipt of the valuation notice in which to lodge their objection to the new assessed value. The onus is on the owner to provide full details of the matters which they consider important for a reconsideration of the assessed value. Objections are dealt with by the Department of Natural Resources and Mines with a written decision be made as soon as reasonably practicable.

If the landowner is dissatisfied with the decision on the objection by the Department the matter may be appealed to the Land Court. The appeal must be lodged on the prescribed form within 42 days of the issue of the decision on objection. The grounds of appeal are restricted to those stated by the appellant on the form of appeal. Should the decision of the Land Court not be acceptable to either party further redress is available through the Land Appeal Court, the Court of Appeal and finally the High Court of Australia. The grounds of these latter appeals are, however, restricted to points of law only and appellants must seek leave to appeal to the High Court.

Exemptions

Under the Local Government Act 1993 all land is rateable other than the following categories:

- vacant state land;
- land occupied by the state or a government entity (other than a non-exempt government owned corporation), except land under a lease from a private person;
- land in a state forest or timber reserve, other than land occupied under an occupational permit or stock grazing permit;
- Aboriginal land under the Aboriginal land Act 1991 or land under the Torres Strait Islander Land Act 1991, other than land used for commercial or residential purposes;
- strategic port land occupied by a port authority, the state, or a government entity;
- existing or new rail corridor land;
- a regulation may be made to exempt from rating land used for religious, charitable, educational or public purposes.

Tax base

Figure 8.1 illustrates the growth in the level of unimproved values for the state over the period 1971-2003. Figure 8.2 highlights the growth in the number of rateable parcels.

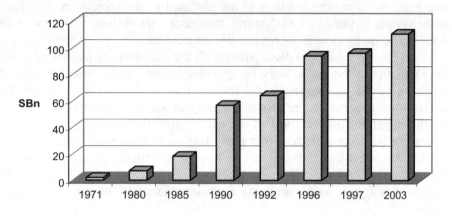

Figure 8.1   Growth in unimproved values for the state

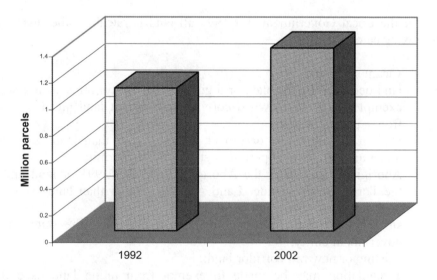

Figure 8.2   Number of rateable parcels

Local government

There are three levels of government in Australia: federal, State (Territory) and local. In Queensland, there are 125 local councils along with a number of Aboriginal and Torres Strait Islander community councils. Councils vary in size and by the range of services they provide, for example Brisbane City has a population of just less than one million, whereas, Isisford Shire has a population of approximately 270 people; Cook Shire has a land area more than half the size of Victoria. Local government within Queensland is responsible for the carrying out of a wide variety of functions beneficial to their local community. Historically, local government had a narrow range of defined functions. The expression 'roads, rates and rubbish' has been used to describe these functions. However, over the years the range of functions has been expanding and, under the Local Government Act 1993, local governments are given a broad general competence power to enable them to provide most services a local community may need or desire. Therefore, it is necessary for a local government to be able to raise its 'own' revenue to fund the major part of its expenditures on services and facilities. The following represent the main services which local government have primary responsibility for:

- preventive health;
- recreation;
- community development;
- social and cultural development;
- town development;
- road network;
- stormwater drainage;
- water supply;
- sewerage;
- solid waste management.

Revenue raising powers

The powers of local government to raise revenue may be classified in a number of ways. One possible way to understand their powers is to distinguish between taxing powers and powers which are, in essence contractual. The taxing powers are delegated in legislation by the State government and include the authority to impose a rate, charge, or fee other than under a contractual arrangement. The principal taxing powers are to be found in the Local Government Act 1993, other State Acts may confer taxing powers on local authorities such as the Integrated Planning Act 1997. The taxing powers may be considered as mandatory or discretionary.

An example of a mandatory power is the power to make a general rate or differential rates under the LGA 1993. Section 561 of that Act requires local governments to make such rates for each financial year. This is distinct from the other taxing powers identified in Section 559(1) which are discretionary.

The taxing powers, such as rating, do not depend upon any agreement between the person charged and the local government for the supply of any service or facility. However, in some cases taxing powers may relate to the supply of specific goods or services, such as utility charges for water, sewerage, cleansing and gas. In other cases they may allow local governments to raise revenue regardless of the cost or level of supply of goods or services to that person.

Contractual charges are charges that depend on the person requesting local government to supply a good or service. Examples of these could include the use of a refuse tip or the sale of quarry materials.

Rates and charges

The Local Government Act 1993 contains powers to make rates at the annual budget meting of the local government and to levy those rates by the issue of a rate notice to the owner of land. Specifically, Section 559(1) provides for the making of the following rates and charges:

- general rate or differential general rates;
- minimum general rates;
- separate rates and charges;
- special rates and charges; and
- utility charges (for water, sewerage, cleansing or gas).

The revenue policy underlies the budget process and fulfils two important functions firstly, it guides the development of revenue alternatives in the budget process and secondly, as an external reporting document to help explain to the community the rationale for the revenue measures adopted. Matters to be contained in the revenue policy would include:

- how rates and charges are decided and the extent the rates and charges relate to relevant costs;
- any rebates and concessions on rates and charges;
- any limitations of increases in rates and charges; and
- the extent physical and social infrastructure costs for new development are to be funded by charges for the development.

General rates

General rates are traditionally the principle source of local government revenue. In the simplest approach general rates are the result of dividing the residual revenue requirement (after deducting other revenue sources) by the total valuation of rateable property in the local authority area. A local government cannot by law levy both a general rate and a differential general rate, it must be one or the other. General rates are used to defray the costs of any or all of the functions of local government.

Differential general rates

It is a discretionary power conferred on local government as to whether they levy either a general rate or a differential general rate. Some local governments consider the cost or benefits of services to land to be too disparate using a single general rate. In some cases objectives for distributing the rate burden may not be able to be achieved using a single general rate. Before a differential rate can be levied rateable land must be categorised into two or more categories with the authority specifying the criteria by which land is placed into each category. The Local Government Act 1993 does not identify any criteria by which a local authority should classify land. It is therefore open to an authority to categorise land according to those criteria hat it considers to be most relevant.

The typical criteria which should be taken into account in developing a differential rating scheme could include the following:

- existing and/or future land use;
- services, facilities or activities available, or which will be made available to the land;
- the consumption of particular local government resources;
- location;
- access to services;
- economic circumstances affecting the land;
- demographic patterns; and
- climatic or environmental issues affecting the land.

A differential rate can be used to fund all of the same functions of local government as the general rate.

Minimum general rates

Rather than levying a general rate on every parcel of rateable land in the area the local authority may consider the making of a minimum general rate. Such a rate allows a local government to collect a fixed sum in respect of those parcels of rateable land which would otherwise pay a lesser amount than the minimum under a general or differential general rate. In practice, local governments should conduct some modelling exercises to assess the product of the general and minimum general rates. The modelling will assess the amount produced by each value band of property valuations.

Special rates and charges

Special rates and charges may be levied in addition to a general rate or differential general rate. Unlike a separate rate or charge a special rate is not levied on all rateable land, but rather on specifically identified rateable land. A special rate or charge may take the form of a rate in the dollar or a fixed amount. Each rate or charge must relate to the provision of a service or a facility.

   One of the most important elements of this type of levy is the clear identification of the land that will avail of the specific benefit. This aspect can be particularly difficult as there may be differences of opinion about where a special benefit starts and ends.

Separate rates and charges

A separate rate or charge is levied equally on all rateable land in the local government area to fund a particular service or facility. The service or facility will benefit the community generally and it is not possible to say that one or more specific parts of the community get the sole benefit of the service.

Utility charges

These types of charges are aimed specifically for the supply of water, gas, sewerage and refuse collection. A wide range of options are normally available to local government in relation to the way these charges are calculated. The options range from charges based on valuation to fully user pay charges, however, there would appear to be a move away from valuation based charges.

General charges

Local government can make charges for those services and facilities supplied by it. Such examples can include giving an approval, consent licence or registration; giving information; receiving an application; and recording a change in ownership.

Revenue limitation measures

Local government has the ability to lessen the impact of rate increases on rateable land caused by non-uniform valuation changes or significant increases in valuations by applying:

*   limitation of increases in rates powers; or
*   averaging powers.

Apart from the above alternatives there are a number of other ways to deal with valuation increases including the use of differential general rates or, on an individual level, the concession powers.

The regulations governing the limitation of increases and averaging powers are contained in the Local Government Act 1993. It should be noted that the application of either measure is discretionary.

Limitation of increase in rate levied

Section 632 of the LGA 1993 confers the power to limit the amount of an increase in rates that would otherwise be levied on land by the application of its rating strategy or where large or rapid valuation increases have occurred. The power effectively enables the amount of rate levied in a financial year to be tied to the amount of rate levied in the preceding financial year. In other words, no increase or the amount of the rate to be levied in the forthcoming year to be no more than a certain percentage.

Local government has the flexibility to apply a percentage limit to land in a part as well as the whole of its area. It can also apply the limitation on some but not necessarily all rates e.g. on the general rates but not on other rates. Each rate may have a different increase applied e.g. general 8 per cent, special rate 4 per cent. However, in practice, to set different increases for different rates may well be administratively complex. The important issue for local governments which choose to use this power is determining an equitable and logical basis for its application.

In applying this strategy local governments need to be aware that there are circumstances that affect land valuations which, when properly considered, may lead to the conclusion that a limit should not be applied. For example it might not be prudent to apply a limit to a property where the valuation has risen dramatically as a result of a rezoning decision where the land may be utilised for a higher use.

Averaging of valuations

Where there is a marked increase in the valuations in all or part of the local government area since the last valuation a local government may decide to average valuations for rating purposes. The purpose of this is to alleviate the impact of significant rises in unimproved values so that rates do not increase dramatically. Valuations can be averaged over a two or three year period (sections 555-558 of the LGA 1993). The local government must decide on whether to average valuations over a two or three year period.

An averaged valuation can be used as the basis for the application of a general or differential general rate. If averaging is used, it must apply throughout the whole area. Where the averaged value is calculated as being equal to or higher than the current valuation, the current valuation must be applied to calculate the amount of rates levied. This ensures that averaging does not result in a higher valuation being used as the basis for rating, which would be the case if the valuation for a parcel declined rather than increased over the averaging period.

Where a local government chooses to average over three years, the average value of each parcel of land which has had the required number of valuations is calculated by dividing the sum of the valuations used by three. The following simple formula can be used:

$$\frac{a+b+c}{3}$$

where:

a, b and c are the first, second and third annual valuations respectively.

Not all parcels will have the required number of valuations to apply averaging over either two or three years e.g. newly sub-divided land, or Crown land which has become rateable. In these cases the LGA 1993 prescribes the method for calculating the averaged value. The method is best demonstrated by using a simple example (based on three years of valuations) where;

Effective value of parcel for the current year	$50,000
Total effective value of area in Year 1 (TV1) million	$60
Total effective value of area in Year 2 (TV2) million	$80
Total effective value of area for current year (TCV) million	$100

Average value of parcel = current effective value of parcel x averaging factor

$$= \text{current effective value x } \frac{(TV1 + TV2 + TCV)}{3TCV}$$

$$= \$50,000 \text{ x } \frac{(60m + 80m + 100m)}{3x100m}$$

$$= \$50,000 \text{ x } 0.8$$

$$= \$40,000$$

Therefore the rates to be levied on the parcel will be based on the averaged value of $40,000.

Concessions and reliefs

Owner occupied concession

The owner occupied concession caps the general rate increase on the previous years general rate for owners of property who reside permanently on the property. The main conditions which must be satisfied to obtain relief are:

- the concession is only applicable to domestic properties;
- land must be Category A, that is residential;
- the concession does not apply to any land held in the name of a trust or company.

Potential use

Section 17 of the 1944 Valuation of Land Act provides that in making a valuation of the unimproved value of land exclusively used for purposes of a single dwelling house or for the purposes of farming, any enhancement in that value for the land due to the potential for use as industrial, subdivision or any other purpose shall be disregarded irrespective of whether or not, that potential use is lawful when the valuation is made.

Farming means:

- the business or industry of grazing, dairying, viticulture, forestry, the growing of crops of any kind; or
- any other business or industry involving the cultivation of soils, the gathering in of crops or the rearing of livestock;

if the business or industry represents the dominant use of the land, and:

- has a significant and substantial commercial purpose or character; and
- is engaged in for the purpose of profit on a continuous or repetitive basis.

Valuation

Valuation notices

The Valuation of Land Act 1944 specifically refers to the obligation placed upon the Chief Executive, after completing an annual valuation to advertise in a newspaper circulating he area in respect of which the valuation was made:

- that the valuation has been made;

- that particulars of the valuation will be available for inspection for a period of 21 days commencing on a specified date and at the places and times specified;
- that an owner who is dissatisfied with the valuation of the owners land may lodge an objection.

The notices should be mailed to the individual landowners which would clearly explain the valuation system. The information to be contained in the notices should include the following:

- old value;
- new value;
- valuation date and effective date;
- land use category;
- percentage change in category;
- objection period;
- date and location of display.

Case study

Brisbane City Council

Figure 8.3 illustrates the increase in the number of rateable parcels for
Brisbane over the period 2001 2003.

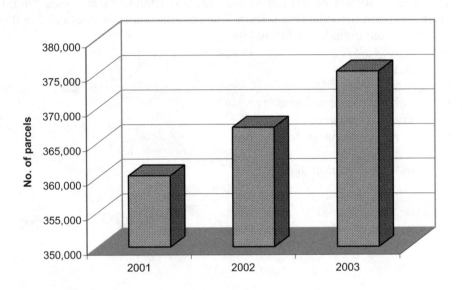

Figure 8.3   Comparison of number of parcels

The residential property sector tends to dominate the tax base in terms of
value. Figure 8.4 illustrates the levels of rateable value between residential,
commercial and industrial and rural property types.

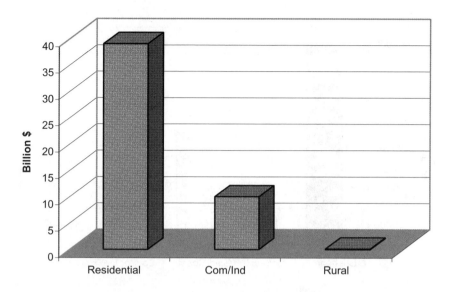

Figure 8.4   Value of parcels by main property types

Brisbane has by far the greatest number of rateable properties in the state. Figure 8.5 shows the number of parcels between several of the main Queensland cities.

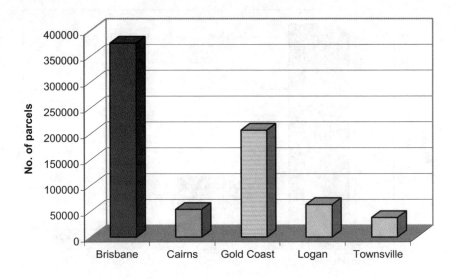

Figure 8.5   Number of rateable land parcels

Sources of revenue

The primary sources of revenue for Brisbane City Council comprises rates and utility charges, fees, and grants. Figure 8.6 illustrates the relative importance of each of the revenue categories. Rates and utility charges represented 64 per cent of the total operating income for the council.

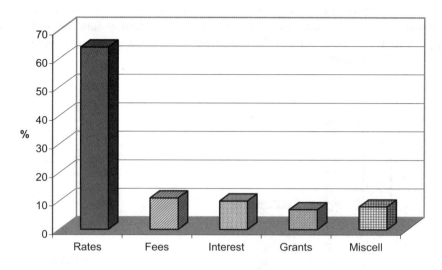

Figure 8.6   Principal revenue sources

As Figure 8.6 highlights there is an important reliance on rates as the main revenue source.

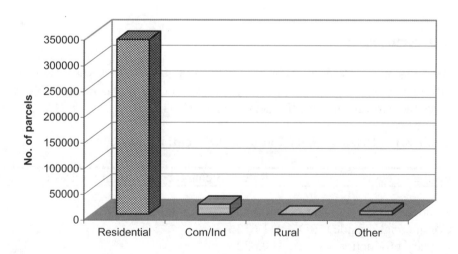

Figure 8.7   Distribution of rateable properties by property type

Figure 8.7 illustrates an analysis of the land use parcels within the Brisbane City Council area. It is clear that the majority of rateable properties are residential.

Figure 8.8 illustrates the relative breakdown of the division of rates contributed by the main land use categories. Residential land provides for approximately 56 per cent of the total rates revenue whilst commercial land provides 30 per cent.

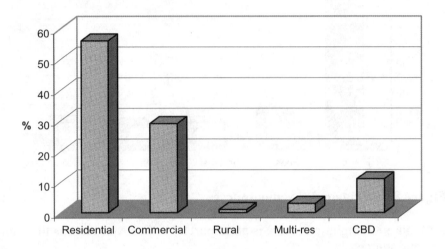

Figure 8.8   Revenue share by property type

Differential rates

Brisbane City Council operate a differential rating system whereby different types of property have specific rate in the dollar rates. Table 8.1 gives the various rates for financial year 2003-04.

Table 8.1   Brisbane City Council: differential rates 2003-2004

Rating category	Rate in $ charged on unimproved value
Residential	0.6569 cents in the $
Commercial outside CBD	1.6736
Primary production	0.8328
Multi residential	0.8092
CBD commercial	2.4368
Mixed residential	1.6736
Other uses	0.6588

Source: Brisbane City Council Budget 2003-04

Critical review

Basis of valuation

Since the turn of the century local government rates in Queensland have been levied on the unimproved capital value of properties. Meaning the value of the land literally without any improvements of any kind (but with all existing amenities). The existing definition of unimproved value requires the valuer to make two basic assumptions, the first being that the estate is a fee simple one and the other being that the land at the date of valuation is in its natural state i.e. without either visible or invisible improvements, in other words both unimproved and undeveloped. The making of the second of these assumptions means that the determination of the unimproved value of improved land under the existing definition requires the valuer in most cases to attempt the impossible task of ascertaining the original state and condition of the land, at a point in time when there is no longer any evidence as to that state and condition. This requirement introduces unnecessary uncertainty and complexity in the valuation process, and provokes differences, disputes and litigation between the valuing authority and the owner.

For valuers the difficulties and anomalies associated with this definition of land, however are increasing with the passage of time and urban development. For example, improvements such as levelling, clearing and filling carried out many years previously are becoming virtually impossible to identify. Other states have adopted the concept of 'site value'. This means the value of land including improvements which have merged with it over time because they have become permanent; require no maintenance; and for all practical purposes have merged with the land and become invisible. For the purposes of assessing the rateable value of land, such improvements should be deemed to have merged with the land after a period of ten years or upon its prior sale. The BCC Chalk Report (1989), the Smith Review (1990 and the Evans Report (1996) all supported the adoption of 'site value'.

The adoption of the concept of 'site value', in place of unimproved value would have the advantage of eliminating a misleading concept from the rating system. It is clear that the term 'unimproved value' is not generally understood by the taxpaying community and that the hypotheses upon which such a value has to be ascertained are confusing. Therefore, the phrase 'site value' should ideally be adopted in place of unimproved value.

Frequency of revaluations

The current system in force is that of annual valuations throughout the state. However, it is questionable whether such an 'intensive' approach is required for all regions within the state. It is important that a mechanism for prompt valuation is in place to respond to rapid changes in land values. It is nonetheless equally valid only to revalue when it is required. The annual value system may not be entirely appropriate for rural areas where values are more stable and not so influenced by supply and demand. A revaluation cycle of three years would seem reasonable and have the following advantages:

• a sufficient body of sales would have occurred enabling an accurate analysis of market trends across all land use categories;
• this would give sufficient time to inspect all properties.

Annual valuations represent a significant drain on scarce resources with only a limited overall benefit. There is an argument for moving away from annual valuations based on economic and practical grounds. In addition it is not feasible to expect accurate and precise results for annual valuations of the entire state.

Valuation service provision

At present the Department of Natural Resources and Mines (DNRM) provides all valuations for statutory purposes for the entire state under the following legislation:

• The Land Tax Act 1915;
• The Local Government Act 1993;
• The City of Brisbane Act 1924.

The present position of having the responsibility for all the rating valuations within a government department has a number of important advantages including the fact that there is a greater chance of achieving consistency, credibility and impartiality within the assessment process. Within the Department there is a unique knowledge and understanding of the valuation process, there is extensive experience in undertaking such valuations and a vast amount of relevant property related data held by the department.

There are a number of broad principles to be considered particularly that of the role of government in service delivery. In relation to this, whether or not acting as a provider itself, through its own agencies, government should clearly separate and distinguish its role as purchaser from its role as provider (Report of the Queensland Commission of Audit, 1996).

Accredited contract valuers could competently perform the valuations under the directions of the department, who would act as a regulator. There is, however, some concern as to whether the private sector is sufficiently geared up and would have the capacity to perform the valuations in a cost-effective manner.

The option of devolving the valuation process to the municipality is giving the local authority the discretion to contract out its valuation service provision. In this case the Department can compete directly against the private sector for this work. Where valuation services are contracted out to the private sector there is a need to have an independent body within the government to act as a form of controller/regulator. This body would have the functions of co-ordinating the valuation process, maintaining a quality control, supervisory and advisory role.

In the Review of the State's Valuation System (Evans, 1996) the question of valuation service provision was addressed; some 87 per cent of contributors were of the opinion that the valuations for rating purposes should be provided by, or be the responsibility of, the department/government.

Rate limitation

The application of rate increase limitation measures or rate capping can lead to equity problems. The key legal issue is that rate capping can only be undertaken by reference to the amount of rates actually levied on the particular parcel in the previous year. The first and obvious consequence of this is that rate capping is not possible in respect of a parcel which first comes into existence (as a result of subdivision or boundary alteration) in a particular year. This can produce anomalies; a developing urban area may contain some parcels which were sub-divided in the previous financial year and other parcels which are adjacent to and materially identically to the first parcels, but which were created in the current financial year. Rate capping can only be applied to the first class of parcel and not the second. If capping is applied this would have the result of identical parcels paying different amounts of rates due solely to the capping scheme.

The application of a rate cap may produce an unintended windfall if external factors such as rezoning have substantially increased land valuation for the current financial year as compared to the valuation I the preceding year. Ideally rate capping is better suited in local government areas where stable property market conditions apply where there are no special factors which affect or cause changes in the valuation of the land.

References

Bridge Committee (1960), '*Report by the Committee of Inquiry on certain matters arising under the Valuation of Land Act 1916-1951*', New South Wales.
Chalk Committee (1989), '*Report by the Committee of Inquiry into Valuation and Rating*', Brisbane, Queensland.
Department of Natural Resources and Mines (2004), '*Annual Report*', Queensland Government, Australia.
Evans, L. (1996), '*Review of the State's Valuation System*' (1996), Department of Natural Resources, Queensland.
DLGPSR (2004), '*Population Growth: Highlights and Trends*', Department of Local Government, Planning, Sport and Recreation, Queensland Government.
Kirby, A. (1997), 'Computer Assisted Mass Appraisal: the Queensland Experience', in W.J. McCluskey and A.S. Adair (eds), *Computer Assisted Mass Appraisal: an International Review*, Ashgate Publishing Limited, Aldershot, England, pp. 187-209.
McCluskey, W.J. and Franzsen, R.C.D. (2001), '*Land Value Taxation: A Case Study Approach*', research paper for the Lincoln Institute of Land Policy, Cambridge, Massachusetts, United States.
Slack, E. (2004), 'Property Taxation in Australia', in R.M. Bird and E. Slack (eds), *International Handbook of Land and Property Taxation*, Edward Elgar Publishing Limited, UK, pp. 91-97.
Trickett, J. (1982), 'Unimproved Value in Queensland', *The Valuer*, July, pp. 237-238.

Legislation referred to:

The Land Tax Act 1915.
The Local Government Act 1993.
The City of Brisbane Act 1924.
Valuation of Land Act 1944.

Chapter 9

Land Value Taxation – Concluding Remarks

Riël C.D. Franzsen and William J. McCluskey

Introduction

In the context of this overview of seven jurisdictions where land value taxation is (or was until recently) still extensively used, one statement that can be made with some confidence: When a land-value based system functions well in practice, it is neither superior nor inferior to any other ad valorem system.

Historic developments

The introduction of land value taxation in Australia can indeed be traced back to its "particular philosophical attraction to those responsible for the development of a largely undeveloped state". Henry George's ideas regarding land value taxation were most apposite in the context of a country like Australia and New Zealand at the end of the 19th Century. From Australia and New Zealand it spread to Fiji and also South Africa. South Africa's property tax legislation was taken as the example for property taxation in Botswana, Lesotho, Namibia, Swaziland and Zimbabwe (Southern Rhodesia as it then was) – in other words countries in southern Africa where land value taxation is presented as a statutory option. As indicated in the chapter on Kenya, land-value taxation also spread from South Africa to East Africa.

Early unsuccessful experiences with an annual rental value system (based on the British example) in Jamaica and Kenya necessitated an alternative.

In all of these jurisdictions a capital improved value system which could be perceived to penalise development was also perceived to be unacceptable, hence the option to tax land in its unimproved state only. In young, developing colonies or ex-colonies evidence of land values was readily available (or at least probably more so than for any other ad valorem tax base) and the political environment susceptible to this form of taxation.

Tax base

Land tenure

In the context of tenure insecurity and boundary disputes some countries opt to levy a tax on the owner or occupier of improvements, which are more readily measurable and identifiable with a potential taxpayer, than the land on which the improvements are situated. For example, in Tanzania, where all land has been nationalised and is deemed to be a national asset, and in Sierra Leone, where tenure security is problematic, the tax base is respectively the capital value and annual value of buildings and other improvements. However, as indicated by the Jamaica case study, a legal cadastre is not a prerequisite for a fiscal cadastre.

In Australia, Fiji, Kenya, New Zealand and South Africa an accurate system of registration of title (in most instances the Torrens system) and/or deeds were in place at the time and at least within the areas where property taxes were introduced. This made the introduction of a tax on land values and attractive option.

In all seven jurisdictions studied the land value tax is predominantly or exclusively levied in respect of freehold land. In New Zealand, however, it is indeed levied on Maori land. Problems experienced with the imposition of property taxes on communal land generally relate to the identification of an appropriate taxpayer and effectively enforcing a tax where the land cannot in the final instance be seized and sold to recoup unpaid taxes.

Multiple tax bases

It is noteworthy that in Australia, Kenya, New Zealand and South Africa legislation allows for local choice as regards the tax base. However, in Kenya the practice is to use site value only. It has been argued that the prevalence of illegal improvements, the value of some structures, as well as the pace at which improvements are affixed to land, would make it difficult to introduce a system based on capital improved values. To some extent this also applies to Jamaica.

In South Africa the new property tax dispensation will provide for one uniform national system (capital improved values). However since early in the 20th Century municipalities had, and utilised, their statutory right of choosing a tax base.

In New Zealand and in some states in Australia (for example Victoria), local councils still avail themselves of the opportunity to choose a system. As the Australian, New Zealand and South African case studies indicate, there is, however, a trend to discard land value as tax base. The preference is for capital improved value. Probably the most plausible explanation for this is the difficulty and increasing artificiality of separation of land and improvements in heavily built-up environments, the availability of accurate data regarding capital values and the capacity to regularly do general valuations and, in the interim, maintain the accuracy of valuation rolls through supplementary valuations.

Rural and agricultural land

In respect of all the jurisdictions discussed, except Kenya and Fiji, rural land is included in the tax base. To the extent that agricultural land is located within the boundaries of a taxing authority, it is taxable in all jurisdictions, except Kenya. A variety of relief mechanisms are used to ensure that farm land is not taxed too heavily. These include:

•   Deferral of non-agriculture related value (New Zealand);
•   Differential rates (Western Australia);
•   Disregarding potential use, in other words limiting taxable value to current use (Queensland);
•   Preferential rates (Fiji and South Africa);
•   Rebates (Jamaica).

Valuation and assessment

Any ad valorem system – to remain legitimate and just – requires regular revaluations. This presupposes adequate capacity and availability of skills in the critical area of valuation. Where capacity constraints are prevalent, development generally, but especially when coupled with rapid urbanisation, can put severe pressures on accurate recordkeeping on buildings and other improvements (e.g. identification, development and diversification) for valuation purposes – as is the case in Jamaica, Fiji and Kenya. Migration to capital improved values under these conditions may prove counterproductive. It is therefore insightful that Fiji is not contemplating to change the tax base to either capital improved value or annual value, but to rather focus more acutely on valuation methodology and service delivery.

Whether the value of land or the value of improvements is taken as the residual value in circumstances where a developed parcel is to be valued, the most difficult task faced by valuers in respect of a land-value system is a defendable value where vacant land sales are few or absent altogether.

Australian jurisdictions and New Zealand suggest that land value as tax base is perfectly suited for the use of CAMA and GIS – in both urban and rural environments. In both Queensland and Western Australia all rateable parcels are annually valued.

Tax rates

In respect of any ad valorem system, a proper relation between assessed values reflected in the valuation roll and the rate (or rates) struck in relation to these values is critical. Bahl (1998) argues that one of the problems with land value taxation is the fact that it is generally only efficient as a source of revenue at relatively high nominal rates. This is especially true if revaluations are not regularly undertaken.

In both Fiji and Kenya the uniform rates applying equally to high-value properties in the central business district and low-value residential properties are causing tension. In the other jurisdictions this problem is to some extent overcome by utilising differential tax rates (or in South Africa, through liberal rebates). Presently, however, the Fijian and Kenyan systems do not allow for differential tax rates.

There seems to be a growing trend to make use of differential rates to counter some of the problems associated with a less buoyant and narrower tax base that excludes improvements. These are often used to engineer higher rates on especially commercial and industrial properties – as these properties generally do not vote in local elections, and generally put more pressure to bear on municipal services and infrastructure. In some instances a higher differential rate is also used to penalise unimproved properties as opposed to improved and occupied properties.

A problem which would be common to any system of ad valorem property tax, but is probably more accentuated in respect of a narrower-based land value system, relates to the use of too low tax rates and/or tax rates that are nor adjusted annually or at least regularly. For example, even though Jamaica uses progressive rates, these are only adjusted with a general revaluation. By setting rates annually, as is done in, for example, Australia, New Zealand and South Africa, increasing revenue requirements could be met through gradual tax rate increases during the life span of any valuation roll.

Tax administration

Sometimes the poor performance of a property tax system is blamed on the nature of the tax base, when in actual fact it could be traced back to unrealistically low tax rates and/or weak administration generally. Although annual rental value or capital improved value may provide a more buoyant tax base, systems utilising these bases will not necessarily outperform a system based on land value if one or more of the following problems are systemic:

- poor base coverage (i.e. with numerous exclusions, exemptions and properties not reflected or properly recorded in a land registry or deeds office;
- poor valuation coverage due to lack of professional skills and capacity (endemic in many developing countries using one or more forms of ad valorem taxation);
- poor billing and collection; or
- the lack or utilisation of proper enforcement mechanisms.

However, given an environment where tax rates are appropriately struck and tax administration is good, a land value tax may not necessarily outperform any other ad valorem property tax system. In Australia and New Zealand where base coverage is comprehensive and valuations undertaken regularly – if not annually – and the administration of the tax is well in hand, there are still pressures on land value as tax base.

In the case of Queensland the problem seems to relate to the archaic definition of "unimproved land" in that state, whereas in Western Australia and New Zealand the trend to move towards annual rental values and capital improved values respectively, is predominantly flowing from a paucity of reliable data in heavily built-up environments (such as central business districts). The latter probably being the most often used arguments against a land-value tax, it is not surprising that is also one of the arguments levelled against site rating in South Africa, Kenya and Fiji.

Conclusions

Paradoxically it has in some jurisdictions been argued that land value as a tax base is easier to explain to taxpayers whereas in others that it is more complicated. It is probably accurate to state that taxpayers in more developed countries may generally have a better appreciation of whatever tax base is used, but would most likely equate their monthly or annual property tax bill to the services they receive in return. In short: Taxpayer satisfaction probably relates better to the level of local services than an intimidate knowledge of the valuation and assessment processes and methodologies.

What is clearly illustrated by almost a century of experience in New Zealand, Western Australia and Queensland (and until the new property tax becomes fully operational in South Africa), is that a land-value system can perform well and realise significant levels of revenue (often in excess of 50% of own revenues on aggregate), if coupled with:

- the skills and capacity to undertake regular revaluations;
- differential tax rates to address equity concerns;
- general taxpayer satisfaction with the standards and range of locally-funded services.

References

Bahl, R.W. (1998), 'Land vs Property Taxes in Developing and Transition Countries' in D. Netzer (ed.), *Land Value Taxation: Can it and Will it Work Today?*, Lincoln Institute of Land Policy, Cambridge, MA, United States, pp. 141-171.

Index

Land Value Taxation